# Proofs of a Conspiracy

# The Americanist Classics

. . . *reaches for its manuscripts to every corner of the earth, and to every era of man's culture. For the ideals represented by America at its best have been acclaimed alike by the Roman Cicero two thousand years ago; by the Frenchman Bastiat a hundred years ago; and by the Korean Syngman Rhee only yesterday.*

. . . *is published for readers of every clime and color and creed, and of every nationality. An American or a German or an Egyptian or a Japanese or an Australian; a Catholic or a Protestant or a Jew or a Mohammedan or a Buddhist; each alike can be or become a good americanist, in the fundamental meaning of that term which these volumes will strengthen and support.*

. . . *seeks to make readily available, in a uniform and inexpensive format, a growing series of great books that define many battle lines in the long war between freedom and slavery. The first fully recorded engagement in that war was between the constructive forces of Athenian individualism and the destructive forces of Spartan collectivism. Those prototypes find their recurrent spiritual reincarnation today in the bitter contemporary struggle between the americanist and the communist systems.*

*For the americanist, always and everywhere, education is the basic strategy, and truth is the vital weapon. It is the purpose of this series to supply searchlights and alarm bells, and weaponry and the will to win, for those who believe that Bryant's admonition must be heeded in every age:*

> *"Not yet, O Freedom! close thy lids in slumber, for thine enemy never sleeps."*

# Proofs of a Conspiracy
## By John Robison, A.M.

1739- 1805-

Originally published in 1798
with a new Introduction by
**THE PUBLISHERS**

**THE AMERICANIST CLASSICS**

Published by WESTERN ISLANDS ★ BOSTON ★ LOS ANGELES

PROOFS OF A CONSPIRACY,

A Western Islands book,
is reissued in this reprint series
as a book and thesis of historical interest
and of significance in understanding
the current ideological contest.

Except for choosing a modern typeface
and changing the typographically
old fashioned "s" which looked much
like an "f" and which confuses the eye of
today's reader, we have tried to reproduce
this 1798 book exactly as it was first
printed (except for substituting a modern
typeface). This faithfulness to the original
includes inconsistencies in spelling, in
capitalizing and other matters of editorial
"style" and even obvious typographical errors.

Introduction to the Americanist Classics edition
Copyright © 1967 by Western Islands
Belmont, Massachusetts, 02178
Manufactured in the United States of America

# Contents

# INTRODUCTION TO THE
# AMERICANIST CLASSICS EDITION

Very few people are aware that the intense drama of our twentieth century—the life and death struggle between capitalism and Communism, freedom and slavery—has its origins in the late eighteenth century. All Americans are aware that the Declaration of Independence was written in 1776. Few are aware that Adam Smith's *Wealth of Nations,* which provided the ideological foundation for capitalism and for the Industrial Revolution, was published in 1776. And fewer still are aware that in that same year, 1776, Adam Weishaupt, a professor of Canon law at Ingolstadt University in Germany, founded the Illuminati Order, a conspiratorial organization which embodied all of the goals, aims, and methods of what we now call Communism. All history books will tell you of the first event. A good many will tell you of the second. But practically none will even allude to the last. Why? When you know the answer to that question you know history better than the historians.

The two prime source books for our knowledge of Adam Weishaupt's Illuminati conspiracy are Professor John Robison's *Proofs of a Conspiracy,* first published in 1798, and the Abbé Augustin Barruel's impressive four-volume study, *Memoirs Illustrating the History of Jacobinism,* published in 1799, some months after the first appearance of Robison's book. Both men—one a Professor of Natural Philosophy at Edinburgh University, the other a French clergyman—writing in different countries and in different languages, without the one knowing the other, basically covered the same subject matter and came to the very same conclusions. Thus, we have two excellent works which tell us virtually all we need to know about the origin of history's most diabolical, long-range conspiracy.

While Barruel's work is the more extensive, better documented, and perhaps more painstakingly accurate, Professor Robison's book is the more literate, sophisticated and reflective. Its documentation is extensive, but its intellectual scope is its chief delight, for Robison, in this work, is more than merely a historian; he is a philosopher, moralist, social commentator, wise observer of human foibles, scientist, critic, and stylist.

Robison had all of the virtues of the enlightened, rational, scientific, humane and religious spirit which characterized the founders of our own country and which represented the flower of eighteenth century English intellect. He had traveled widely in the old and new worlds, was one of the century's leading teachers of science—then known as "natural philosophy"—and he knew many of the major men of achievement in all the sciences. He was a close friend of James Watt, the inventor of the steam engine, who described Robison when the latter died in 1805 at the age of 66 as "a man of the clearest head and the most science of anybody I have ever known."

Professor Robison was a member of the distinguished circle of intellectuals who at that time enhanced the reputation of the University of Edinburgh. In fact, in 1783, Robison was elected general secretary of the Royal Society of Edinburgh. In short, Robison was one of the leading intellects of his time, deeply interested in every aspect of man's attainments, both scientific and moral, in civilized society.

The French Revolution, with its incredible atrocities, its militant atheism, its reign of terror, its wanton destruction of civilized values, was the major event which shook Europe during Robison's mature years. Its shock was particularly painful because it occurred when science, rationality and enlightenment were making incredible strides. Yet the Revolution, brought on in the name of all of these, plus "liberty, equality and fraternity," resulted in the beheading by guillotine of such scientific geniuses as Antoine Lavoisier, who was well known and greatly admired by his English colleagues.

Men of genuine learning in Europe were well aware that the French Revolution had been preceded by a long period of intense intellectual agitation, in which the very foundations of civilized society were seriously questioned. Ideas and doctrines advocating the abolition of all religion, the overthrow of all civil governments, the creation of utopian world citizenship and the abolition of private property, were to be found in books, tracts and pamphlets, written often at the risk of provoking the authorities. But the main haven for the free expression of such revolutionary ideas on the Continent were certain Masonic lodges, which, departing from the simpler practices of English Freemasonry, had become forums where diverse opinions on morals, religion and politics could be and were freely expressed. This development *was a peculiarly French innovation,* but it was adopted by numbers of Masonic lodges in many other parts of Europe, particularly Germany.

Because Freemasonry concerned itself with fundamental philosophical and mystical questions, it was bound to be a gathering place for the philosophically and mystically inclined, especially at that time in history when philosophy was in great ferment. But even more important, the lodges provided the brethren with full protection from the authorities by maintaining their rule of secrecy. Robison, a former Mason himself, found that "this impunity had gradually encouraged men of licentious principles to become more bold, and to teach doctrines subversive of all our notions of morality."

Let us be quick to say that Freemasonry in England, America and elsewhere was historically, and today is, quite another kind and its members characterized by high standards of morality and spirituality.

But it was not surprising that a man like Adam Weishaupt, a professor of considerable renown at Ingolstadt University, driven by an incredible and diabolical ambition to rule the world—no less—would be attracted to the Masonic lodges, where he could find secrecy, protection, and a few like-minded colleagues. Weishaupt was not a military man bent on conquering the world via large armies; nor was he a crude gangster who could organize and lead a band of thieves. Weishaupt was an intellectual, a professor of law at a noted university with the arrogant self-conceit of the mentally superior who feel that they should be running the world and everyone in it. And so he devised an ingenious vehicle for world conquest—a secret Order—which would prove immensely attractive to other mentally superior beings of a similar frame of mind. He called it the Illuminati Order and *grafted it, at selected points, onto Freemasonry—like a fungus.*

The ostensible purpose of the Order was to bring universal happiness to the human race. The idea was, in Weishaupt's words to "form a durable combination of the most worthy persons, who should work together in removing the obstacles to human happiness, become terrible to the wicked, and give their aid to all the good without distinction, and should by the most powerful means, first fetter, and by fettering, lessen vice; means which at the same time should promote virtue, by rendering the inclination to rectitude, hitherto too feeble, more powerful and engaging. Would not such an association be a blessing to the world?"

To be more explicit, the Illuminati Order was built around the novel idea that the end—the happiness of the human race—justified the means!

That the Order was intended to embrace the entire world was evidenced by Weishaupt's own definition quoted in the Larousse *Grand Dictionnaire* published in 1873, in which he said that the goal of the Order was to "unite, by way of one common higher interest and by a lasting bond, men from all parts of the globe, from all social classes and from all religions, despite the diversity of their opinions and passions, to make them love this common interest and bond to the point where, together or alone, they act as one individual."

Members of the secret Order pledged blind obedience to their superiors and only knew about the organization what their immediate superiors would tell them. Their oath read in part: "I bind myself to perpetual silence and unshaken loyalty and submission to the Order, in the persons of my Superiors; here making a faithful and complete surrender of my private judgment, my own will, and every narrow-minded employment of my power and influence." Members were required to spy on one another and submit reports and autobiographies which could compromise them should they decide to leave the Order.

The ultimate despotic purpose of the Illuminati Order was kept secret. Only by degrees—going from the lower "Nursery" degrees of *Preparation, Novice, Minerval* and *Illuminatus Minor* to the higher "Mysteries" of *Priest, Regent, Magus* and *Rex*—could the initiated learn of the true mysteries and purposes of the Order. And each step of the way was very carefully plotted and planned by Weishaupt and his colleagues, so that the squeamish and gullible never rose higher than the lowest degrees, while the bold, ruthless and cynical, those ready and willing to dispense with religion, morality, patriotism and any other hindrances, rose to the top.

It was through this process of selection and careful inculcation that Weishaupt, in a mere decade, was able to gather into his Order the cleverest and most diabolical minds in Europe. The true purpose of the Order was to rule the world. To achieve this it was necessary for the Order to destroy all religions, overthrow all governments, and abolish private property. In order to accomplish this it would be necessary to convince enough people that religion, governments, and private property were the real obstacles to human happiness. *This is exactly what the Communists have been doing since 1848!*

Please note that Robison makes it clear that the Illuminati Order was quite *distinct and separate from Freemasonry*. Freemasonry had existed long before Weishaupt had come on the scene. But because the Illuminati *used parts of Freemasonry as a cover,* Robison found it necessary to explain how and why this state of affairs came about. Thus, the first part of the book deals with Freemasonry and provides an examination of the Masonic movement in the places and at the time the Illuminati Order came into being. He gives some of the history of Freemasonry and how it was developed in France, where it had been brought from England. Most important, however, he documents and traces the ideological evolution within the French lodges, which were eventually to become the Jacobin Clubs of revolutionary fame.

With the background on French Freemasonry given, Robison then examines the state of Freemasonry in Germany, where the Illuminati aberration originated. He describes the schisms within German Freemasonry, the great fascination with mysteries, the widespread influence of deism—the philosophy that the universe is creating God rather than the reverse—and such utopian ideas imported from France as Cosmo-politism, or world citizenship, and finally the strong influence of French Masonic practices and doctrines through the Lodge of Lyons, the mother lodge of a segment of Masonry known as the *Grand Orient de la France.*

One of the lodges in Germany affiliated with the Lodge of Lyons was the Lodge Theodore of Munich. It was in this lodge—to which Weishaupt belonged—that the Illuminati Order was organized by him as a secret organization within a secret organization. It took a number of years before the existence of this secret society within a secret society came to light. Its revolutionary doctrines were so zealously propagated that it couldn't be completely hidden for very long. In 1783, a Bavarian Court of Enquiry began its investigation of the Illuminati Order. Much of what we know today about Weishaupt's secret conspiracy is a result of this investigation.

The second chapter of Robison's book, undoubtedly the most fascinating, is devoted to reviewing the evidence uncovered by the authorities, and it is here that we discover that Weishaupt's entire program and methodology was virtually identical with what was later to become known as Communism.

In the third chapter of the book, entitled *The German Union,* Robison attempts to reveal how after the Bavarian Court of Enquiry exposed and banned the Illuminati Order and its leaders, the Order went underground and emerged as a network of Reading Societies throughout Germany. The goal of this literary network was to monopolize the writing, publication, reviewing and distribution of all literature, more effectively to control the minds of the readers. In this chapter, one sees more clearly than ever how the conspiracy used the printed word as its ultimate weapon in subverting the minds of the people.

The fourth chapter of the book demonstrates how all of the foregoing worked to culminate in the horror of the French Revolution, in which Illuminati doctrines and methodology provided the necessary engines of destruction and how members of the Order became the motormen. The pitiful role played by the Duc d'Orleans, the Grand Master of the Grand Orient de la France, reveals the incredible cleverness and deceit with which the conspirators were able to use one royal dupe and his fortune to destroy the monarchy as well as himself.

The final portion of the book is devoted to Professor Robison's General Reflections. He discusses morality and religion, politics and the nature of civilized society, the structure of the British government, the role of women and how the Illuminati planned to use them, the dangers of secret societies, human nature, education, and finally, why he was compelled to write this book. It is all worth reading very carefully, and rereading, for it brims with knowledge and wisdom, and is as pertinent today as it was when it was first published.

What is the value of Robison's work today? First, it sheds light on an important period in history which has been greatly distorted by historians and novelists. It tells us a great deal about the origins of that conspiracy which, by now, has the world almost completely within its grasp. It teaches us how little the conspiracy has changed in either its methods or ideology, and how successful it has been in mesmerizing the masses and covering its tracks. But most important is the revelation that this was a conspiracy conceived, organized, and activated by professionals and intellectuals, many of them brilliant but cunning and clever, who decided to put their minds in the service of total evil; a conspiracy conceived not by Masons as Masons, but by evil men *using* Freemasonry as a vehicle for their own purposes. It is also highly significant that it required another intellectual—Professor Robison—to expose the conspiracy.

It is obvious that this conspiracy, appealing to the conceit of half-baked intellectuals, would attract educators, writers, philosophers, publishers, and clergymen. Their counterparts who run America today—like the Galbraiths, the Rostows, the Kennans, the Bundy's, the Littells, the Lippmanns—have the same self-conceit, the same arrogance which seems to characterize the overly bright and overly sadistic in any age and any civilization. But the Illuminati offered an even more attractive inducement than its long-range goal: it offered immediate and assured success. For, through its connections and intrigues, the conspiracy was able to place its selected members in positions of influence and power where they could enjoy all the glories of worldly success, provided they used that success to work unceasingly for the advancement of the Order. As Weishaupt explains, once the candidate has achieved the exalted degree of *Illuminatus Minor,* his superiors "will assist him in bringing his talents into action, and will place him in situations most favorable for their exertion, so that he may be *assured* of success."

One tends to think of professors, philosophers, and writers as sitting in their ivory towers, perfectly harmless to the world. Robison and history prove otherwise. Activist scholars and professors like Karl Marx and Weishaupt have had a profound influence in shaping the kind of irrational world we live in. From Woodrow Wilson—himself a professor—to Lyndon Johnson, we have had nothing but Presidents surrounded by professors and scholars, who seem to owe their allegiance to one idea only—that of world government. All of which brings to mind Weishaupt's plan to surround the ruling authorities with members of his Order. He writes: "These powers are despots, when they do not conduct themselves by its [the Order's] principles; and it is therefore our duty to surround them with its members, so that the profane may have no access to them. Thus we are able most powerfully to promote its interests. If any person is more disposed to listen to Princes than to the Order, he is not fit for it, and must rise no higher. We must do our utmost to procure the advancement of Illuminati into all important civil offices."

Did the Illuminati Order survive beyond its exposure by the Bavarian authorities in 1783? Robison is convinced that it did, and that it was still quite alive and kicking and as dangerous as ever when his book was published in 1798. Between that year and the emergence of the Communist movement in 1848, there is a considerable knowledge gap, which, as far as we know, historians have made no attempt to bridge. However, the nature of the Order would lead one to believe that it was quite capable of surviving the most glaring exposure. Such exposure would hardly have frightened away the hard core who knew exactly what they were after.

In the realm of *ideology*, certainly the line from the Illuminati Order to the Communist Manifesto is straight and unbroken, although modified to suit the new conditions of the Industrial Revolution. Weishaupt, it is interesting to note, lived until 1822; moreover, the Catholic Encyclopedia tells us that he finally repented and returned to the Church. Whether he was sincere or not, we shall never know.

The publication of both Robison's and Barruel's works caused a sensation at the time and proved to have a strong influence on public opinion for the few years they were in circulation. The first printing of *Proofs of a Conspiracy* was exhausted in a few days, and several editions followed. Both works were also quickly published in the United States where they had an immediate and widespread impact. Jacobin ideas and influences had already been noted with alarm in the New World and it was known that the

Illuminati had established some lodges in the United States. That the Illuminati would attempt to gain control of the press and publishing industry in this country goes without saying. It was, after all, the hallmark of their method.

It wasn't until 1826 that anti-Illuminati feelings were once more aroused in this country as a result of the disappearance of one William Morgan, an American Freemason, who had written a book revealing Masonic secrets entitled *Illustrations of Freemasonry*. Morgan, apparently, had been abducted and drowned in Lake Ontario. It was alleged that fellow Masons had done it. This caused a nationwide furor, resulting in the creation of an anti-Masonic political party in 1829 by Henry Dana Ward, Thurlow Weed, and William H. Seward. Interest in both Robison's and Barruel's books were revived during that period, with the result that Freemasonry suffered a great loss of membership. The anti-Masonic movement lasted a few years until the furor died down. By 1840, the anti-Masonic party was extinct.

Let it be stressed that the present publication of Robison's work is not intended to open old wounds or create new animosity or distrust toward Freemasonry, whose adherents today certainly number among our staunchest patriots and anti-Communists. The intention is merely to illustrate how a conspiracy of intellectuals, using Freemasonry, got off the ground and grew to its present incredible proportions. The conspirators have long since discarded Freemasonry as their vehicle. If clever conspirators could use—of all groups— so fine a group as the Masons, we must open our minds to consider what infinite possibilities are available to them in our own present day society. Their main habitat these days seems to be the great subsidized universities, tax-free foundations, mass media communication systems, government bureaus such as the State Department, and a myriad of private organizations such as the Council on Foreign Relations. If the publication of this book merely serves to convince enough people that conspiracies of this kind have existed in the past do exist in the present and should be routed out, it will have served its purpose. All men of good will, we hope, anxious to keep freedom alive, will recognize the value, therefore, of this new edition of one of the most interesting books in history.

The Publishers

# PROOFS

OF A

# CONSPIRACY

AGAINST ALL THE

## *RELIGIONS AND GOVERNMENTS*

OF

# EUROPE,

CARRIED ON

### IN THE SECRET MEETINGS

OF

## *FREE MASONS, ILLUMINATI,*

AND

## *READING SOCIETIES,*

COLLECTED FROM GOOD AUTHORITIES,

## By JOHN ROBISON, A. M.

PROFESSOR OF NATURAL PHILOSOPHY, AND SECRETARY TO THE
ROYAL SOCIETY OF EDINBURGH.

*Nam tua res agitur paries cum proximus ardet.*

THE FOURTH EDITION.

TO WHICH IS ADDED, A POSTSCRIPT.

———————

*NEW-YORK:*
Printed and Sold by George Forman, No. 64, Water-Street,
between Coenties and the Old-Slip.
1798.

TO THE RIGHT HONORABLE
## WILLIAM WYNDHAM
SECRETARY AT WAR, &c. &c. &c.

SIR,

IT was with great satisfaction that I learned from a
Friend that you coincided with me in the opinion, that
the information contained in this performance would make
a useful impression on the minds of my Countrymen.

I have presumed to inscribe it with your Name, that I
may publicly express the pleasure which I felt, when I
found that neither a separation for thirty years, nor the
pressure of the most important business, had effaced your
kind remembrance of a College Acquaintance, or abated
that obliging and polite attention with which you favored
me in those early days of life.

The friendship of the accomplished and the worthy is
the highest honor; and to him who is cut off, by want of
health, from almost every other enjoyment, it is an inesti-
mable blessing. Accept, therefore, I pray, of my grate-
ful acknowledgements, and of my earnest wishes for your
Health, Prosperity, and increasing Honor,
With sentiments of the greatest Esteem and Respect,
I am,
SIR,
Your most obedient,
and most humble Servant,
JOHN ROBISON.

EDINBURGH,
September 5, 1797.

QUOD si quis verâ vitam ratione gubernet,
Divitiæ grandes homini sunt, vivere parcè
Æquo animo: neque enim est unquam penuria parvi,
At claros se homines voluérunt atque potentes,
Ut fundamento stabili fortuna maneret,
Et placidam possent opulenti degere vitam:
Nequicquam.—quoniam ad summum succedere honorem
Certantes, iter infestum secêre viaï,
Et tamen e summo quasi fulmen dejicit ictos
Invidia interdum contemptim in Tartara tetra.

Ergo, Regibus occisis, subversa jacebat
Pristina majestas soliorum, et sceptra superba:
Et capitis summi præclarum insigne, cruentum,
Sub pedibus volgi magnum lugebat honorem:
Nam cupidè conculcatur nimis ante metutum.
Res itaque ad summam fæcem, turbasque redibat,
Imperium sibi cum ac summatum quisque petebat.

LUCRETIUS, V. 1153.

# Introduction.

BEING AT a friend's house in the country during some part of the summer 1795, I there saw a volume of a German periodical work, called *Religions Begebenheiten, i. e.* Religious Occurrences; in which there was an account of the various schisms in the Fraternity of Free Masons, with frequent allusions to the origin and history of that celebrated association. This account interested me a good deal, because, in my early life, I had taken some part in the occupations (shall I call them) of Free Masonry; and having chiefly frequented the Lodges on the Continent, I had learned many doctrines, and seen many ceremonials, which have no place in the simple system of Free Masonry which obtains in this country. I had also remarked, that the whole was much more the object of reflection and thought than I could remember it to have been among my acquaintances at home. There, I had seen a Mason Lodge considered merely as a pretext for passing an hour or two in a fort of decent conviviality, not altogether void of some rational occupation. I had sometimes heard of differences of doctrines or of ceremonies, but in terms which marked them as mere frivolities. But, on the Continent, I found them matters of serious concern and debate. Such too is the contagion of example, that I could not hinder myself from thinking one opinion better founded, or one Ritual more apposite and significant, than another; and I even felt something like an anxiety for its being adopted, and a zeal for making it a general practice. I had been initiated in a very splendid Lodge at Liege, of which the Prince Bishop, his Trefonciers, and the chief Noblesse of the State, were members. I visited the French Lodges at Valenciennes, at Brussels, at Aix-la-Chapelle, at Berlin, and Koningsberg;

and I picked up some printed discourses delivered by the Brother-orators of the Lodges. At St. Petersburgh I connected myself with the English Lodge, and occasionally visited the German and Russian Lodges held there. I found myself received with particular respect as a Scotch Mason, and as an Eleve of the *Lodge de la Parfaite Intelligence* at Liege. I was importuned by persons of the first rank to pursue my masonic career through many degrees unknown in this country. But all the splendour and elegance that I saw could not conceal a frivolity in every part. It appeared a baseless fabric, and I could not think of engaging in an occupation which would consume much time, cost me a good deal of money, and might perhaps excite in me some of that fanaticism, or, at least, enthusiasm that I saw in others, and perceived to be void of any rational support. I therefore remained in the English Lodge, contented with the rank of Scotch Master, which was in a manner forced on me in a private Lodge of French Masons, but is not given in the English Lodge. My masonic rank admitted me to a very elegant entertainment in the female *Loge de la Fidelité,* where every ceremonial was composed in the highest degree of elegance, and every thing conducted with the most delicate respect for our fair sisters, and the old song of brotherly love was chanted in the most refined strain of sentiment. I do not suppose that the Parisian Free Masonry of forty-five degrees could give me more entertainment. I had profited so much by it, that I had the honor of being appointed the Brother-orator. In this office I gave such satisfaction, that a worthy Brother sent me at midnight a box, which he committed to my care, as a person far advanced in masonic science, zealously attached to the order, and therefore a fit depositary of important writings. I learned next day that this gentleman had found it convenient to leave the empire in a hurry, but taking with him the funds of an establishment of which her Imperial Majesty had made him the manager. I was desired to keep these writings till he should see me again. I obeyed. About ten years afterward I saw the gentleman on the street in Edinburgh, conversing with a foreigner. As I passed by him, I saluted him softly in the Russian language, but without stopping, or even looking him in the face. He coloured, but made no return. I endeavoured in vain to meet with him, intending to make a proper return for much civility and kindness which I had received from him in his own country.

I now considered the box as accessible to myself, and opened it. I found it to contain all the degrees of the *Parfait Maçon Ecossois,* with the Rituals, Catechisms, and Instructions, and also four other degrees of Free Masonry, as cultivated in the Parisian Lodges. I have kept them with all care, and mean to give them to some respectable Lodge. But as I am bound by no engagement of any kind, I hold myself as at liberty to make such use of them as may be serviceable to the public, without enabling any uninitiated person to enter the Lodges of these degrees.

This acquisition might have roused my former relish for Masonry, had it been merely dormant; but, after so long separation from the *Loge de la Fidelité,* the masonic spirit had evaporated. Some curiosity, however, remained, and some wish to trace this plastic mystery to the pit from which the clay had been dug, which has been moulded into so many different shapes, "some to honor, and some to dishonor." But my opportunities were now gone. I had given away (when in Russia) my volumes of discourses, and some far-fetched and gratuitous histories, and nothing remained but the pitiful work of Anderson, and the *Maçonnerie Adonhiramique devoilée,* which are in every one's hands.

My curiosity was strongly roused by the accounts given in the *Religions Begebenheiten.* There I saw quotations without number; systems and schisms of which I had never heard; but what particularly struck me, was a zeal and fanaticism about what I thought trifles, which astonished me. Men of rank and fortune, and engaged in serious and honorable public employments, not only frequenting the Lodges of the cities where they resided, but journeying from one end of Germany or France to the other, to visit new Lodges, or to learn new secrets or new doctrines. I saw conventions held at Wismar, at Wisbad, at Kohlo, at Brunswick, and at Willemsbad, consisting of some hundreds of persons of respectable stations. I saw adventurers coming to a city, professing some new secret, and in a few days forming new Lodges, and instructing in a troublesome and expensive manner hundreds of brethren.

German Masonry appeared a very serious concern, and to be implicated with other subjects with which I had never suspected it to have any connection. I saw it much connected with many occurrences and schisms in the Christian church; I saw that the Jesuits had several times interfered in it; and that most of the exceptionable innovations and dissentions had arisen about the time that the order of *Loyola* was suppressed; so that it should seem, that these intriguing brethren had attempted to maintain their influence by the help of Free Masonry. I saw it much disturbed by the mystical whims of J. Behmen and Swedenborg—by the fanatical and knavish doctrines of the modern Rosycrucians—by Magicians—Magnetisers—Exorcists, &c. And I observed that these different sects reprobated each other, as not only maintaining erroneous opinions, but even inculcating opinions which were contrary to the established religions of Germany, and contrary to the principles of the civil establishments. At the same time they charged each other with mistakes and corruptions, both in doctrine and in practice; and particularly with falsification of the first principles of Free Masonry, and with ignorance of its origin and its history; and they supported these charges by authorities from many different books which were unknown to me.

My curiosity was now greatly excited. I got from a much-respected friend many of the preceding volumes of the *Religions Begebenheiten,* in hopes of much information from the patient industry of German erudition. This opened a new and very interesting scene; I was frequently sent back to England, from whence all agreed that Free Masonry had been imported into Germany. I was frequently led into France and into Italy. There, and more remarkably in France, I found that the Lodges had become the haunts of many projectors and fanatics, both in science, in religion, and in politics, who had availed themselves of the secrecy and the freedom of speech maintained in these meetings, to broach their particular whims, or suspicious doctrines, which, if published to the world in the usual manner, would have exposed the authors to ridicule, or to censure. These projectors had contrived to tag their peculiar nostrums to the mummery of Masonry, and were even allowed to twist the masonic emblems and ceremonies to their purpose; so that in their hands Free Masonry became a thing totally unlike, and almost in direct opposition to the system (if it may get such a name) imported from England; and some Lodges had become schools of irreligion and licentiousness.

No nation in modern times has so particularly turned its attention to the cultivation of every thing that is refined or ornamental as France, and it has long been the resort of all who hunt after entertainment in its most refined form; the French have come to consider themselves as the instructors of the world in every thing that ornaments life, and feeling themselves received as such, they have formed their manners accordingly—full of the most condescending complaisance to *all who acknowledge* their superiority. Delighted, in a high degree, with this office, they have become zealous missionaries of refinement in every department of human pursuit, and have reduced their apostolic employment to a system, which they prosecute with ardour and delight. This is not groundless declamation, but sober historical truth. It was the professed aim (and it was a magnificent and wise aim) of the great Colbert, to make the court of Louis XIV, the fountain of human refinement, and Paris the Athens of Europe. We need only look at the plunder of Italy by the French army, to be convinced that their low-born generals and statesmen have in this respect the same notions with the Colberts and the Richlieus.

I know no subject in which this aim at universal influence on the opinions of men, by holding themselves forth as the models of excellence and elegance, is more clearly seen than in the care that they have been pleased to take of Free Masonry. It seems indeed peculiarly suited to the talents and taste of that vain and ardent people. Baseless and frivolous, it admits of every form that Gallic refinement can invent, to recommend it to the young, the gay, the luxurious; that class of society which alone deserves their care, because, in one way or another, it leads all other classes of society.

It has accordingly happened, that the homely Free Masonry imported from England has been totally changed in every country of Europe, either by the imposing ascendancy of French brethren, who are to be found every where, ready to instruct the world; or by the importation of the doctrines, and ceremonies, and ornaments of the Parisian Lodges. Even England, the birth-place of Masonry, has experienced the French innovations; and all the repeated injunctions, admonitions, and reproofs of the old Lodges, cannot prevent those in different parts of the kingdom from admitting the French novelties, full of tinsel and glitter, and high-sounding titles.

Were this all, the harm would not be great. But long before good opportunities had occurred for spreading the refinements on the simple Free Masonry of England, the Lodges in France had become places of very serious discussion, where opinions in morals, in religion, and in politics, had been promulgated and maintained with a freedom and a keenness, of which we in this favored land have no adequate notion, because we are unacquainted with the restraints, which, in other countries, are laid on ordinary conversation. In consequence of this, the French innovations in Free Masonry were quickly followed in all parts of Europe, by the admission of similar discussions, although in direct opposition to a standing rule, and a declaration made to every newly received Brother, "that nothing touching the religion or government shall ever be spoken of in the Lodge." But the Lodges in other countries followed the example of France, and have frequently become the rendezvous of innovators in religion and politics, and other disturbers of the public peace. In short, I have found that the covert of a Mason Lodge had been employed in every country for venting and propagating sentiments in religion and politics, that could not have circulated in public without exposing the author to great danger. I found, that this impunity had gradually encouraged men of licentious principles to become more bold, and to teach doctrines subversive of all our notions of morality—of all our confidence in the moral government of the universe—of all our hopes of improvement in a future state of existence—and of all satisfaction and contentment with our present life, so long as we live in a state of civil subordination. I have been able to trace these attempts, made, through a course of fifty years, under the specious pretext of enlightening the world by the torch of philosophy, and of dispelling the clouds of civil and religious superstition which keep the nations of Europe in darkness and slavery. I have observed these doctrines gradually diffusing and mixing with all the different systems of Free Masonry; till, at last, AN ASSOCIATION HAS BEEN FORMED for the express purpose of ROOTING OUT ALL THE RELIGIOUS ESTABLISHMENTS, AND OVERTURNING ALL THE EXISTING GOVERNMENTS OF EUROPE. I have seen this Association exerting itself zealously and systematically, till it has become almost irresistible: And I have seen that the most active leaders in the French Revolution were members of this Association, and conducted their first movements according to its principles, and by means of its instructions and assistance, *formerly requested and obtained:* And, lastly, I have seen that this Association still exists, still works in secret, and that not only several appearances among ourselves show that its emissaries are endeavoring to propagate their detestable doctrines among us, but that the Association has Lodges in Britain corresponding with the mother Lodge at Munich ever since 1784.

If all this were a matter of mere curiosity, and susceptible of no good use, it would have been better to have kept it to myself, than to disturb my neighbours with the knowledge of a state of things which they cannot amend. But if it shall appear that the minds of my countrymen are misled in the very same manner as were those of our continental neighbours—if I can show that the reasonings which make a very strong impression on some persons in this country are the same which actually produced the dangerous association in Germany; and that they had this unhappy influence solely because they were thought to be sincere, and the expressions of the sentiments of the speakers—if I can show that this was all a cheat, and that the Leaders of this Association disbelieved *every word* that they uttered, and every doctrine that they taught; and that their real intention was to abolish *all* religion, overturn every government, and make the world a general plunder and a wreck—if I can show, that the principles which the Founder and Leaders of this Association held forth as the perfection of human virtue, and the most powerful and efficacious for forming the minds of men, and making them good and happy, had no influence on the Founder and Leaders themselves, and that they were, almost without exception, the most insignificant, worthless, and profligate of men; I cannot but think, that such information will make my countrymen hesitate a little, and receive with caution, and even distrust, addresses and instructions which flatter our self-conceit, and which, by buoying us up with the gay prospect of what is perhaps attainable by a change, may make us discontented with our present condition, and forget that there never was a government on earth where the people of a great and luxurious nation enjoyed so much freedom and security in the possession of every thing that is dear and valuable.

When we see that these boasted principles had not that effect on the leaders which they assert to be their native, certain, and inevitable consequences, we will distrust the fine descriptions of the happiness that should result from such a change. And when we see that the methods which were practised by this Association for the express purpose of breaking all the bands of society, were employed solely in order that the leaders might rule the world with uncontroulable power, while all the rest, even of the associated, will be degraded in their own estimation, corrupted in their principles, and employed as mere tools of the ambition of their *unknown superiors;* surely a free-born Briton will not hesitate to reject at once, and without any farther examination, a plan so big with mischief, so disgraceful to its underling adherents, and so uncertain in its issue.

These hopes have induced me to lay before the public a short abstract of the information which I think I have received. It will be short, but I hope sufficient for establishing the fact, that *this detestable Association exists, and its emissaries are busy among ourselves.*

I was not contented with the quotations which I found in the *Religions Begebenheiten,* but procured from abroad some of the chief writings from which they are taken. This both gave me confidence in the quotations from books which I could not procure, and furnished me with more materials. Much, however, remains untold, richly deserving the attention of all those who *feel* themselves disposed to listen to the tales of a possible happiness that may be enjoyed in a society where all the magistrates are wise and just, and all the people are honest and kind.

I hope that I am honest and candid. I have been at all pains to give the true sense of the authors. My knowledge of the German language is but scanty, but I have had the assistance of friends whenever I was in doubt. In compressing into one paragraph what I have collected from many, I have, as much as I was able, stuck to the words of the author, and have been anxious to give his precise meaning. I doubt not but that I have sometimes failed, and will receive correction with deference. I entreat the reader not to expect a piece of good literary composition. I am very sensible that it is far from it—it is written during bad health, when I am not at ease—and I wished to conceal my name—but my motive is, without the smallest mixture of another, to do some good in the only way I am able, and I think that what I say will come with better grace, and be received with more confidence, than any anonymous publication. Of these I am now most heartily sick. I throw myself on my country with a free heart, and I bow with deference to its decision.

The Association of which I have been speaking, is the Order of ILLUMINATI, founded in 1775, by Dr. Adam Weishaupt, professor of Canon law in the university of Ingolstadt, and abolished in 1786 by the Elector of Bavaria, but revived immediately after, under another name, and in a different form, all over Germany. It was again detected, and seemingly broken up; but it had by this time taken so deep root that it still subsists without being detected, and has spread into all the countries of Europe. It took its first rise among the Free Masons, but is totally different from Free Masonry. It was not, however, the mere protection gained by the secrecy of the Lodges that gave occasion to it, but it arose naturally from the corruptions that had gradually crept into that fraternity, the violence of the party-spirit which pervaded it, and from the total uncertainty and darkness that hangs over the whole of that mysterious Association. It is necessary, therefore, to give some account of the innovations that have been introduced into Free Masonry from the time that it made its appearance on the continent of Europe as a mystical Society, possessing secrets different from those of the mechanical employment whose name it assumed, and thus affording entertainment and occupation to persons of all ranks and professions. It is by no means

intended to give a history of Free Masonry. This would
lead to a very long discussion. The patient industry of German erudition has been very seriously employed on this
subject, and many performances have been published, of
which some account is given in the different volumes of the
Religions Begebenheiten, particularly in those for 1779,
1785, and 1786. It is evident, from the nature of the thing,
that they cannot be very instructive to the public; because
the obligation of secrecy respecting the important matters
which are the very subjects of debate, prevents the author
from giving that full information that is required from an
historian, and the writers have not, in general, been persons
qualified for the talk. Scanty erudition, credulity, and enthusiasm, appear in almost all their writings; and they have
neither attempted to remove the heap of rubbish with which
Anderson has disgraced his *Constitutions of Free Masonry*
(the basis of masonic history) nor to avail themselves of informations which history really affords to a sober enquirer.
Their Royal art must never forsooth appear in a state of
infancy or childhood, like all other human acquirements;
and therefore, when they cannot give proofs of its existence in a state of manhood, possessed of all its mysterious
treasures, they suppose what they do not see, and say that
they are concealed by the oath of secrecy. Of such instructions I can make no use, even if I were disposed to
write a history of the Fraternity. I shall content myself with
an account of such particulars as are admitted by all the
masonic parties, and which illustrate or confirm my general
proposition, making such use of the accounts of the higher
degrees in my possession as I can, without admitting the
profane into their Lodges. Being under no tie of secrecy
with regard to these, I am with-held by discretion alone
from putting the public in possession of all their mysteries.

# CHAP. I.

## Schisms in Free Masonry.

THERE IS undoubtedly a dignity in the art of building, or in architecture, which no other art possesses, and this, whether we consider it in its rudest state, occupied in raising a hut, or as practised in a cultivated nation, in the erection of a magnificent and ornamented temple. As the arts in general improve in any nation, this must always maintain its pre-eminence; for it employs them all, and no man can be eminent as an architect who does not possess a considerable knowledge of almost every science and art already cultivated in his nation. His great works are undertakings of the most serious concern, connect him with the public, or with the rulers of the state, and attach to him the practitioners of other arts, who are wholly occupied in executing his orders: His works are the objects of public attention, and are not the transient spectacles of the day, but hand down to posterity his invention, his knowledge, and his taste. No wonder then that he thinks highly of his profession, and that the public should acquiesce in his pretensions, even when in some degree extravagant.

It is not at all surprising, therefore, that the incorporated architects in all cultivated nations should arrogate to themselves a pre-eminence over the similar associations of other tradesmen. We find traces of this in the remotest antiquity. The Dionysiacs of Asia Minor were undoubtedly an association of architects and engineers, who had the exclusive privilege of building temples, stadia, and theatres, under the mysterious tutelage of Bacchus, and distinguished from the uninitiated or profane inhabitants by the science which they possessed, and by many private signs and tokens, by which they recognized each other. This association came into Ionia from Syria, into which country it had come from Persia, along with that style of architecture that we call

Grecian. We are also certain that there was a similar trading association, during the dark ages, in Christian Europe, which monopolized the building of great churches and castles, working under the patronage and protection of the Sovereigns and Princes of Europe, and possessing many privileges. Circumstances, which it would be tedious to enumerate and discuss, continued this association later in Britain than on the Continent.

But it is quite uncertain when and why persons who were not builders by profession first sought admission into this Fraternity. The first distinct and unequivocal instance that we have of this is the admission of Mr. Ashmole, the famous antiquary, in 1648, into a Lodge at Warrington, along with his father-in-law Colonel Mainwaring. It is not improbable that the covert of secrecy in those assemblies had made them courted by the Royalists, as occasions of meeting. Nay, the Ritual of the Master's degree seems to have been formed, or perhaps twisted from its original institution, so as to give an opportunity of founding the political principles of the candidate, and of the whole Brethren present. For it bears so easy an adaptation to the death of the King, to the overturning of the venerable constitution of the English government of three orders by a mean democracy, and its re-establishment by the efforts of the loyalists, that this would start into every person's mind during the ceremonial, and could hardly fail to show, by the countenances and behaviour of the Brethren, how they were affected. I recommend this hint to the consideration of the Brethren. I have met with many particular facts, which convince me that this use had been made of the meetings of Masons, and that at this time the Jesuits interfered considerably, insinuating themselves into the Lodges, and contributing to encrease that religious mysticism that is to be observed in all the ceremonies of the order. This society is well known to have put on every shape, and to have made use of every mean that could promote the power and influence of the order. And we know that at this time they were by no means without hopes of re-establishing the dominion of the Church of Rome in England. Their services were not scrupled at by the distressed Royalists, even such as were Protestants, while they were highly prized by the Sovereign. We also know that Charles II. was made a Mason, and frequented the Lodges. It is not unlikely, that besides the amusement of a vacant hour, which was always agreeable to him, he had pleasure in the meeting with his loyal friends, and in the occupations of the Lodge, which recalled to his mind their attachment and services. His brother and successor James II. was of a more serious and manly cast of mind, and had little pleasure in the frivolous ceremonies of Masonry. He did not frequent the Lodges. But, by this time, they were the resort of many persons who were not of the profession, or members of the trading corporation. This circumstance, in all probability, produced the denominations of FREE and ACCEPTED Masons. A person who has the privilege of working at any incorporated trade, is said to be a *freeman* of that trade. Others were *accepted* as Brethren, and admitted to a kind of honorary freedom, as is the case in many other trades and incorporations, without having (as far as we can learn for certain) a legal title to earn a livelihood by the exercise of it.

The Lodges being in this manner frequented by persons of various professions, and in various ranks of civil society, it cannot be supposed that the employment in those meetings related entirely to the ostensible profession of Masonry. We have no authentic information by which the public can form any opinion about it. It was not till some years after this period that the Lodges made open profession of the cultivation of general benevolence, and that the grand aim of the Fraternity was to enforce the exercise of all the social virtues. It is not unlikely that this was an after thought. The political purposes of the association being once obtained, the conversation and occupations of the members must take some particular turn, in order to be generally acceptable. The establishment of a fund for the relief of unfortunate Brethren did not take place till the very end of last century; and we may presume that it was brought about by the warm recommendations of some benevolent members, who would naturally enforce it by addresses to their assembled Brethren. This is the probable origin of those philanthropic discourses which were delivered in the Lodges by one of the Brethren as an official task. Brotherly love was the general topic, and this, with great propriety, when we consider the object aimed at in those addresses. Nor was this object altogether a novelty. For while the manners of society were yet but rude, Brother Masons, who were frequently led by their employment far from home and from their friends, stood in need of such helps, and might be greatly benefited by such an institution, which gave them introduction and citizenship wherever they went, and a right to share in the charitable contributions of Brethren who were strangers to them. Other incorporated trades had similar provisions for their poor. But their poor were townsmen and neighbours, well known to them. There was more persuasion necessary in this Fraternity, where the objects of our immediate beneficence were not of our acquaintance. But when the Lodges consisted of many who were not Masons, and who had no particular claim to good offices from a stranger, and their number might be great, it is evident that stronger persuasions were now necessary, and that every topic of philanthropy must now be employed. When the funds became considerable, the effects naturally took the public eye, and recommended the Society to notice and respect. And now the Brethren were induced to dwell on the same topic, to join in the commendations bestowed on the Society, and to say that universal beneficence was the great aim of the Order. And this is all that could be said in public, without infringing the obligation to secrecy. The inquisitive are always prying and teazing, and this is the only point on which a Brother is at liberty to speak. He will therefore do it with affectionate zeal, till perhaps he has heated his own fancy a little, and overlooks the inconsistency of this universal beneficence and philanthropy with the exclusive and monopolizing spirit of an Association, which not only confines its benevolence to its own Members (like any other charitable association) but hoards up in its bosom inestimable secrets, whose natural tendency, they say, is to form the heart to this generous and kind conduct, and inspire us with love to all mankind. The profane world cannot see the beneficence of concealing from public view a principle or a motive which so powerfully induces a Mason to be good and kind. The Brother says that publicity would rob it of its force, and we must take him at his word; and our curiosity is so much the more excited to learn what are the secrets which have so singular a quality.

Thus did the Fraternity conduct themselves, and thus

were they considered by the public, when it was carried over from England to the continent; and here, it is to be particularly remarked, that all our Brethren abroad profess to have received the Mystery of Free Masonry from Britain. This is surely a puzzle in the history; and we must leave it to others to reconcile this with the repeated assertions in Anderson's book of Constitutions, "That the Fraternity existed all over the world," and the numberless examples which he adduces of its exertions in other countries; nay, with his repeated assertions, "that it frequently was near perishing in Britain, and that our Princes were obliged to send to France and other countries, for leading men, to restore it to its former energy among us." We shall find by and by that this is not a point of mere historical curiosity, but that much hinges on it.

In the mean time, let us just remember, that the plain tale of Brotherly love had been polished up to protestations of universal benevolence, and had taken place of loyalty and attachment to the unfortunate Family of Stuart, which was now totally forgotten in the English Lodges. The Revolution had taken place, and King James, with many of his most zealous adherents, had taken refuge in France.

But they took Free Masonry with them to the continent, where it was immediately received by the French, and was cultivated with great zeal in a manner suited to the taste and habits of that highly polished people. The Lodges in France naturally became the rendezvous of the adherents to their banished King, and the means of carrying on a correspondence with their friends in England. At this time also the Jesuits took a more active hand in Free Masonry than ever. They insinuated themselves into the English Lodges, where they were caressed by the Catholics, who panted after the re-establishment of their faith, and tolerated by the Protestant royalists, who thought no concession too great a compensation for their services. At this time changes were made in some of the masonic symbols, particularly in the tracing of the Lodge, which bear evident marks of Jesuitical interference.

It was in the Lodges held at St. Germain's that the degree of *Chevalier Maçon Ecoffois* was added to the three SYM-

BOLICAL degrees of English Masonry. The constitution, as imported, appeared too coarse for the refined taste of our neighbours, and they must make Masonry more like the occupation of a gentleman. Therefore, the English degrees of Apprentice, Fellowcraft, and Master, were called *symbolical,* and the whole Fraternity was considered either as typical of something more elegant, or as a preparation for it. The degrees afterwards superadded to this leave us in doubt which of these views the French entertained of our Masonry. But at all events, this rank of Scotch Knight was called the *first* degree of the *Maçon Parfait.* There is a device belonging to this Lodge which deserves notice. A lion, wounded by an arrow, and escaped from the stake to which he had been bound, with the broken rope still about his neck, is represented lying at the mouth of a cave, and occupied with mathematical instruments which are lying near him. A broken crown lies at the foot of the stake. There can be little doubt but that this emblem alludes to the dethronement, the captivity, the escape, and the asylum of James II. and his hopes of re-establishment by the help of the loyal Brethren. This emblem is worn as the gorget of the Scotch Knight. It is not very certain, however when this degree was added, whether immediately after King James's Abdication, or about the time of the attempt to set his son on the British Throne. But it is certain, that in 1716, this and still higher degrees of Masonry were much in vogue in the Court of France. The refining genius of the French, and their love of show, made the humble denominations of the English Brethren disgusting; and their passion for military rank, the only character that connected them with the Court of an absolute monarch, made them adapt Free Masonry to the same scale of public estimation, and invent ranks of *Maçons Chevaliers* ornamented with titles, and ribbands, and stars. These were highly relished by that vain people; and the price of reception, which was very high, became a rich fund, that was generously applied to relieve the wants of the banished British and Irish adherents of the unfortunate Family who had taken refuge among them. Three new degrees of *Novice, Eleve,* and *Chevalier,* were soon added, and the *Parfait Maçon* had now seven receptions to go through, for each of which a handsome contribution was made. Afterwards, when the first beneficent purpose of this contribution ceased to exist, the finery that now glittered in all the Lodges made a still more craving demand for reception-money, and ingenuity was set to work to invent new baits for the Parfait Maçon. More degrees of chivalry were added, interspersed with degrees of *Philosophe, Pellerin, Clairvoyant,* &c. &c. till some Parisian Lodges had forty-five ranks of Masonry, having fifteen orders of chivalry. For a Knighthood, with a Ribband and a Star, was a *bonne bouche,* given at every third step. For a long while these degrees of chivalry proceeded on some faint analogies with several orders of chivalry which had been erected in Europe. All of these had some reference to some mystical doctrines of the Christian Church, and were, in fact, contrivances of the Church of Rome for securing and extending her influence on the laymen of rank and fortune, whom she retained in her service by these play-things. The Knights Templars of Jerusalem, and the Knights of the Desert, whose office it was to protect pilgrims, and to defend the holy city, afforded very apt models for Masonic mimicry, because the Temple of Solomon, and the Holy Sepulchre, always shared the same fate. Many contended doctrines of the theologians had also their Chevaliers to defend them.

In all this progressive mummery we see much of the hand of the Jesuits, and it would seem that it was encouraged by the church. But a thing happened which might easily have been foreseen. The Lodges had become familiar with this kind of invention; the professed object of many *real* Orders of Knighthood was often very whimsical, or very refined and far-fetched, and it required all the finesse of the clergy to give it some slight connection with religion or morality. The Masons, protected by their secrecy, ventured to go farther. The declamations in the Lodges by the Brother orator, must naturally resemble the compositions of the ancient sophists, and consist of wire-drawn dissertations on the social duties, where every thing is amplified and strained to hyperbole, in their far-fetched and fanciful explanations of the symbols of Masonry. Thus accustomed to allegory, to fiction, to finesse, and to a sort of innocent hypocrisy, by which they cajoled themselves into a notion that this child's-play had at bottom a serious and important meaning, the zealous champions of Free Masonry found no inclination to check this inventive spirit or circumscribe its flights. Under the protection of Masonic secrecy, they planned schemes of a different kind, and instead of more Orders of Chivalry directed against the enemies of their faith, they formed associations in opposition to the ridiculous and oppressive ceremonies and superstitions of the church. There can be no doubt, that in those hidden assemblies, a free communication of sentiment was highly relished and much indulged. It was soon suspected that such use was made of the covert of a Mason Lodge; and the church dreaded the consequences, and endeavored to suppress the Lodges. But in vain. And when it was found, that even auricular confession, and the spiritual threatenings of the church, could not make the Brethren break their oath of secrecy; a full confidence in their security made these free-thinking Brethren bring forward, with all the eagerness of a missionary, such sentiments as they were afraid to hazard in ordinary society. This was long suspected; but the rigours of the church only served to knit the Brethren more firmly together, and provoked them to a more eager exercise of their bold criticisms. The Lodges became schools of scepticism and infidelity, and the spirit of conversion or proselytism grew every day stronger. Cardinal Dubois had before this time laboured with all his might to corrupt the minds of the courtiers, by patronising, directly and indirectly, all sceptics who were otherwise men of talents. He gave the young courtiers to understand that if he should obtain the reins of government, they should be entirely freed from the bigotry of Louis XIV, and the oppression of the church, and should have the free indulgence of their inclinations. His own plans were disappointed by his death; but the Regent Orleans was equally indulgent, and in a few years there was hardly a man in France who pretended to knowledge and reflection, who did not laugh at all religion. Amidst the almost infinite number of publications from the French presses, there is hardly a dozen to be found whose author attempts to vindicate religion from the charges of universal superstition and falsehood. And it must be acknowledged that little else was to be seen in the established religion of the kingdom. The people found nothing in Christianity but a never-ceasing round of insignificant and troublesome ceremonies, which consumed their time, and furnished a fund for supporting a set of lordly and oppressive dignitaries, who declared in the plainest manner their own disbelief of their religion, by their total disregard of common decency, by their continual residence at court, and by absolute neglect, and even the most haughty and oppressive treatment, of the only part of their order that took any concern about the religious sentiments of the nation, namely, the Curés or parish-priests. The monks appeared only as lazy drones; but the parish-priests instructed the people, visited the sick, reconciled the offender and the offended, and were the great mediators between the landlords and their vassals, an office which endeared them more to the people than all the other circumstances of their profession. And it is remarkable, that in all the licentious writings and bitter satyrical tales of the philosophic freethinkers, such as Voltaire, who never fails to have a taunting hit at the clergy, the Curé is generally an amiable personage, a charitable man, a friend to the poor and unfortunate, a peace-maker, and a man of piety and worth. Yet these men were kept in a state of the most slavish and cruel subjection by the higher orders of the clergy, and all hopes of advancement cut off. Rarely, hardly ever, does it happen, that a Curé becomes a Bishop. The Abbés step into every line of preferment. When such procedure is observed by a whole nation, what opinion can be formed but that the whole is a vile cheat? This however was the case in France, and therefore infidelity was almost universal. Nor was this overstrained freedom or licentiousness confined to religious opinions. It was perhaps more naturally directed to the restraints arising from civil subordination. The familiar name of Brother could not but tickle the fancy of those of inferior rank, when they found themselves set cheek by jowl with persons whom they cannot approach out of doors but with cautious respect; and while these men of rank have their pride lulled a little, and perhaps their hearts a little softened by the slang and sentimental declamation on the topic of Brotherly love and Utopian felicity, the others begin to fancy the happy days arrived, and the light of philanthropy beaming from the east and illuminating the Lodge. The Garret Pamphleteer enjoys his fancied authority as Senior Warden, and conducts with affectionate solemnity the young nobleman, who pants for the honor of Mastership, and he praises the trusty Brother who has guarded him in his perilous journies round the room. What topic of declamation can be more agreeable than the equality of

the worthy Brethren? and how naturally will the Brother
Orator, in support of this favorite topic, slide into all the
common-place pictures of human society, freed from all the
anxieties attending civil distinction, and passing their days in
happy simplicity and equality. From this state of the fancy,
it is hardly a step to descant on the propriety, the expediency, and at last, the justice of this arrangement of civil
society; and in doing this, one cannot avoid taking notice
of the great obstructions to human felicity which we see in
every quarter, proceeding from the abuses of those distinctions of rank and fortune  which have arisen in the
world: and as the mischiefs and horrors of superstition are
topics of continual declamation to those who wish to throw
off the restraints of religion; so the oppression of the rulers
of this world, and the sufferings of talents and worth in
inferior stations, will be no less greedily listened to by all
whose notions of morality are not very pure, and by all
who would be glad to have the enjoyments of the wealthy without the trouble of labouring for them. Free Masonry may
be affirmed to have a natural tendency to foster such levelling wishes; and we cannot doubt but that great liberties
are taken with those subjects in the Lodges, especially in
countries where the distinctions of rank and fortune are
strongly expressed and noticed.

But it is not a matter of mere probability that the Mason
Lodges were the seminaries of these libertine instructions.
We have distinct proof of it, even in some of the French
degrees. In the degree called the *Chevalier de Soleil,* the
whole instruction is aimed against the established religion
of the kingdom. The professed object is the emancipation
from error, and the discovery of truth. The inscription in
the east is *Sageffe,* that in the north is *Liberal,* that in the
south is *Fermeté,* and in the west it is *Caution;* terms which
are very significant. The *Tres Venerable* is Adam; the Senior Warden is Truth, and all the Brethren are Children of
Truth. The process of reception is very well contrived: the
whole ritual is decent and circumspect, and nothing occurs
which can alarm the most timid. Brother Truth is asked,
What is the hour? He informs Father Adam, that among
men it is the hour of darkness, but that it is mid-day in the
Lodge. The candidate is asked, Why he has knocked at the
door, and what is become of the eight companions (he is

one of the *Elûs*)? He says, that the world is in darkness,
and his companions and he have lost each other; that
*Hesperus*, the star of Europe, is obscured by clouds of incense, offered up by superstition to despots, who have made
themselves gods, and have retired into the inmost recesses
of their palaces, that they may not be recognised to be
men, while their priests are deceiving the people, and causing them to worship these divinities. This and many similar
sentiments are evident allusions to the pernicious doctrine
of the book called *Origine du Despotisme Oriental*, where
the religion of all countries is considered as a mere engine
of state; where it is declared that reason is the only light
which nature has given to man; and that our anxiety about
futurity has made us imagine endless torments in a future
world; and that princes, taking advantage of our weakness,
have taken the management of our hopes and fears, and
directed them so as to suit their own purposes; emancipation
from the fear of death is declared the greatest of all deliver-
ances; questions are put to the candidate, tending to discover whether and how far he may be trusted, and what
sacrifices he is willing to make in search after truth.

This shape given to the plastic mysteries of Masonry
was much relished, and in a very short time this new path
was completely explored, and a new series of degrees was
added to the list, viz. the *Novice,* and the *Elu de la Verité,*
and the *Sublime Philosophe.* In the progress through these
degrees, the Brethren must forget that they have formerly
been *Chevaliers de l'Orient, Chevaliers de l' Aigle,* when the
symbols were all explained as typical of the life and immortality brought to light by the gospel. Indeed they are
taught to class this among the other clouds which have
been dispelled by the sun of reason. Even in the *Chevalerie
de l' Aigle* there is a two-fold explanation given of the symbols, by which a lively imagination may conceive the whole
history and peculiar doctrines of the New Testament, as
being typical of the final triumph of reason and philosophy
over error. And perhaps this degree is the very first step
in the plan of ILLUMINATION.

We are not to suppose that this was carried to extremity
at once. But it is certain, that before 1743 it had become
universal, and that the Lodges of Free Masons had become

the places for making proselytes to every strange and obnoxious doctrine. *Theurgy, Cosmogony, Cabala,* and many whimsical and mythical doctrines which have been grafted on the distinguishing tenets and the pure morality of the Jews and Christians, were subjects of frequent discussion in the Lodges. The celebrated Chevalier Ramsay was a zealous apostle in this mission. Affectionately attached to the family of Stuart, and to his native country, he had co-operated heartily with those who endeavoured to employ Masonry in the service of the Pretender, and, availing himself of the pre-eminence given (at first perhaps as a courtly compliment) to Scotch Masonry, he laboured to shew that it existed, and indeed arose, during the Crusades, and that there really was either an order of chivalry whose business it was to rebuild the Christian churches destroyed by the Saracens; or that a fraternity of Scotch Masons were thus employed in the east, under the protection of the Knights of St. John of Jerusalem. He found some facts which were thought sufficient grounds for such an opinion, such as the building of the college of these Knights in London, called the Temple, which was actually done by the public Fraternity of Masons who had been in the holy wars. It is chiefly to him that we are indebted for that rage for Masonic chivalry which distinguishes the French Free Masonry. Ramsay's singular religious opinions are well known, and his no less singular enthusiasm. His eminent learning, his elegant talents, his amiable character, and particularly his estimation at court, gave great influence to every thing he said on a subject which was merely a matter of fashion and amusement. Whoever has attended much to human affairs, knows the eagerness with which men propagate all singular opinions, and the delight which attends their favorable reception. None are more zealous than the apostles of infidelity and atheism. It is in human nature to catch with greediness any opportunity of doing what lies under general restraint. And if our apprehensions are not completely quieted, in a case where our wishes lead us strongly to some favorite but hazardous object, we are conscious of a kind of self-bullying. This naturally gets into our discourse, and in our eagerness to get the encouragement of joint adventurers, we enforce our tenets with an energy, and even a violence, that is very inconsistent with the subject in hand. If I am an Atheist, and my neighbour a

Theist, there is surely nothing that should make me violent in my endeavors to rid him of his error. Yet how violent were the people of this party in France.

These facts and observations fully account for the zeal with which all this patch-work addition to the simple Free Masonry of England was prosecuted in France. It surprises us, Britons, who are accustomed to consider the whole as a matter of amusement for young men, who are glad of any pretext for indulging in conviviality. We generally consider a man advanced in life with less respect, if he shows any serious attachment to such things. But in France, the civil and religious restraints on conversation made these secret assemblies very precious; and they were much frequented by men of letters, who there found an opportunity of expressing in safety their dissatisfaction with those restraints, and with that inferiority of rank and condition to which they were subjected, and which appeared to themselves so inadequate to their own talents and merits. The *Avocats de Parlement,* the unbeneficed Abbés, the young men of no fortune, and the *soi-disant* philosophers, formed a numerous band, frequented the Lodges, and there discussed every topic of religion and politics. Specimens of this occupation appeared from time to time in Collections of Discourses delivered by the *Frere Orateur.* I once had in my possession two volumes of these discourses, which I now regret that I left in a Lodge on the continent, when my relish for Free Masonry had forsaken me. One of these is a discourse by Brother Robinet, delivered in the *Loge des Chevaliers Bienfaisants de la Sainte Cité* at Lyons, at a visitation by the Grand Master the *Duc de Chartres,* afterwards *Orleans* and *Egalité.* In this discourse we have the germ and substance of his noted work, the *Systeme de la Nature, ou l'Homme moral et physique.* In another discourse, delivered by Brother Condorcet in the *Loge des Philalethes at Strasbourg,* we have the outlines of his posthumous work, *Le Progres de l'Esprit humain;* and in another, delivered by Mirabeau in the *Loge des Chevaliers Bienfaisants* at Paris, we have a great deal of the levelling principles, and cosmopolitism,* which he thundered from

*Citizenship of the World, from the Greek words *Cosmos,* world, and *Polis,* a city.

the tribunes of the National Assembly. But the most remarkable performances of this kind are, the *Archives Mystico-Hermetiques,* and the *Des Erreurs, et de la Verité.* The first is considered as an account historical and dogmatical, of the procedure and system of the *Loge des Chevaliers Bienfaisants* at Lyons. This was the most zealous and systematical of all the cosmopolitical Lodges in France. It worked long under the patronage of its Grand Master the *Duc de Chartres,* afterwards *Orleans,* and at last *Ph. Egalité.* It sent out many affiliated Lodges, which were erected in various parts of the French dominions. The daughter Lodges at Paris, Strasbourg, Lille, Thoulouse, took the additional title of *Philalethes.* There arose some schisms, as may be expected, in an Association where every man is encouraged to broach and to propagate any the most singular opinion. These schisms were continued with some heat, but were in a great measure repaired in Lodges which took the name of *Amis reunis de la Verité.* One of this denomination at Paris became very eminent. The mother Lodge at Lyons extended its correspondence into Germany, and other foreign countries, and sent constitutions or systems, by which the Lodges conducted their operations.

I have not been able to trace the steps by which this Lodge acquired such an ascendency; but I see, that in 1769 and 1770, all the refined or philosophical Lodges in Alsace and Lorraine united, and in a convention at Lyons, formally put themselves under the patronage of this Lodge, cultivated a continual correspondence, and considered themselves as professing one Masonic Faith, sufficiently distinguishable from that of other Lodges. What this was we do not very distinctly know. We can only infer it from some historical circumstances. One of its favorite daughters, the Lodge *Theodor von der guten Rath,* at Munich, became so remarkable for discourses dangerous to church and state, that the Elector of Bavaria, after repeated admonitions during a course of five or six years, was obliged to suppress it in 1786. Another of its suffragan Lodges at Regensburgh became exceedingly obnoxious to the state, and occasioned several commotions and insurrections. Another, at Paris, gradually refined into the Jacobin club—And in the year 1791, the Lodges in Alsace and Lorraine, with those of Spire and Worms, invited Custine into Germany, and delivered Mentz into his hands.

When we reflect on these historical facts, we get some key to the better understanding of the two performances which I mentioned as descriptive of the opinions and occupations of this sect of Free Masons. The *Archives Mystico-Hermetiques* exhibit a very strange mixture of Mysticism, Theosophy, Cabalistic whim, real Science, Fanaticism, and Freethinking, both in religion and politics. They must not be considered as an account of any settled system, but rather as annals of the proceedings of the Lodge, and abstracts of the strange doctrines which made their successive appearance in the Lodge. But if an intelligent and cautious reader examine them attentively, he will see, that the book is the work of one hand, and that all the wonders and oddities are caricatured, so as to engross the general attention, while they also are twisted a little, so that in one way or another they accord with a general spirit of licentiousness in morals, religion, and politics. Although every thing is expressed decently, and with some caution and moderation, atheism, materialism, and discontent with civil subordination, pervade the whole. It is a work of great art. By keeping the ridicule and the danger of superstition and ignorance continually in view, the mind is captivated by the relief which free enquiry and communication of sentiment seems to secure, and we are put off our guard against the risk of delusion, to which we are exposed when our judgment is warped by our passions.

The other book, "Des Erreurs et de la Verité," came from the same school, and is a sort of holy scripture, or at least a Talmud among the Free Masons of France. It is intended only for the initiated, and is indeed a mystery to any other reader. But as it was intended for spreading the favorite opinions of some enthusiastic Brethren, every thing is said that does not directly betray the secrets of the Order. It contains a system of Theosophy that has often appeared in the writings of philosophers, both in ancient and modern times. "All the intelligence and moral sentiment that appears in the universe, either directly, as in the minds of men, or indirectly, as an inference from the marks of design that we see around us, some of which show us that men have acted, and many more that some other intelligence has acted, are considered as parts or portions of a general mass of intelligence which exists in the universe, in the same manner as matter exists in it. This intelligence has an inscrutable connection with the material part of the universe, perhaps resembling the connexion, equally unsearchable, that subsists between the mind and body of man; and it may be considered as the *Soul of the World*. It is this substance, the natural object of wonder and respect, that men have called God, and have made the object of religious worship. In doing so they have fallen into gross mistakes, and have created for themselves numberless unfounded hopes and fears, which have been the source of superstition and fanaticism, the most destructive plagues that have ever afflicted the human race. The Soul of Man is separated from the general mass of intelligence by some of the operations of nature, which we shall never understand, just as water is raised from the ground by evaporation, or taken up by the root of a plant. And as the water, after an unsearchable train of changes, in which it sometimes makes part of a flower, sometimes part of an animal, &c. is at last reunited, in its original form, to the great mass of waters, ready to run over the same circle again; so the Soul of Man, after performing its office, and exhibiting all that train of intellectual phenomena that we call human life, is at last swallowed up in the great ocean of intelligence." The author then breaks out

> "Felix qui potuit rerum cognoscere causas,
> Atque metus omnes et inexorabile fatum
> Subjecit pedibus, strepitumque Acherontis avari."

For he has now got to his asylum. This deity of his may be the object of wonder, like every thing great and incomprehensible, but not of worship, as the moral Governor of the universe. The hopes are at an end, which rest on our notions of the immortality and individuality of the human soul, and on the encouragement which religion holds forth to believe, that improvement of the mind in the course of this life, by the exercise of wisdom and of virtuous dispositions, is but the beginning of an endless progress in all that can give delight to the rational and well-disposed mind. No relation now subsists between man and Deity that can warm the heart. But, as this is contrary to some natural propensity in the human mind, which in all ages and nations has panted after some connection with Deity, the author strives to avail himself of some cold principles of symmetry in the works of nature, some ill-supported notions of propriety, and other such considerations, to make this *anima mundi* an object of love and respect. This is done in greater detail in another work, *Tableau des rapports entre l'Homme, Dieu, et l'Univers,* which is undoubtedly by the same hand. But the intelligent reader will readily see, that such incongruous things cannot be reconciled, and that we can expect nothing here but sophistry. The author proceeds, in the next place, to consider man as related to man, and to trace out the path to happiness in this life. Here we have the same overstrained morality as in the other work, the same universal benevolence, the same lamentations over the miserable state of mankind, resulting from the oppression of the powerful, the great ones of the earth, who have combined against the happiness of mankind, and have succeeded, by debasing their minds, so that they have become willing slaves. This could not have been brought about without the assistance of superstition. But the princes of this world enlisted into their service the priests, who exerted themselves in darkening the understandings of men, and filled their minds with religious terrors. The altar became the chief pillar of the throne, and men were held in complete subjection. Nothing can recover them from this abject state but knowledge. While this dispels their fears, it will also show them their rights, and the way to attain them.

It deserves particularly to be remarked, that this system of opinions (if such an inconsistent mass of assertions can be called a system) bears a great resemblance to a performance of Toland's, published in 1720, called *Pantheisticon, seu Celebratio Sodalitii Socratici.* It is an account of the principles of a Fraternity which he calls Socratica, and the Brothers Pantheistæ. They are supposed to hold a Lodge, and the author gives a ritual of the procedure in this Lodge; the ceremonies of opening and shutting of the Lodge, the admission of Members into its different degrees, &c. Reason is the Sun that illuminates the whole, and Liberty and Equality are the objects of their occupations.

We shall see afterwards that this book was fondly pushed into Germany, translated, commented, and misrepresented, so as to take off the attention from the real spirit of the book, which is intentionally wrapped up in cabala and enigma. Mirabeau was at much pains to procure it notice; and it must therefore be considered as a treasure of the cosmo-political opinions of the Association of *Chevaliers Bienfaisants, Philalethes,* and *Amis Reunis,* who were called the *improved* Lodges, working under the D. de Chartres—of these there were 266 in 1784. This will be found a very important remark. Let it also be recollected afterwards, that this Lodge of Lyons sent a deputy to a grand Convention in Germany in 1772, viz. Mr. Willermooz, and that the business was thought of such importance, that he remained there two years.

The book *Des Erreurs et de la Verité,* must therefore be considered as a classical book of these opinions. We know that it originated in the *Loge des Chev. Bienfaisants* at Lyons. We know that this Lodge stood as it were at the head of French Free Masonry, and that the fictitious Order of Masonic Knights Templars was formed in this Lodge, and was considered as the model of all the rest of this mimic chivalry. They proceeded so far in this mummery, as even to have the clerical tonsure. The Duke of Orleans, his son, the Elector of Bavaria, and some other German Princes, did not scruple at this mummery in their own persons. In all the Lodges of reception, the Brother Orator never failed to declaim on the topics of superstition, blind to the exhibition he was then making, or indifferent as to the vile hypocrisy of it. We have, in the lists of Orators and Office-bearers, many names of persons, who have had an opportunity at last of proclaiming their sentiments in public. The Abbé Sieyes was of the Lodge of Philalethes at Paris, and also at Lyons. Lequinio, author of the most profligate book that ever disgraced a press, the *Prejuges vaincus par la Raison,* was warden in the Lodge *Compacte Sociale.* Despremenil, Bailly, Fauchet, Maury, Mounier, were of the same system, though in different Lodges. They were called Martinists, from a St. Martin, who formed a schism in the system of the *Chevaliers Bienfaisants,* of which we have not any very precise account. Mercier, gives some account of it in his *Tableau de Paris,* and in his *Année* 1888.

The breach alarmed the Brethren, and occasioned great heats. But it was healed, and the Fraternity took the name of *Misa du Renis,* which is an anagram of *des Amis Reunis.* The Bishop of Autun, the man so bepraised as the benevolent Citizen of the World, the friend of mankind and of good order, was Senior Warden of another Lodge at Paris, established in 1786 (I think chiefly by Orleans and himself) which afterwards became the Jacobin Club. In short, we may assert with confidence, that the Mason Lodges in France were the hot-beds, where the seeds were soon, and tenderly reared, of all the pernicious doctrines which soon after choaked every moral or religious cultivation, and have made the Society worse than a waste, have made it a noisome marsh of human corruption, filled with every rank and poisonous weed.

These Lodges were frequented by persons of all ranks, and of every profession. The idle and the frivolous found amusement, and glittering things to tickle their satiated fancies. There they became the dupes of the declamations of the crafty and licentious Abbés, and writers of every denomination. Mutual encouragement in the indulgence of hazardous thoughts and opinions which flatter our wishes or propensities is a lure which few minds can resist. I believe that most men have felt this in some period of their lives. I can find no other way of accounting for the company that I have sometimes seen in a Mason Lodge. The Lodge *de la Parfaite Intelligence* at Liege, contained, in December 1770, the Prince Bishop, and the greatest part of his Chapter, and all the Office-bearers were dignitaries of the church; yet a discourse given by the Brother Orator was as poignant a satire on superstition and credulity, as if it had been written by Voltaire. It was under the auspices of this Lodge that this collection of discourses, which I mentioned above, was published, and there is no fault found with Brother Robinet; nor Brother Condorcet. Indeed the Trefonciers of Liege were proverbial even in Brabant, for their Epicurism in the most extensive sense of the word.

Thus was corruption spread over the kingdom under the mask of moral instruction. For these discourses were full of the most refined and strained morality, and florid paintings of Utopian felicity, in a state where all are Brothers and citizens of the world. But alas! these wire-drawn principles seem to have had little influence on the hearts, even of those who could best display their beauties. Read the tragedies of Voltaire, and some of his grave performances in prose—What man is there who seems better to know his Master's will? No man expresses with more propriety, with more exactness, the feelings of a good mind. No man seems more sensible of the immutable obligation of justice and of truth. Yet this man, in his transactions with his book-sellers, with the very men to whom he was immediately indebted for his affluence and his fame, was repeatedly, nay, incessantly, guilty of the meanest, the vilest tricks. When he sold a work for an enormous price to one book-seller (even to Cramer, whom he really respected) he took care that a surreptitious edition should appear in Holland, almost at the same moment. Proof-sheets have been traced from Ferney to Amsterdam. When a friend of Cramer's expostulated with Voltaire on the injustice of this conduct, he said, grinning, *Oh le bon Cramer—eh bien—il n'a que d'etre du parti*—he may take a share—he will not give me a livre the less for the first piece I offer him. Where shall we see more tenderness, more honor, more love of every thing that is good and fair, than in Diderot's *Pere de Famille*. —Yet this man did not scruple to sell to the Empress of Russia an immense library, which he did not possess, for an enormous price, having got her promise that it should remain in his possession in Paris during his life. When her ambassador wanted to see it, after a year or two's payments, and the visitation could be no longer staved off, Diderot was obliged to set off in a hurry, and run through all the book-sellers shops in Germany, to help him to fill his empty shelves. He had the good fortune to save appearances—but the trick took air, because he had been niggardly in his attention to the ambassador's secretary. This, however, did not hinder him from honoring his Imperial pupil with a visit. He expected adoration, as the light of the world, and was indeed received by the Russian courtiers with all the childish fondness that they feel for every Parisian mode. But they did not understand him, and as he did not like to lose money at play they did not long court his company. He found his pupil too clearsighted. *Ces philosophes*, said she, *sont beaux, vûs de loin; mais de plus prés, le diamant pardit crystal*. He had contrived a poor story, by which he hoped to get his daughter married in parade, and portioned by her Majesty—but it was seen through, and he was disappointed.

When we see the inefficacy of this refined humanity on these two apostles of philosophical virtue, we see ground for doubting of the propriety and expediency of trusting entirely to it for the peace and happiness of a state, and we should be on our guard when we listen to the florid speeches of the Brother Orator, and his congratulations on the emancipation from superstition and oppression, which will in a short time be effectuated by the *Chevaliers Bienfaisants*, the *Philalethes,* or any other sect of cosmo-political Brethren.

I do not mean by all this to maintain, that the Mason Lodges were the sole corrupters of the public mind in France.—No.—In all nations that have made much progress in cultivation, there is a great tendency to corruption, and it requires all the vigilance and exertions of magistrates, and of moral instructors, to prevent the spreading of licentious principles and maxims of conduct. They arise naturally of themselves, as weeds in a rich soil; and, like weeds, they are pernicious, only because they are, where they should not be, in a cultivated field. Virtue is the cultivation of the human soul, and not the mere possession of good dispositions; all men have these, and occasionly exhibit them. But virtue supposes exertion; and, as the husbandman must be incited to his laborious task by some cogent motive, so must man be prompted to that exertion which is necessary on the part of every individual for the very existence of a great society: For man is indolent, and he is luxurious; he wishes for enjoyment, and this with little trouble. The less fortunate envy the enjoyments of others, and repine at their own inability to obtain the like. They see the idle in affluence. Few, even of good men, have the candour, nay, I may call it the wisdom, to think on the activity and the labour which had procured these comforts to the rich, or to their ancestors; and to believe that they are idle only because they are wealthy, but would be active if they were needy. Such spontaneous reflections cannot be expected in persons who are engaged in unceasing labour, to procure a very moderate share (in their estimation at least) of the comforts of life. Yet such reflections would, in the main, be just, and surely they would greatly tend to quiet the minds of the unsuccessful.

This excellent purpose may be greatly forwarded by a national establishment for moral instruction and admonition; and if the public instructors should add all the motives to virtuous moderation which are suggested by the considerations of genuine religion, every advice would have a tenfold influence. Religious and moral instructions are therefore, in their own nature, unequivocal supports to that moderate exertion of the authority arising from civil subordination, which the most refined philanthropist or cosmopolite acknowledges to be necessary for the very existence of a great and cultivated society. I have never seen a scheme of Utopian happiness that did not contain some system of education, and I cannot conceive any system of education of which moral instruction is not a principal part. Such establishments are dictates of nature, and obtrude themselves on the mind of every person who begins to form plans of civil union. And in all existing societies they have indeed been formed, and are considered as the greatest corrector and soother of those discontents that are unavoidable in the minds of the unsuccessful and the unfortunate. The magistrate, therefore, whose professional habits lead him frequently to exert himself for the maintenance of public peace, cannot but see the advantages of such stated remembrancers of our duty. He will therefore support and cherish this public establishment, which so evidently assists him in his beneficent and important labours.

But all the evils of society do not spring from the discontents and the vices of the poor. The rich come in for a large and a conspicuous share. They frequently abuse their advantages. Pride and haughty behaviour on their part rankle in the breasts, and affect the tempers of their inferiors, already fretted by the hardships of their own condition. The rich also are luxurious; and are often needy. Grasping at every mean of gratification, they are inattentive to the rights of inferiors whom they despise, and, despising, oppress. Perhaps their own superiority has been acquired by injustice. Perhaps most sovereignties have been acquired by oppression. Princes and Rulers are but men; as such, they abuse many of their greatest blessings. Observing that religious hopes make the good resigned under the hardships of the present scene, and that its terrors frequently restrain the bad; they avail themselves of these observations, and support religion as an engine of state, and a mean of their own security. But they are not contented with its real advantages; and they are much more afraid of the resentment and the crimes of the offended profligate, than of the murmurs of the suffering worthy. Therefore they encourage superstition, and call to their aid the vices of the priesthood. The priests are men of like passions as other men, and it is no ground of peculiar blame that they also frequently yield to the temptations of their situation. They are encouraged to the indulgence of the love of influence natural to all men, and they heap terror upon terror, to subdue the minds of men, and darken their understandings. Thus, the most honorable of all employments, the moral instruction of the state, is degraded to a vile trade, and is practised with all the deceit and rapacity of any other trade; and religion, from being the honor and the safeguard of a nation, becomes its greatest disgrace and curse.

When a nation has fallen into this lamentable state, it is extremely difficult to reform. Although nothing would so immediately and so completely remove all ground of complaint, as the re-establishing private virtue, this is of all others the least likely to be adopted. The really worthy, who see the mischief where it really is, but who view this life as the school of improvement, and know that man is to be made perfect through suffering, are the last persons to complain. The worthless are the most discontented, the most noisy in their complaints, and the least scrupulous about the means of redress. Not to improve the nation, but to advance themselves, they turn the attention to the abuses of power and influence. And they begin their attack where they think the place most defenceless, and where perhaps they expect assistance from a discontented garrison. They attack superstition, and are not at all solicitous that true religion shall not suffer along with it. It is not, perhaps, with any direct intention to ruin the state, but merely to obtain indulgence for themselves, and the cooperation of the wealthy. They expect to be listened to by many who wish for the same indulgence; and thus it is that religious free-thinking is generally the first step of anarchy and revolution. For in a corrupted state, persons of all ranks have the same licentious wishes, and if superstitious, fear be really an ingredient of the human mind, it requires some *struggle* to shake it off. Nothing is so effectual as mutual encouragement, and therefore all join against priestcraft; even the rulers forget their interest, which should lead them to support it. In such a state, the pure morality of true religion vanishes from the sight. There is commonly no remains of it in the religion of the nation, and therefore all goes together.

Perhaps there never was a nation where all those co-operating causes had acquired greater strength than in France. Oppressions of all kinds were at a height. The luxuries of life were enjoyed exclusively by the upper classes, and this in the highest degree of refinement; so that the desires of the rest were whetted to the utmost. Religion appeared in its worst form, and seemed calculated solely for procuring establishments for the younger sons of the insolent and useless noblesse. The morals of the higher orders of the clergy and of the laity were equally corrupted. Thousands of literary men were excluded by their station from all hopes of advancement to the more respectable offices in the church. These vented their discontents as far as there was safety, and were encouraged by many of the upper classes, who joined them in their satires on the priesthood. The clergy opposed them, it is true, but feebly, because they could not support their opposition by examples of their own virtuous behaviour, but were always obliged to have recourse to the power of the church, the very object of hatred and disgust. The whole nation became infidel, and when in a few instances a worthy Cure uttered the small still voice of true religion, it was not heard amidst the general noise of satire and reproach. The misconduct of administration, and the abuse of the public treasures, were every day growing more impudent and glaring, and exposed the government to continual criticism. But it was still too powerful to suffer this to proceed to extremities; while therefore infidelity and loose sentiments of morality passed unpunished, it was still very hazardous to publish any thing against the state. It was in this respect chiefly, that the Mason Lodges contributed to the dissemination of dangerous opinions, and they were employed for this purpose all over the kingdom. This is not an assertion hazarded merely on account of its probability. Abundant proof will appear by and by, that the most turbulent characters in the nation frequented the Lodges. We cannot doubt, but that under this covert they indulged their factious dispositions; nay, we shall find the greatest part of the Lodges of France, converted, in the course of a very few weeks, into corresponding political societies.

But it is now time to turn our eyes to the progress of Free Masonry in Germany and the north of Europe; there it took a more serious turn. Free Masonry was imported into Germany somewhat later than into France. The first German Lodge that we have any account of, is that at Cologne, erected in 1716, but very soon suppressed. Before the year 1725 there were many, both in Protestant and Catholic Germany. Those of Wetzlar, Frankfort on the Mayne, Brunswick, and Hamburg, are the oldest, and their priority is doubtful. All of them received their institution from England, and had patents from a mother Lodge in London. All seem to have got the mystery through the same channel, the banished friends of the Stuart family. Many of these were Catholics, and entered into the service of Austria and the Catholic princes.

The true hospitality, that is no where more conspicuous than in the character of the Germans, made this institution a most agreeable and useful passport to these gentlemen; and as many of them were in military stations, and in garrison, they found it a very easy matter to set up Lodges in all parts of Germany. These afforded a very agreeable pastime to the officers, who had little to occupy them, and were already accustomed to a subordination which did not affect their vanity on account of family distinctions. As the Ensign and the General were equally gentlemen, the allegory or play of universal Brotherhood was neither novel nor disgusting. Free Masonry was then of the simplest form, consisting of the three degrees of Apprentice, Fellow-craft, and Master. It is remarkable, that the Germans had been long accustomed to the word, the sign, and the gripe of the Masons, and some other handicraft trades. In many parts of Germany there was a distinction of operative Masons into Wort-Maurers and Schrift-Maurers. The Wort-Maurers had no other proof to give of their having been regularly brought up to the trade of builders, but the word and signs; the Schrift-Maurers had written indentures to shew. There are extant and in force, borough-laws, enjoining the Masters of Masons to give employment to journeymen who had the proper words and sign. In particular it appears, that some cities had more extensive privileges in this respect than others. The word given at Wetzlar, the feat of the great council of revision for the empire, entitled the possessor to work over the whole empire. We may infer from the processes and decisions in some of those municipal courts, that a master gave a word and token for each year's progress of his apprentice. He gave the word of the incorporated Imperial city or borough on which he depended, and also a word peculiar to himself, by which all his own pupils could recognise each other. This mode of recognisance was probably the only document of education in old times, while writing was confined to a very small part of the community. When we reflect on the nature of the German empire, a confederation of small independent states, we see that this profession cannot keep pace with the other mechanic arts, unless its practitioners are invested with greater privileges than others. Their great works exceed the strength of the immediate neighbourhood, and the workmen must be brought together from a distance. Their association must therefore be more cared for by the public.

When English Free Masonry was carried into Germany, it was hospitably received. It required little effort to give it respectability, and to make it the occupation of a gentleman, and its secrets and mysteries were not such novelties as in France. It spread rapidly, and the simple topic of Brotherly love was sufficient for recommending it to the honest and hospitable Germans. But it soon took a very different turn. The German character is the very opposite of frivolity. It tends to seriousness, and requires serious occupation. The Germans are eminent for their turn for investigation; and perhaps they indulge this to excess. We call them plodding and dull, because we have little relish for enquiry for its own sake. But this is surely the occupation of a rational nature, and deserves any name but stupidity. At the same time it must be acknowledged, that the spirit of enquiry requires regulation as much as any propensity of the human mind. But it appears that the Germans are not nice in their choice of their objects; it appears that singularity, and wonder, and difficulty of research, are to them irresistible recommendations and incitements.. They have always exhibited a strong hankering after every thing that is wonderful, or solemn, or terrible; and in spite of the great progress which men have made in the course of these two last centuries, in the knowledge of nature, a progress too in which we should be very unjust if we did not acknowledge that the Germans have been generally in the foremost ranks, the gross absurdities of magic, exorcism, witchcraft, fortune-telling, transmutation of metals, and universal medicine, have always had their zealous partizans, who have listened with greedy ears to the nonsense and jargon of fanatics and cheats; and though they every day saw examples of many who had been ruined or rendered ridiculous by their credulity, every new pretender to secrets found numbers ready to listen to him, and to run over the same course.

Free Masonry, professing mysteries, instantly roused all these people, and the Lodges appeared to the adventurers who wanted to profit by the enthusiasm or the avarice of their dupes, the fittest places in the world for the scene of their operations. The Rosycrucians were the first who availed themselves of the opportunity. This was not the Society which had appeared formerly under that name, and was now extinct; but a set of Alchymists, pretenders to the transmutation of metals and the universal medicine, who, the better to inveigle their votaries, had mixed with their own tricks a good deal of the absurd superstitions of that sect, in order to give a greater air of mystery to the whole, to protract the time of instruction, and to afford more room for evasions, by making so many difficult conditions necessary for perfecting the grand work, that the unfortunate gull, who had thrown away his time and his money, might believe that the failure was owing to his own incapacity or unfitness for being the possessor of the grand secret. These cheats found it convenient to make Masonry one of their conditions, and by a small degree of art, persuaded their pupils that they were the only true Masons. These Rosycrucian Lodges were soon established, and became numerous, because their mysteries were addressed, both to the curiosity, the sensuality, and the avarice of men. They became a very formidable band, adopting the constitution of the Jesuits, dividing the Fraternity into circles, each under the management of its own superior, known to the president, but unknown to the individuals of the Lodges. These superiors were connected with each other in a way known only to themselves, and the whole was under one General. At least this is the account which they wish to be believed. If it be just, nothing but the absurdity of the ostensible motives of their occupations could have prevented this combination from carrying on schemes big with hazard to the peace of the world. But the Rosycrucian Lodges have always been considered by other Free Masons as bad Societies, and as gross schismatics. This did not hinder, however, their alchemical and medical secrets from being frequently introduced into the Lodges of simple Free Masonry; and in like manner, exorcism, or ghost-raising, magic, and other gross superstitions, were often held out in their meetings as attainable mysteries, which would be immense acquisitions to the Fraternity, without any necessity of admitting along with them the religious deliriums of the Rosycrucians.

In 1743, a Baron Hunde, a gentleman of honorable character and independent fortune, was in Paris, and got acquainted with the Earl of Kilmarnock and some other gentlemen who were about the Pretender, and learned from them that they had some wonderful secrets in their Lodges. He was admitted, through the medium of that nobleman, and of a Lord Clifford, and his Masonic patent was signed *George* (said to be the signature of Kilmarnock). Hunde had attached himself to the fortunes of the Pretender, in hopes (as he says himself) of rising in the world under his protection. The mighty secret was this. "When the Order of Knights Templars was abolished by Philip the Fair, and cruelly persecuted, some worthy persons escaped, and took refuge in the Highlands of Scotland, where they concealed themselves in caves. These persons possessed the true secrets of Masonry, which had always been in that Order, having been acquired by the Knights, during their services in the east, from the pilgrims whom they occasionally protected or delivered. The *Chevaliers de la Rose-Croix* con-

tinued to have the same duties as formerly, though robbed
of their emoluments. In fine, every true Mason is a Knight
Templar." It is very true that a clever fancy can accommodate the ritual of reception of the *Chevalier de l' Epée,* &c.
to something like the institution of the Knights Templars,
and perhaps this explanation of young Zerobabel's pilgrim-
age, and of the rebuilding of the Temple by Ezra, is the
most significant explanation that has been given of the
meagre symbols of Free Masonry.

When Baron Hunde returned to Germany, he exhibited
to some friends his extensive powers for propagating this
system of Masonry, and made a few Knights. But he was
not very active. Probably the failure of the Pretender's attempt to recover the throne of his ancestors had put an
end to Hunde's hopes of making a figure. In the mean time
Free Masonry was cultivated with zeal in Germany, and
many adventurers found their advantage in supporting particular schisms.

But in 1756, or 1757, a complete revolution took place.
The French officers who were prisoners at large in Berlin,
undertook, with the assurance peculiar to their nation, to
instruct the simple Germans in every thing that embellishes
society. They said, that the homespun Free Masonry, which
had been imported from England, was fit only for the unpolished minds of the British; but that in France it had
grown into an elegant system, fit for the profession of Gentlemen. Nay, they said, that the English were ignorant of
true Masonry, and possessed nothing but the introduction
to it; and even this was not understood by them. When the
ribbands and stars, with which the French had ornamented
the Order, were shown to the Germans, they could not resist the enchantment. A Mr. Rosa, a French commissary,
brought from Paris a complete waggonload of Masonic ornaments, which were all distributed before it had reached
Berlin, and he was obliged to order another, to furnish the
Lodges of that city. It became for a while a most profitable
business to many French officers and commissaries dispersed over Germany, having nothing else to do. Every
body gaped for instruction, and these kind teachers were
always ready to bestow it. In half a year Free Masonry
underwent a complete revolution all over Germany, and

Chevaliers multiplied without number. The Rosaic system was a gospel to the Mason and the poor British system was despised. But the new Lodges of Berlin, as they had been the teachers of the whole empire, wanted also to be the governors, and insisted on complete subjection from all the others. This startled the Free Masons at a distance, and awakened them from their golden dreams. Now began a struggle for dominion and for independency. This made the old Lodges think a little about the whole affair. The result of this was a counter revolution. Though no man could pretend that he understood the true meaning of Free Masonry, its origin, its history, or its real aim, all saw that the interpretations of their hieroglyphics, and the rituals of the new degrees imported from France, were quite gratuitous. It appeared, therefore, that the safest thing for them was an appeal to the birth-place of Masonry. They sent to London for instructions. There they learned, that nothing was acknowledged for genuine unsophisticated Masonry but the three degrees; and that the mother Lodge of London alone could, by her instructions, prevent the most dangerous schisms and innovations. Many Lodges, therefore, applied for patents and instructions. Patents were easily made out, and most willingly sent to the zealous Brethren; and these were thankfully received and paid for. But instruction was not so easy a matter. At that time we had nothing but the book of constitutions, drawn up about 1720, by Anderson and Desaguilliers, two persons of little education, and of low manners, who had aimed at little more than making a pretext, not altogether contemptible, for a convivial meeting. This, however, was received with respect. We are apt to smile at grave men's being satisfied with such coarse and scanty fare. But it was of use, merely because it gave an ostensible reason for resisting the despotism of the Lodges of Berlin. Several respectable Lodges, particularly that of Frankfort on the Mayne, that of Brunswick, that of Wetzlar, and the Royal York of Berlin, resolutely adhered to the English system, and denied themselves all the enjoyment of the French degrees, rather than acknowledge the supremacy of the Rosaic Lodges of Berlin.

About the year 1764 a new revolution took place. An adventurer, who called himself Johnson, and passed himself for an Englishman, but who was really a German or Bo-

hemian named Leucht, said that he was ambassador from
the Chapter of Knights Templars at Old Aberdeen in Scotland, sent to teach the Germans what was true Masonry.
He pretended to transmute metals, and some of the Brethren declared that they had seen him do it repeatedly. This
reached Baron Hunde and brought back all his former enthusiasm. There is something very dark in this part of the
history; for in a little Johnson told his partisans that the
only point he had to inform them of was, that Baron Hunde
was the Grand Master of the 7th province of Masonry,
which included the whole of Germany, and the royal dominions of Prussia. He showed them a map of the Masonic
Empire arranged into provinces, each of which had distinguishing emblems. These are all taken from an old forgotten and insignificant book, *Typotii Symbola Divina et
Humana*, published in 1601. There is not the least trace in
this book either of Masonry or Templars, and the emblems
are taken out without the smallest ground of selection.
Some inconsistency with the former magnificent promises
of Johnson startled them at first, but they acquiesced and
submitted to Baron Hunde as Grand Master of Germany.
Soon after Johnson turned out to be a cheat, escaped, was
taken, and put in prison, where he died. Yet this seems not
to have ruined the credit of Baron Hunde. He erected
Lodges, gave a few simple instructions, all in the system of
English Masonry, and promised, that when they had approved themselves as good Masons, he would then impart
the mighty secret. After two or three years of noviciate, a
convention was held at Altenberg; and he told them that
his whole secret was, *that every true Mason was a Knight
Templar*. They were astonished, and disappointed; for they
expected in general that he would teach them the philosopher's stone, or ghost-raising, or magic. After much discontent, falling out, and dispute, many Lodges united in
this system, made somewhat moderate and palatable, under
the name of the STRICT DISCIPLINARIANS, *Strickten Observanz*. It was acceptable to many, because they insisted that
they were really Knights, properly consecrated, though without temporalities; and they seriously set themselves about
forming a fund which should secure the order in a landed
property and revenue, which would give them a respectable
civil existence. Hunde declared that his whole estate should
devolve on the Order. But the vexations which he after-

wards met with, and his falling in love with a lady who prevailed on him to become Roman Catholic, made him alter this intention. The Order went on, however, and acquired considerable credit by the serious regularity of their proceedings; and, although in the mean time a new apostle of Mysteries, a Dr. Zinzendorff, one of the *Strict Observanz*, introduced a new system, which he said was from Sweden, distinguished by some of the mystical doctrines of the Swedenborgh sect, and though this system obtained the Royal patronage, and a National Lodge was established at Berlin by patent, still the *Tempelorden*, or *Orden des Stricten Observanz*, continued to be very respectable. The German gentry were better pleased with a Grand Master of their own choosing, than with any imposed on them by authority.

During this state of things, one Stark, a Protestant divine, well known in Germany by his writings, made another trial of public faith. One Gugomos (a private gentleman, but who would pass for son to a King of Cyprus) and one Schropfer, keeper of a coffee-house at Nuremberg, drew crowds of Free Masons around them, to learn ghost-raising, exorcism, and alchymy. Numbers came from a great distance to Weisbad to see and learn these mysteries, and Free Masonry was on the point of another revolution. Dr. Stark was an adept in all these things, and contended with Cagliostro in Courland for the palm of superiority. He saw that this deception could not long stand its ground. He therefore came forward, at a convention at Braunschweig in 1772, and said to the Strict Disciplinarians or Templars, That he was of their Order, but of the spiritual department, and was deputed by the Chapter of K—m—d—t in Scotland, where he was Chancellor of the Congregation, and had the name of Archidemides, *Eques ab Aquila fulva:* That this Chapter had the superintendance of the Order: That they alone could consecrate the Knights, or the unknown superiors; and that he was deputed to instruct them in the real principles of the Order, and impart its inestimable secrets, which could not be known to Baron Hunde, as he would readily acknowledge when he should converse with him. Johnson, he said, had been a cheat, and probably a murderer. He had got some knowledge from papers which he must have stolen from a missionary, who had disappeared, and was probably killed. Gugomos and Schropfer must have had some similar information; and Schropfer had even deceived him for a time. He was ready to execute his commission, upon their coming under the necessary obligations of secrecy and of submission. Hunde (whose name in the Order was the *Eques ab Ense*) acquiesced at once, and proposed a convention, with full powers to decide and accept. But a Schubart, a gentleman of character, who was treasurer to the Templar Masons, and had an employment which gave him considerable influence in the Order, strongly dissuaded them from such a measure. The most unqualified submission to unknown superiors, and to conditions equally unknown, was required previous to the smallest communication, or any knowledge of the powers which Archidemides had to treat with them. Many meetings were held, and many attempts were made to learn something of this spiritual court, and of what they might expect from them. Dr. Stark, Baron Weggensak, Baron Von Raven, and some others of his coadjutors in the Lodges at Koningsberg in Prussia, and at Wismar, were received into the Order. But in vain—nothing was obtained from these ghostly Knights but some insignificant ceremonials of receptions and consecrations. Of this kind of novelties they were already heartily sick; and though they all panted after the expected wonders, they were so much frightened by the unconditional submission, that they could come to no agreement, and the secrets of the Scotch Congregation of K— m—d—t still remain with Dr. Stark. They did, however, a sensible thing; they sent a deputation to Old Aberdeen, to enquire after the caves where their venerable mysteries were known, and their treasures were hid. They had, as they thought, merited some more confidence; for they had remitted annual contributions to these unknown superiors, to the amount of some thousands of rix-dollars. But alas, their ambassadors found the Free Masons of Old Aberdeen ignorant of all this, and as eager to learn from the ambassadors what was the true origin and meaning of Free Masonry, of which they knew nothing but the simple tale of Old Hiram. This broke Stark's credit; but he still insisted on the reality of his commission, and said that the Brethren at Aberdeen were indeed ignorant, but that he had never said otherwise; their expectations from that quarter had rested on the scraps purloined by Johnson. He reminded them of a thing well known to themselves; that one of them had been sent for by a dying nobleman to receive papers on this subject, and that his visit having been delayed a few hours by an unavoidable accident, he found all burnt but a fragment of a capitulary and a thing in cypher, part of which he (Dr. Stark) had explained to them. They had employed another gentleman, a H. Wachter, to make similar enquiries in Italy, where Schropfer and others (even Hunde) had told them great secrets were to be obtained from the Pretender's secretary Approsi, and others. Wachter told them, that all this was a fiction, but that he had seen at Florence some Brethren from the Holy Land, who really possessed wonderful secrets, which he was willing to impart, on proper conditions. These, however, they could not accede to; but they were cruelly tortured by seeing Wachter, who had left Germany in sober circumstances, now a man of great wealth and expence. He would not acknowledge that he had got the secret of gold-making from the Asiatic Brethren; but said that no man had any right to ask him how he had come by his fortune. It was enough that he behaved honorably, and owed no man any thing. He broke off all connections with them, and left them in great distress about their Order, and panting after his secrets. *Risum teneatis amici.*

Stark, in revenge for the opposition he had met with from Schubart, left no stone unturned to hurt him with his Brethren, and succeeded, so that he left them in disgust. Hunde died about this time. A book appeared, called, *The Stumbling Block and Rock of Offence,* which betrayed (by their own confession) the whole secrets of the Order of Templars, and soon made an end of it, as far as it went beyond the simple English Masonry.

Thus was the faith of Free Masons quite unhinged in Germany. But the rage for mysteries and wonder was not in the least abated; and the habits of these secret assemblies were becoming every day more craving. Dissension and schism was multiplying in every quarter; and the Institution, instead of being an incitement to mutual complaisance and Brotherly love, had become a source of contention, and of bitter enmity. Not satisfied with defending the propriety of its own Institutions, each System of Free

Masonry was busy in enticing away the partisans of other Systems, shut their Lodges against each other, and proceeded even to vilify and persecute the adherents of every System but their own.

These animosities arose chiefly from the quarrel about precedency, and the arrogance (as it was thought) of the patent Lodge of Berlin, in pretending to have any authority in the other parts of the Empire. But these pretensions were not the result of mere vanity. The French importers of the new degrees, always true to the glory of their nation, hoped by this means to secure the dependence even of this frivolous Society; perhaps they might foresee political uses and benefits which might arise from it. One thing is worth notice: The French Lodges had all emanated from the great Confederation under the Duke de Chartres, and, even if we had no other proof, we might presume that they would cultivate the same principles that characterised that Sect. But we are certain that infidelity and laxity of moral principles were prevalent in the Rosaic Lodges, and that the observation of this corruption had offended many of the sober, oldfashioned Lodges, and was one great cause of any check that was given to the brilliant Masonry of France. It is the observation of this circumstance, in which they all resembled, and which soon ceased to be a distinction, because it pervaded the other Lodges, that induced me to expatiate more on this history of Free Masonry in Germany, than may appear to my readers to be adequate to the importance of Free Masonry in the general subject-matter of these pages. But I hope that it will appear in the course of my narration that I have not given it greater value than it deserves.

About this very time there was a great revolution of the public mind in Germany, and scepticism, infidelity and irreligion, not only were prevalent in the minds and manners of the wealthy and luxurious, and of the profligate of lower ranks, but began to appear in the productions of the press. Some circumstances, peculiar to Germany, occasioned these declensions from the former acquiescence in the faith of their forefathers to become more uniform and remarkable than they would otherwise have been. The Confessions of Germany are the Roman Catholic, the Lutheran (which they call Protestant) and the Calvinist (which they call Reformed). These are professed in many small contiguous principalities, and there is hardly one of them in which all the three have not free exercise. The desire of making proselytes is natural to all serious professors of a rational faith, and was frequently exercised. The Roman Catholics are supposed by us to be particularly zealous; and the Protestants (Lutherans and Calvinists) were careful to oppose them by every kind of argument, among which those of ridicule and reproach were not spared. The Catholics accused them of infidelity respecting the fundamental doctrines of Christianity which they professed to believe, and even with respect to the doctrines of natural religion. This accusation was long very slightly supported; but, of late, by better proofs. The spirit of free inquiry was the great boast of the Protestants, and their only support against the Catholics, securing them both in their religious and civil rights. It was therefore supported by their governments. It is not to be wondered at that it should be indulged to excess, or improperly, even by serious men, liable to error, in their disputes with the Catholics. In the progress of this contest, even their own Confession did not escape criticism, and it was asserted that the Reformation which those Confessions express was not complete. Further Reformations were proposed. The Scriptures, the foundation of our faith, were examined by clergymen of very different capacities, dispositions, and views, till by explaining, correcting, allegorising, and otherwise twisting the Bible, men's minds had hardly any thing left to rest on as a doctrine of revealed religion. This encouraged others to go farther, and to say that revelation was a solecism, as plainly appeared by the irreconcileable differences among these Enlighteners (so they were called) of the public, and that man had nothing to trust to but the dictates of natural reason. Another set of writers, proceeding from this as a point already settled, proscribed all religion whatever, and openly taught the doctrines of materialism and atheism. Most of those innovations were the work of Protestant divines, from the causes that I have mentioned. Teller, Semler, Eberhardt, Leffing, Bahrdt, Riem, and Shultz, had the chief hand in all these innovations. But no man contributed more than Nicholai, an eminent and learned bookseller in Berlin. He has been for many years the publisher of a periodical work, called the General German Library (*Algemein deutsche Bibliothek*) consisting of original dissertations, and reviews of the writings of others. The great merit of this work, on account of many learned dissertations which appear in it, has procured it great influence on that class of readers whose leisure or capacity did not allow them a more profound kind of reading. This is the bulk of readers in every country. Nicholai gives a decided preference to the writings of the Enlighteners, and in his reviews treats them with particular notice, makes the public fully acquainted with their works, and makes the most favorable comments; whereas the performances of their opponents, or more properly speaking, the defenders of the National Creeds, are neglected, omitted, or barely mentioned, or they are criticised with every severity of ridicule and reproach. He fell upon a very sure method of rendering the orthodox writers disagreeable to the public, by representing them as the abetters of superstition; and as secret Jesuits. He asserts, that the abolition of the Order of *Loyola* is only apparent. The Brethren still retain their connection, and most part of their property, under the secret patronage of Catholic Princes. They are, therefore, in every corner, in every habit and character, working with unwearied zeal for the restoration of their empire. He raised a general alarm, and made a journey through Germany, hunting for Jesuits, and for this purpose, became Free Mason and Rosycrucian, being introduced by his friends Gedicke and Biester, clergymen, publishers of the *Berlin Monatschrift*, and most zealous promoters of the new doctrines. This favor he has repaid at his return, by betraying the mysteries of the Lodges, and numberless falsehoods. His journey was published in several volumes, and is full of frightful Jesuitisms. This man, as I have said, found the greatest success in his method of slandering the defenders of Bible-Christianity, by representing them as concealed Jesuits. But, not contented with open discussion, he long ago published a sort of romance, called *Sebaldus Nothanker*, in which these divines are introduced under feigned names, and made as ridiculous and detestable as possible. All this was a good trading job, for sceptical and free-thinking writings have every where a good market; and Nicholai was not only reviewer, but publisher, having presses in different cities of the Empire. The immense literary manufacture of Germany, far exceeding that of any nation of Europe, is carried on in a very particular way. The books go in sheets to the great fairs of Leipsic and Frankfort, twice a year. The booksellers meet there, and see at one glance the state of literature; and having speculated and made their bargains, the books are instantly dispersed through every part of the Empire, and appear at once in all quarters. Although every Principality has an officer for licensing, it is impossible to prevent the currency of a performance, although it may be prohibited; for it is to be had by the carrier at three or four miles distance in another state. By this mode of traffic, a plot may be formed, and actually has been formed, for giving any particular turn to the literature of the country. There is an excellent work printed at Bern by the author Heinzmann, a bookseller, called, *Appeal to my Country, concerning a Combination of Writers, and Booksellers, to rule the Literature of Germany, and form the public mind into a contempt for the religion and civil establishments of the Empire*. It contains a historical account of the publications in every branch of literature for about thirty years. The author shows, in the most convincing manner, that the prodigious change from the former satisfaction of the Germans on those subjects to their present discontent and attacks from every quarter, is neither a fair picture of the prevailing sentiments, nor has been the simple operation of things, but the result of a combination of trading Infidels.

I have here somewhat anticipated (for I hope to point out the sources of this combination,) because it helps to explain or illustrate the progress of infidelity and irreligion that I was speaking of. It was much accelerated by another circumstance. One *Basedow*, a man of talents and learning, set up, in the Principality of Anhalt-Dessau, a PHILANTHROPINE, or academy of general education, on a plan extremely different from those of the Universities and Academies. By this appellation, the founder hoped to make parents expect that much attention would be paid to the morals of the pupils; and indeed the programs or advertisements by which Basedow announced his institution to the public, described it as the professed seminary of practical Ethics. Languages, sciences, and the ornamental exercises, were here considered as mere accessories, and the great aim was to form the young mind to the love of mankind and of virtue, by a plan of moral education which was very specious and unexceptionable. But there was a circumstance which greatly obstructed the wide prospects of the founder. How were the religious opinions of the youth to be cared for? Catholics, Lutherans, and Calvinists, were almost equally numerous in the adjoining Principalities; and the exclusion of any two of these communions would prodigiously limit the proposed usefulness of the institution. Basedow was a man of talents, a good scholar, and a persuasive writer. He framed a set of rules, by which the education should be conducted, and which, he thought, should make every parent easy; and the plan is very judicious and manly. But none came but Lutherans. His zeal and interest in the thing made him endeavour to interest others; and he found this no hard matter. The people of condition, and all sensible men, saw that it would be a very great advantage to the place, could they induce men to send their children from all the neighbouring states. What we wish, we readily believe to be the truth; and Basedow's plan and reasonings appeared complete, and had the support of all classes of men. The moderate Calvinists, after some time, were not averse from them, and the literary manufacture of Germany was soon very busy in making pamphlets, defending, improving, attacking and reprobating the plans. Innumerable were the projects for moderating the differences between the three Christian communions of Germany, and making it possible for the members of them all, not only to live amicably among each other, and to worship God in the same church, but even to communicate together. This attempt naturally gave rise to much speculation and refinement; and the proposals for amendment of the formulas and the instructions from the pulpit were prosecuted with so much keenness, that the ground-work, Christianity, was refined and refined, till it vanished altogether, leaving Deism, or Natural, or, as it was called, Philosophical Religion, in its place. I am not much mistaken as to historical fact, when I say, that the astonishing change in religious doctrine which has taken place in Protestant Germany within these last thirty years was chiefly occasioned by this scheme of Basedow's. The pre-disposing causes existed, indeed, and were general and powerful, and the disorder had already broken out. But this specious and enticing object first gave a title to Protestant clergymen to put to their hand without risk of being censured.

Basedow corrected, and corrected again, but not one Catholic came to the Philanthropine. He seems to have thought that the best plan would be, to banish all positive religion whatever, and that he would then be sure of Catholic scholars. Cardinal Dubois was so far right with respect to the first Catholic pupil of the church. He had recommended a man of his own stamp to Louis XIV. to fill some important office. The monarch was astonished, and told the Cardinal, that "that would never do, for the man was a Jansenist; *Eh! que non, Sire,*" said the Cardinal, "*il n'est qu' Athée;*" all was safe, and the man got the priory. But though all was in vain, Basedow's Philanthropine at Dessau got a high character. He published many volumes on education that have much merit.

It were well had this been all. But most unfortunately, though most naturally, writers of loose moral principles and of wicked hearts were encouraged by the impunity which the sceptical writers experienced, and ventured to publish things of the vilest tendency, inflaming the passions and justifying licentious manners. These maxims are congenial with irreligion and Atheism, and the books found a quick market. It was chiefly in the Prussian States that this went on. The late King was, to say the best of him, a naturalist, and, holding this life for his all, gave full liberty to his subjects to write what they pleased, provided they did not touch on state matters. He declared, however, to a minister of his court, long before his death, that "he was extremely sorry that his indifference had produced such effects; that he was sensible it had greatly contributed to hurt the peace and mutual good treatment of his subjects;" and he said, "that he would willingly give up the glory of his best fought battle, to have the satisfaction of leaving his people in the same state of peace and satisfaction with their religious establishments, that he found them in at his accession to the throne." His successor Frederick William found that things had gone much too far, and determined to support the church establishment in the most peremptory manner; but at the same time to allow perfect freedom of thinking and conversing to the professors of every christian faith, provided it was enjoyed without disturbing the general peace, or any encroachment on the rights of those already supported by law. He published an edict to this effect, which is really a model worthy of imitation in every country. This was the epoch of a strange revolution. It was attacked from all hands, and criticisms, satires, slanders, threatenings, poured in from every quarter. The independency of the neighbouring states, and the monarch's not being a great favorite among several of his neighbours, permitted the publication of these pieces in the adjoining principalities, and it was impossible to prevent their circulation even in the Prussian States. His edict was called an unjustifiable tyranny over the consciences of men; the dogmas supported by it, were called absurd superstitions; the King's private character, and his opinions in religious matters, were treated with little reverence, nay, were ridiculed and scandalously abused. This field of discussion being thus thrown open, the writers did not confine themselves to religious matters. After flatly denying that the prince of any country had the smallest right to prescribe, or even direct the faith of his subjects, they extended their discussions to the rights of princes in general; and now they fairly opened their trenches, and made an attack in form on the constitutions of the German confederacy, and after the usual approaches, they set up the standard of universal citizenship on the very ridge of the glacis, and summoned the fort to surrender. The most daring of these attacks was a collection of anonymous letters on the constitution of the Prussian States. It was printed (or said to be so) at Utrecht; but by comparing the faults of some types with some books printed in Berlin, it was supposed by all to be the production of one of Nicholai's presses. It was thought to be the composition of Mirabeau. It is certain that he wrote a French translation, with a preface and notes, more impudent than the work itself. The monarch was declared to be a tyrant; the people are addressed as a parcel of tame wretches crouching under oppression. The people of Silesia are represented as still in a worse condition, and are repeatedly called to rouse themselves, and to rise up and assert their rights. The King is told, that there is a combination of philosophers (*conjuration*) who are leagued together in defence of truth and reason, and which no power can withstand; that they are to be found in every country, and are connected by mutual and solemn engagement, and will put in practice every mean of attack. Enlightening, instruction, was the general cry among the writers. The triumph of reason over error, the overthrow of superstition and slavish fear, freedom from religious and political prejudices, and the establishment of liberty and equality, the natural and unalienable rights of man, were the topics of general declamation; and it was openly maintained, that secret societies, where the communication of sentiment should be free from every restraint, was the most effectual mean for instructing and enlightening the world.

And thus it appears, that Germany has experienced the same gradual progress, from Religion to Atheism, from decency to dissoluteness, and from loyalty to rebellion, which has had its course in France. And I must now add, that this progress has been effected in the same manner, and by the same means; and that one of the chief means of seduction has been the Lodges of the Free Masons. The French, along with their numerous chevaleries, and stars, and ribbands, had brought in the custom of haranguing in the Lodges, and as human nature has a considerable uniformity every where, the same topics became favorite subjects of declamation that had tickled the ear in France; there were the same corruptions of sentiments and manners among the luxurious or profligate, and the same incitements to the utterance of these sentiments, wherever it could be done with safety; and I may say, that the zealots in all these tracts of free-thinking were more serious, more grave, and fanatical. These are not assertions *apriori*. I can produce proofs. There was a Baron Knigge residing at that time in the neighbourhood of Frankfort, of whom I shall afterwards have occasion frequently to speak. This man was an enthusiast in Masonry from his youth, and had run through every possible degree of it. He was dissatisfied with them all, and particularly with the frivolity of the French chivalry; but he still believed that Masonry contained invaluable secrets. He imagined that he saw a glimpse of them in the cosmo-political and sceptical discourses in their Lodges; he sat down to meditate on these, and soon collected his thoughts, and found that those French orators were right without knocking it; and that Masonry was pure natural religion and universal citizenship, and that this was also true Christianity. In this faith he immediately began his career of Brotherly love, and published three volumes of sermons; the first and third published at Frankfort, and the second at Heidelberg, but without his name. He published also a popular system of religion. In all these publications, of which there are extracts in the *Religions Begebenheiten,* Christianity is considered as a mere allegory, or a Masonic type of natural religion; the moral duties are spun into the common-place declamations of universal benevolence; and the attention is continually directed to the absurdities and horrors of superstition, the sufferings of the poor, the tyranny and oppression of the great, the tricks of the priests, and the indolent simplicity and patience of the laity and of the common people. The happiness of the patriarchal life, and sweets of universal equality and freedom, are the burden of every paragraph; and the general tenor of the whole is to make men discontented with their condition of civil subordination, and the restraints of revealed religion.

All the proceedings of Knigge in the Masonic schisms show that he was a zealous apostle of cosmo-politism, and that he was continually dealing with people in the Lodges who were associated with him in propagating these notions among the Brethren; so that we are certain that such conversations were common in the German Lodges.

When the reader considers all these circumstances, he will abate of that surprise which naturally affects a Briton, when he reads accounts of conventions for discussing and fixing the dogmatic tenets of Free Masonry. The perfect freedom, civil and religious, which we enjoy in this happy country, being familiar to every man, we indulge it with calmness and moderation, and secret assemblies hardly differ from the common meetings of friends and neighbours. We do not forget the expediency of civil subordination, and of those distinctions which arise from secure possession of our rights, and the gradual accumulation of the comforts of life in the families of the sober and industrious. These have, by prudence and a respectable œconomy, preserved the acquisitions of their ancestors. Every man feels in his own breast the strong call of nature to procure for himself and his children, by every honest and commendable exertion, the means of public consideration and respect. No

man is so totally without spirit, as not to think the better
of his condition when he is come of creditable parents, and
has creditable connections; and without thinking that he
is in any respect generous, he presumes that others have
the same sentiments, and therefore allows the moderate expression of them, without thinking it insolence or haughti-
ness. All these things are familiar, are not thought of, and
we enjoy them as we enjoy ordinary health, without per-
ceiving it. But in the same manner as a young man who
has been long confined by sickness, exults in returning
health, and is apt to riot in the enjoyment of what he so
distinctly feels; so those who are under continual check in
open society, feel this emancipation in these hidden assemblies, and indulge with eagerness in the expression of sentiments which in public they must smother within their own
breast. Such meetings, therefore, have a zest that is very
alluring, and they are frequented with avidity. There is no
country in Europe where this kind of enjoyment is so poignant as in Germany. Very insignificant principalities have
the same rank in the General Federation with very extensive dominions. The internal constitution of each petty
state being modelled in nearly the same manner, the official
honors of their little courts become ludicrous and even farcical. The Geheim Hofrath, the Hofmareschal, and all the
Kammerhers of a Prince, whose dominions do not equal
the estates of many English Squires, cause the whole to
appear like the play of children, and must give frequent
occasion for discontent and ridicule, Mason Lodges even
keep this alive. The fraternal equality professed in them is
very flattering to those who have not succeeded in the
scramble for civil distinctions. Such persons become the
most zealous Masons, and generally obtain the active offices in the Lodges, and have an opportunity of treating
with authority persons whom in public society they must
look up to with some respect.

These considerations account, in some measure, for the
importance which Free Masonry has acquired in Germany.
For a long while the hopes of learning some wonderful
secret made a German Baron think nothing of long and
expensive journies in quest of some new degree. Of late,
the cosmo-political doctrines encouraged and propagated
in the Lodges, and some hopes of producing a Revolution

in society, by which men of talents should obtain the management of public affairs, seem to be the cause of all the zeal with which the order is still cherished and promoted. In a periodical work, published at Neuwied, called *Algemein Zeitung der Freymaurerey*, we have the list of the Lodges in 1782, with the names of the Office-bearers. Four-fifths of these are clergymen, professors, persons holding offices in the common-law courts, men of letters by trade, such as reviewers and journalists, and other pamphleteers; a class of men, who generally think that they have not attained that rank in society to which their talents entitle them, and imagine that they could discharge the important offices of the state with reputation to themselves and advantage to the public.

The miserable uncertainty and instability of the Masonic faith, which I described above, was not altogether the effect of mere chance, but had been greatly accelerated by the machinations of Baron Knigge, and some other Cosmo-political Brethren whom he had called to his assistance. Knigge had now formed a scheme for uniting the whole Fraternity, for the purpose of promoting his Utopian plan of universal benevolence in a state of liberty and equality. He hoped to do this more readily by completing their embarrassment, and shewing each system how imfirm its foundation was, and how little chance it had of obtaining a general adherence. The *Stricten Observanz* had now completely lost its credit, by which it had hoped to get the better of all the rest. Knigge therefore proposed a plan to the Lodges of Frankfort and Wetzlar, by which all the systems might, in some measure, be united, or at least be brought to a state of mutual forbearance and intercourse. He proposed that the English system should be taken for the ground-work, and to receive all and only those who had taken the three symbolical degrees, as they were now generally called. After thus guarding this general point of faith, he proposed to allow the validity of every degree or rank which should be received in any Lodge, or be made the character of any particular system. These Lodges, having secured the adherence of several others, brought about a general convention at Willemsbad in Hainault, where every different system should communicate its peculiar tenets. It was then hoped, that after an examination of them all, a constitution might be formed, which comprehended every thing that was most worthy of selection, and therefore be far better than the accommodating system already described. By this he hoped to get his favorite scheme introduced into the whole Order, and Free Masons made zealous Citizens of the World. I believe he was sincere in these intentions, and had no intention to disturb the public peace. The convention was accordingly held, and lasted a long while, the deputies consulting about the frivolities of Masonry, with all the seriousness of state-ambassadors. But there was a great shyness in their communications; and Knigge was making but small progress in his plan, when he met with another Mason, the Marquis of Constanza, who in an instant converted him, and changed all his measures, by showing him that he (Knigge) was only doing by halves what was already accomplished by another Society, which had carried it to its full extent. They immediately set about undoing what he had been occupied with, and heightened as much as they could the dissentions, already sufficiently great, and, in the mean time, got the Lodges of Frankfort and Wetzlar, and several others, to unite, and pick out the best of the things they had obtained by the communications from the other systems, and they formed a plan of what they called, the *Eclectic or Syncritic Masonry of the United Lodges* of Germany. They composed a constitution, ritual, and catechism, which has merit, and is indeed the completest body of Free Masonry that we have.

Such was the state of this celebrated and mysterious Fraternity in Germany in 1776. The spirit of innovation had seized all the Brethren. No man could give a tolerable account of the origin, history, or object of the Order, and it appeared to all as a lost or forgotten mystery. The symbols seemed to be equally susceptible of every interpretation, and none of these seemed entitled to any decided preference.

# CHAP. II.

## The Illuminati.

I AM now arrived at what I should call the great epoch of Cosmo-politism, the scheme communicated to Baron Knigge by the *Marchese di Constanza*. This obliges me to mention a remarkable Lodge of the Eclectic Masonry, erected at Munich in Bavaria, in 1775, under the worshipful Master, Professor Baader. It was called *The Lodge Theodore of Good Counsel*. It had its constitutional patent from the Royal York at Berlin, but had formed a particular system of its own, by instructions from the *Loge des Chevaliers Bienfaisants* at Lyons, with which it kept up a correspondence. This respect to the Lodge at Lyons had arisen from the preponderance acquired in general by the French party in the convention at Willemsbad. The deputies of the Rosaic Lodges, as well as the remains of the Templars, and *Stricten Observanz,* all looking up to this as the mother Lodge of what they called the *Grand Orient de la France,* consisting (in 1782) of 266 improved Lodges, united under the *D. de Chartres.* Accordingly the Lodge at Lyons sent Mr. Willermooz as deputy to this convention at Willemsbad. Refining gradually on the simple British Masonry, the Lodge had formed a system of practical morality, which it asserted to be the aim of genuine Masonry, saying, that a true Mason, and a man of upright heart and active virtue, are synonymous characters, and that the great aim of Free Masonry is to promote the happiness of mankind by every mean in our power. In pursuance of these principles, the Lodge Theodore professedly occupied itself with œconomical, statistical, and political matters, and not only published from time to time discourses on such subjects by the Brother Orator, but the Members considered themselves as in duty bound to propagate and inculcate the same doctrines out of doors.

Of the zealous members of the Lodge Theodore the most conspicuous was Dr. Adam Weishaupt, Professor of Canon Law in the university of Ingolstadt. This person had been educated among the Jesuits; but the abolition of their order made him change his views, and from being their pupil, he became their most bitter enemy. He had acquired a high reputation in his profession, and was attended not only by those intended for the practice in the law-courts, but also by the young gentlemen at large, in their course of general education; and he brought numbers from the neighbouring states to this university, and gave a *ton* to the studies of the place. He embraced with great keenness this opportunity of spreading the favorite doctrines of the Lodge, and his auditory became the seminary of Cosmopolitism. The engaging pictures of the possible felicity of a society where every office is held by a man of talents and virtue, and where every talent is set in a place fitted for its exertion, forcibly catches the generous and unsuspecting minds of youth, and in a Roman Catholic state, far advanced in the habits of gross superstition (a character given to Bavaria by its neighbours) and abounding in monks and idle dignitaries, the opportunities must be frequent for observing the inconsiderate dominion of the clergy, and the abject and indolent submission of the laity. Accordingly Professor Weishaupt says, in his Apology for Illuminatism, that Deism, Infidelity, and Atheism are more prevalent in Bavaria than in any country he was acquainted with. Discourses, therefore, in which the absurdity and horrors of superstition and spiritual tyranny were strongly painted, could not fail of making a deep impression. And during this state of the minds of the auditory the transition to general infidelity and irreligion is so easy, and so inviting to sanguine youth, prompted perhaps by a latent wish that the restraints which religion imposes on the expectants of a future state might be found, on enquiry, to be nothing but groundless terrors; that I imagine it requires the most anxious care of the public teacher to keep the minds of his audience impressed with the reality and importance of the great truths of religion, while he frees them from the shackles of blind and absurd superstition. I fear that this celebrated instructor had none of this anxiety, but was satisfied with his great success in the last part of this task, the emancipation of his young hearers from the terrors of superstition. I suppose also that this was the more agreeable to him, as it procured him the triumph over the Jesuits, with whom he had long struggled for the direction of the university.

This was in 1777. Weishaupt had long been scheming the establishment of an Association or Order, which, in time, should govern the world. In his first fervour and high expectations, he hinted to several Ex-Jesuits the probability of their recovering, under a new name, the influence which they formerly possessed, and of being again of great service to society, by directing the education of youth of distinction, now emancipated from all civil and religious prejudices. He prevailed on some to join him, but they all retracted but two. After this disappointment Weishaupt became the implacable enemy of the Jesuits; and his sanguine temper made him frequently lay himself open to their piercing eye, and drew on him their keenest resentment, and at last made him the victim of their enmity.

The Lodge Theodore was the place where the above-mentioned doctrines were most zealously propagated. But Weishaupt's emissaries had already procured the adherence of many other Lodges; and the Eclectic Masonry had been brought into vogue chiefly by their exertions at the Willemsbad convention. The Lodge Theodore was perhaps less guarded in its proceedings, for it became remarkable for the very bold sentiments in politics and religion which were frequently uttered in their harangues; and its members were noted for their zeal in making proselytes. Many bitter pasquinades, satires, and other offensive pamphlets were in secret circulation, and even larger works of very dangerous tendency, and several of them were traced to that Lodge. The Elector often expressed his disapprobation of such proceedings, and sent them kind messages, desiring them to be careful not to disturb the peace of the country, and particularly to recollect the solemn declaration made to every entrant into the Fraternity of Free Masons, "That no subject of religion or politics shall ever be touched on in the Lodge;" a declaration which alone could have procured his permission of any secret assembly whatever, and on the sincerity and honor of which he had reckoned when he gave his sanction to their establishment. But repeated accounts of the same kind increased the alarm, and the Elector ordered a judicial enquiry into the proceedings of the Lodge Theodore.

It was then discovered that this and several associated Lodges were the nursery or preparation-school for another Order of Masons, who called themselves the ILLUMINATED, and that the express aim of this Order was to abolish Christianity, and overturn all civil government. But the result of the enquiry was very imperfect and unsatisfactory. No Illuminati were to be found. They were unknown in the Lodge. Some of the members occasionally heard of certain candidates for illumination called MINERVALS, who were sometimes seen among them. But whether these had been admitted, or who received them, was known only to themselves. Some of these were examined in private by the Elector himself. They said that they were bound by honor to secrecy: But they assured the Elector, on their honor, that the aim of the Order was in the highest degree praiseworthy, and useful both to church and state: But this could not allay the anxiety of the profane public; and it was repeatedly stated to the Elector, that members of the Lodge Theodore had unguardedly spoken of this Order as one that in time must rule the world. He therefore issued an order forbidding, during his pleasure, all secret assemblies, and shutting up the Mason Lodges. It was not meant to be rigorously enforced, but was intended as a trial of the deference of these Associations for civil authority. The Lodge Theodore distinguished itself by pointed opposition, continuing its meetings; and the members, out of doors, openly reprobated the prohibition as an absurd and unjustifiable tyranny.

In the beginning of 1783, four professors of the Marianen Academy, founded by the widow of the late Elector, viz. Utschneider, Cossandey, Renner, and Grunberger, with two others, were summoned before the Court of Enquiry, and questioned, on their allegiance, respecting the Order of the Illuminati. They acknowledged that they belonged to it, and when more closely examined, they related several circumstances of its constitution and principles. Their declarations were immediately published, and were very unfavorable. The Order was said to abjure Christianity, and to refuse admission into the higher degrees to all who adhered to any of the three confessions. Sensual pleasures were restored to the rank they held in the Epicurean philosophy. Self-murder was justified on Stoical principles. In the Lodges death was declared an eternal sleep; patriotism and loyalty were called narrow-minded prejudices, and incompatible with universal benevolence; continual declamations were made on liberty and equality as the unalienable rights of man. The baneful influence of accumulated property was declared an insurmountable obstacle to the happiness of any nation whose chief laws were framed for its protection and increase. Nothing was so frequently discoursed of as the propriety of employing, for a good purpose, the means which the wicked employed for evil purposes; and it was taught, that the preponderancy of good in the ultimate result consecrated every mean employed; and that wisdom and virtue consisted in properly determining this balance. This appeared big with danger; because it appeared that nothing would be scrupled at, if we could make it appear that the Order could derive advantage from it, because the great object of the Order was held as superior to every consideration. They concluded by saying that the method of education made them all spies on each other and on all around them. But all this was denied by the Illuminati. Some of them were said to be absolutely false; and the rest were said to be mistakes. The apostate professors had acknowledged their ignorance of many things. Two of them were only Minervals, another was an Illuminatus of the lowest class, and the fourth was but one step farther advanced. Pamphlets appeared on both sides, with very little effect. The Elector called before him one of the superiors, a young nobleman, who denied these injurious charges, and said that they were ready to lay before his Highness their whole archives and all constitutional papers.

Notwithstanding all this, the government had received such an impression of the dangerous tendency of the Order, that the Elector issued another edict, forbidding all hidden assemblies; and a third, expressly abolishing the Order of Illuminati. It was followed by a search after their papers. The Lodge Theodore was immediately searched, but none were to be found. They said now that they had burnt them all, as of no use, since that Order was at an end.

It was now discovered, that Weishaupt was the head and founder of the Order. He was deprived of his Professor's chair, and banished from the Bavarian States; but with a pension of 800 florins, which he refused. He went to Regensburg, on the confines of Switzerland. Two Italians, the Marquis Constanza and Marquis Savioli, were also banished, with equal pensions (about L. 40) which they accepted. One Zwack, a counsellor, holding some law-office, was also banished. Others were imprisoned for some time. Weishaupt went afterwards into the service of the D. of Saxe Gotha, a person of a romantic turn of mind, and whom we shall again meet with. Zwack went into the service of the Pr. de Salms, who soon after had so great a hand in the disturbances in Holland.

By destroying the papers, all opportunity was lost for authenticating the innocence and usefulness of the Order. After much altercation and paper war, Weishaupt, now safe in Regensburg, published an account of the Order, namely, the account which was given to every *Novice* in a discourse read at his reception. To this were added, the statutes and the rules proceeding, as far as the degree of *Illuminatus Minor,* inclusive. This account he affirmed to be conform to the real practice of the Order. But this publication did by no means satisfy the public mind. It differed exceedingly from the accounts given by the four professors. It made no mention of the higher degrees, which had been most blamed by them. Besides, it was alleged, that it was all a fiction, written in order to lull the suspicions which had been raised (and this was found to be the case, except in respect of the very lowest degree.) The real constitution was brought to light by degrees, and shall be laid before the reader, in the order in which it was gradually discovered, that we may the better judge of things not fully known by the conduct of the leaders during the detection. The first account given by Weishaupt is correct, as far as I shall make use of it, and shows clearly the methods that were taken to recommend the Order to strangers.

The Order of ILLUMINATI appears as an accessory to

Free Masonry. It is in the Lodges of Free Masons that the Minervals are found, and there they are prepared for Illumination. They must have previously obtained the three English degrees. The founder says more. He says that his doctrines are the only true Free Masonry. He was the chief promoter of the *Eclectic System*. This he urged as the best method for getting information of all the explanations which have been given of the Masonic Mysteries. He was also a *Strict Observanz,* and an adept Rosycrucian. The result of all his knowledge is worthy of particular remark, and shall therefore be given at large.

"I declare," says he, "and I challenge all mankind to contradict my declaration, that no man can give any account of the Order of Free Masonry, of its origin, of its history, of its object, nor any explanation of its mysteries and symbols, which does not leave the mind in total uncertainty on all these points. Every man is entitled, therefore, to give any explanation of the symbols, and any system of the doctrines, that he can render palatable. Hence have sprung up that variety of systems which for twenty years have divided the Order. The simple tale of the English, and the fifty degrees of the French, and the Knights of Baron Hunde, are equally authentic, and have equally had the support of intelligent and zealous Brethren. These systems are in fact but one. They have all sprung from the Blue Lodge of Three degrees; take these for their standard, and found on these all the improvements by which each system is afterwards suited to the particular object which it keeps in view. There is no man, nor system, in the world, which can show by undoubted succession that it should stand at the head of the Order. Our ignorance in this particular frets me. Do but consider our short history of 120 years.— Who will show me the Mother Lodge? Those of London we have discovered to be self-erected in 1716. Ask for their archives. They tell you they were burnt. They have nothing but the wretched sophistications of the Englishman Anderson, and the Frenchman Desaguilliers. Where is the Lodge of York, which pretends to the priority, with their King Bouden, and the archives that he brought from the East? These too are all burnt. What is the Chapter of Old Aberdeen, and its Holy Clericate? Did we not find it unknown, and the Mason Lodges there the most ignorant of all the ignorant, gaping for instruction from our deputies? Did we not find the same thing at London? And have not their missionaries been among us, prying into our mysteries, and eager to learn from us what is true Free Masonry? It is in vain, therefore, to appeal to judges; they are no where to be found; all claim for themselves the sceptre of the Order; all indeed are on an equal footing. They obtained followers, not from their authenticity, but from their conduciveness to the end which they proposed, and from the importance of that end. It is by this scale that we must measure the mad and wicked explanations of the Rosycrucians, the Exorcists, and Cabalists. These are rejected by all good Masons, because incompatible with social happiness. Only such systems as promote this are retained. But alas, they are all sadly deficient, because they leave us under the dominion of political and religious prejudice; and they are as inefficient as the sleepy dose of an ordinary sermon.

"But I have contrived an explanation which has every advantage; is inviting to Christians of every communion; gradually frees them from all religious prejudices; cultivates the social virtues; and animates them by a great, a feasible, and *speedy* prospect of universal happiness, in a state of liberty and moral equality, freed from the obstacles which subordination, rank, and riches, continually throw in our way. My explanation is accurate, and complete, my means are effectual, and irresistible. Our secret Association works in a way that nothing can withstand, *and man shall soon be free and happy*.

"This is the great object held out by this Association: and the means of attaining it is Illumination, enlightening the understanding by the sun of reason, which will dispel the clouds of superstition and of prejudice. The proficients in this Order are therefore justly named the Illuminated. And of all Illumination which human reason can give, none is comparable to the discovery of what we are, our nature, our obligations, what happiness we are capable of, and what are the means of attaining it. In comparison with this, the most brilliant sciences are but amusements for the idle and luxurious. To fit man by Illumination for active virtue, to engage him to it by the strongest motives, to render the attainment of it easy and certain, by finding employment for every talent, and by placing every talent in its proper sphere of action, so that all, without feeling any extraordinary effort, and in conjunction with and completion of ordinary business, shall urge forward, with united powers, the general task. This indeed will be an employment suited to noble natures, grand in its views, and delightful in its exercise.

"And what is this general object? THE HAPPINESS OF THE HUMAN RACE. Is it not distressing to a generous mind, after contemplating what human nature is capable of, to see how little we enjoy? When we look at this goodly world, and see that every man *may* be happy, but that the happiness of one depends on the conduct of another; when we see the wicked so powerful, and the good so weak; and that it is in vain to strive, singly and alone, against the general current of vice and oppression; the wish naturally arises in the mind, that it were possible to form a durable combination of the most worthy persons, who should work together in removing the obstacles to human happiness, become terrible to the wicked, and give their aid to all the good without distinction, and should by the most powerful means, first fetter, and by fettering, lessen vice; means which at the same time should promote virtue, by rendering the inclination to rectitude, hitherto too feeble, more powerful and engaging. Would not such an association be a blessing to the world?

"But where are the proper persons, the good, the generous, and the accomplished, to be found? and how, and by what strong motives, are they to be induced to engage in a task so vast, so incessant, so difficult, and so laborious? This Association must be gradual. There *are* some such persons to be found in every society. Such noble minds will be engaged by the heart-warming object. The first task of the Association must therefore be to form the young members. As these multiply and advance, they become the apostles of beneficence, and the work is now on foot, and advances with a speed encreasing every day. The slightest observation shows that nothing will so much contribute to increase the zeal of the members as secret union. We see with what keenness and zeal the frivolous business of Free

Masonry is conducted, by persons knit together by the secrecy of their union. It is needless to enquire into the causes of this zeal which secrecy produces. It is an universal fact, confirmed by the history of every age. Let this circumstance of our constitution therefore be directed to this noble purpose, and then all the objections urged against it by jealous tyranny and affrighted superstition will vanish. The Order will thus work silently, and securely; and though the generous benefactors of the human race are thus deprived of the applause of the world, they have the noble pleasure of seeing their work prosper in their hands."

Such is the aim, and such are the hopes of the Order of the Illuminated. Let us now see how these were to be accomplished. We cannot judge precisely of this, because the account given of the constitution of the Order by its founder includes only the lowest degree, and even this is suspected to be fictitious. The accounts given by the four Professors, even of this part of the Order, make a very different impression on the mind, although they differ only in a few particulars.

The only ostensible members of the Order were the Minervals. They were to be found only in the Lodges of Free Masons. A candidate for admission must make his wish known to some Minerval; he reports it to a Superior, who, by a channel to be explained presently, intimates it to the Council. No notice is farther taken of it for some time. The candidate is carefully observed in silence, and if thought unfit for the Order, no notice is taken of his solicitation. But if otherwise, the candidate receives privately an invitation to a conference. Here he meets with a person unknown to him, and, previous to all further conference, he is required to peruse and to sign the following oath.

"I N. N. hereby bind myself, by mine honor and good name, forswearing all mental reservation, never to reveal, by hint, word, writing, or in any manner whatever, even to my most trusted friend, any thing that shall now be said or done to me respecting my wished-for-reception, and this whether my reception shall follow or not; I being previously assured that it shall contain nothing contrary to religion, the state, nor good manners. I promise, that I shall make no intelligible extract from any papers which shall be shewn me now or during my noviciate. All this I swear, as I am, and as I hope to continue, a Man of Honor."

The urbanity of this protestation must agreeably impress the mind of a person who recollects the dreadful imprecations which he made at his reception into the different ranks of Free Masonry. The candidate is then introduced to an *Illuminatus Dirigens,* whom perhaps he knows, and is told that this person is to be his future instructor. There is now presented to the candidate, what they call a table, in which he writes his name, place of birth, age, rank, place of residence, profession, and favorite studies. He is then made to read several articles of this table. It contains, 1st. a very concise account of the Order, its connection with Free Masonry, and its great object, the promoting the happiness of mankind by means of instruction and confirmation in virtuous principles. 2d. Several questions relative to the Order. Among these are, "What advantages he hopes to derive from being a member? What he most particularly wishes to learn? What delicate questions relative to the life, the prospects, the duties of man, as an individual, and as a citizen, he wishes to have particularly discussed to him? In what respects he thinks he can be of use to the Order? Who are his ancestors, relations, friends, correspondents, or enemies? Whom he thinks proper persons to be received into the Order, or whom he thinks unfit for it, and the reasons for both opinions. To each of these questions he must give some answer in writing.

The Novice and his Mentor are known only to each other; perhaps nothing more follows upon this; if otherwise, the Mentor appoints another conference, and begins his instructions, by giving him in detail certain portions of the constitution, and of the fundamental rules of the Order. Of these the Novice must give a weekly account in writing. He must also read, in the Mentor's house, a book containing more of the instructions of the Order; but he must make no extracts. Yet from this reading he must derive all his knowledge; and he must give an account in writing of his progress. All writings received from his Superiors must be returned with a stated punctuality. These writings consist chiefly of important and delicate questions,

suited, either to the particular inclination, or to the peculiar
taste which the candidate had discovered in his subscriptions of the articles of the table, and in his former rescripts,
or to the direction which the Mentor wishes to give to his
thoughts.

Enlightening the understanding, and the rooting out of
prejudices, are pointed out to him as the principal tasks of
his noviciate. The knowledge of himself is considered as
preparatory to all other knowledge. To disclose to him,
by means of the calm and unbiassed observation of his
instructor, what is his own character, his most vulnerable
side, either in respect of temper, passions, or prepossessions,
is therefore the most essential service that can be done him.
For this purpose there is required of him some account of
his own conduct on occasions where he doubted of its
propriety; some account of his friendships, of his differences of opinion, and of his conduct on such occasions.
From such relations the Superior learns his manner of
thinking and judging, and those propensities which require
his chief attention.

Having made the candidate acquainted with himself, he
is apprised that the Order is not a speculative, but an active
association, engaged in doing good to others. The knowledge of human character is therefore of all others the most
important. This is acquired only by observation, assisted
by the instructions of his teacher. Characters in history are
proposed to him for observation, and his opinion is required. After this he is directed to look around him, and to
notice the conduct of other men; and part of his weekly
rescripts must consist of accounts of all interesting occurrences in his neigbourhood, whether of a public or private
nature. Cossandey, one of the four Professors, gives a particular account of the instructions relating to this kind of
science. "The Novice must be attentive to trifles: For, in
frivolous occurrences a man is indolent, and makes no effort
to act a part, so that his real character is then acting alone.
Nothing will have such influence with the Superiors in
promoting the advancement of a candidate as very copious
narrations of this kind, because the candidate, if promoted,
is to be employed in an active station, and it is from this
kind of information only that the Superiors can judge of

his fitness. These characteristic anecdotes are not for the instruction of the Superiors, who are men of long experience, and familiar with such occupation. But they inform the Order concerning the talents and proficiency of the young member. Scientific instruction, being connected by system, is soon communicated, and may in general be very completely obtained from the books which are recommended to the Novice, and acquired in the public seminaries of instruction. But knowledge of character is more multifarious and more delicate. For this there is no college, and it must therefore require longer time for its attainment. Besides, this assiduous and long continued study of men, enables the possessor of such knowledge to act with men, and by his knowledge of their character, to influence their conduct. For such reasons this study is continued, and these rescripts are required, during the whole progress through the Order, and attention to them is recommended as the only mean of advancement. Remarks on Physiognomy in these narrations are accounted of considerable value." So far Mr. Cossandey.

During all this trial, which may last one, two, or three years, the Novice knows no person of the Order but his own instructor, with whom he has frequent meetings, along with other Minervals. In these conversations he learns the importance of the Order, and the opportunities he will afterwards have of acquiring much hidden science. The employment of his unknown Superiors naturally causes him to entertain very high notions of their abilities and worth. He is counselled to aim at a resemblance to them by getting rid by degrees of all those prejudices or prepossessions which checked his own former progress; and he is assisted in this endeavour by an invitation to a correspondence with them. He may address his Provincial Superior, by directing his letter *Soli,* or the General by *Primo,* or the Superiors in general by *Quibus licet.* In these letters he may mention whatever he thinks conducive to the advancement of the Order; he may inform the Superiors how his instructor behaves to him; if assiduous or remiss, indulgent or severe. The Superiors are enjoined by the strongest motives to convey these letters wherever addressed. None but the General and Council know the result of all this; and all are enjoined to keep themselves and their proceedings unknown to all the world.

If three years of this Noviciate have elapsed without further notice, the Minerval must look for no further advancement; he is found unfit, and remains a Free Mason of the highest class. This is called a *Sta bene*.

But should his Superiors judge more favorably of him, he is drawn out of the general mass of Free Masons, and becomes *Illuminatus Minor*. When called to a conference for this purpose, he is told in the most serious manner, that "it is vain for him to hope to acquire wisdom by mere systematic instruction; for such instruction the Superiors have no leisure. Their duty is not to form speculators, but active men, whom they must *immediately* employ in the service of the Order. He must therefore grow wise and able entirely by the unfolding and exertion of his own talents. His Superiors have already discovered what these are, and know what service he may be capable of rendering the Order, provided he now heartily acquiesces in being thus honorably employed. They will assist him in bringing his talents into action, and will place him in the situations most favorable for their exertion, so that he may be *assured* of success. Hitherto he has been a mere scholar, but his first step farther carries him into action; he must therefore now consider himself as an instrument in the hands of his Superiors, to be used for the noblest purposes." The aim of the Order is now more fully told him. It is, in one sentence, "to make of the human race, without any distinction of nation, condition, or profession, one good and happy family." To this aim, demonstrably attainable, every smaller consideration must give way. This may sometimes require sacrifices which no man standing alone has fortitude to make; but which become light, and a source of the purest enjoyment, when supported and encouraged by the countenance and co-operation of the united wise and good, such as are the Superiors of the Order. If the candidate, warmed by the alluring picture of the possible happiness of a virtuous Society, says that he is sensible of the propriety of this procedure, and still wishes to be of the Order, he is required to sign the following obligation.

"I, N. N. protest before you, the worthy Plenipotentiary of the venerable Order into which I wish to be admitted, that I acknowledge my natural weakness and inability, and that I, with all my possessions, rank, honors, and titles which I hold in political society, am, at bottom, only a man; I can enjoy these things only through my fellow-men, and through them also I may lose them. The approbation and consideration of my fellow-men are indispensibly necessary, and I must try to maintain them by all my talents. These I will never use to the prejudice of universal good, but will oppose, with all my might, the enemies of the human race, and of political society. I will embrace every opportunity of saving mankind, by improving my understanding and my affections, and by imparting all important knowledge, as the good and statutes of this Order require of me. I bind myself to perpetual silence and unshaken loyalty and submission to the Order, in the persons of my Superiors; here making a faithful and complete surrender of my private judgment, my own will, and every narrow-minded employment of my power and influence. I pledge myself to account the good of the Order as my own, and am ready to serve it with my fortune, my honor, and my blood. Should I, through omission, neglect, passion, or wickedness, behave contrary to this good of the Order, I subject myself to what reproof or punishment my Superiors shall enjoin. The friends and enemies of the Order shall be my friends and enemies; and with respect to both I will conduct myself as directed by the Order, and am ready, in every lawful way, to devote myself to its increase and promotion, and therein to employ all my ability. All this I promise, and protest, without secret reservation, according to the intention of the Society which require from me this engagement. This I do as I am, and as I hope to continue, a Man of Honor."

A drawn sword is then pointed at his breast, and he is asked, Will you be obedient to the commands of your Superiors? He is threatened with unavoidable vengeance, from which no potentate can defend him, if he should ever betray the Order. He is then asked, 1. What aim does he wish the Order to have? 2. What means he would choose to advance this aim? 3. Whom he wishes to keep out of the Order? 4. What subjects he wishes not to be discussed in it?

Our candidate is now ILLUMINATUS MINOR. It is needless to narrate the mummery of reception, and it is enough to say, that it nearly resembles that of the *Masonic Chevalier du Soleil,* known to every one much conversant in Masonry. Weishaupt's preparatory discourse of reception is a piece of good composition, whether considered as argumentative (from topics, indeed, that are very gratuitous and fanciful) or as a specimen of that declamation which was so much practised by Libanius and the other Sophists, and it gives a distinct and captivating account of the professed aim of the Order.

The *Illuminatus Minor* learns a good deal more of the Order, but by very sparing morsels, under the same instructor. The task has now become more delicate and difficult. The chief part of it is the rooting out of prejudices in politics and religion; and Weishaupt has shown much address in the method which he has employed. Not the most hurtful, but the most easily refuted, were the first subjects of discussion, so that the pupil gets into the habits of victory; and his reverence for the systems of either kind is diminished when they are found to have harboured such untenable opinions. The proceedings in the Eclectic Lodges of Masonry, and the harangues of the Brother Orators, teemed with the boldest sentiments both in politics and religion. Enlightening, and the triumph of reason, had been the *ton* of the country for some time past, and every institution, civil and religious, had been the subject of the most free criticism. Above all, the Cosmo-politism, which had been imported from France, where it had been the favorite topic of the enthusiastical œconomists, was now become a general theme of discussion in all societies of cultivated men. It was a subject of easy and agreeable declamation; and the Literati found in it a subject admirably fitted for showing their talents, and ingratiating themselves with the young men of fortune, whose minds, unsuspicious as yet and generous, were fired with the fair prospects set before them of universal and attainable happiness. And the pupils of the Illuminati were still more warmed by the thought that they were to be the happy instruments of accomplishing all this. And though the doctrines of universal liberty and equality, as imprescriptible rights of man, might sometimes startle those who possessed the advantage of fortune, there were thousands of younger sons, and of men of talents without fortune, to whom these were agreeable sounds. And we must particularly observe, that those who were now the pupils were a set of picked subjects, whose characters and peculiar biases were well known by their conduct during their noviciate as Minervals. They were therefore such as, in all probability, would not boggle at very free sentiments. We might rather expect a partiality to doctrines which removed some restraints which formerly checked them in the indulgence of youthful passions. Their instructors, who have thus relieved their minds from several anxious thoughts, must appear men of superior minds. This was a notion most carefully inculcated; and they could see nothing to contradict it: for except their own Mentor, they knew none; they heard of Superiors of different ranks, but never saw them; and the same mode of instruction that was practised during their noviciate was still retained. More particulars of the Order were slowly unfolded to them, and they were taught that their Superiors were men of distinguished talents, and were Superiors for this reason alone. They were taught, that the great opportunities which the Superiors had for observation, and their habits of continually occupying their thoughts with the great objects of this Order, had enlarged their views, even far beyond the narrow limits of nations and kingdoms, which they hoped would one day coalesce into one great Society, where consideration would attach to talents and worth alone, and that pre-eminence in these would be invariably attended with all the enjoyments of influence and power. And they were told that they would gradually become acquainted with these great and venerable Characters, as they advanced in the Order. In earnest of this, they were made acquainted with one or two Superiors, and with several Illuminati of their own rank. Also, to whet their zeal, they are now made instructors of one or two Minervals, and report their progress to their Superiors. They are given to understand that nothing can so much recommend them as the success with which they perform this task. It is declared to be the best evidence of their usefulness in the great designs of the Order.

The baleful effects of general superstition, and even of any peculiar religious prepossession, are now strongly inculcated, and the discernment of the pupils in these matters is learned by questions which are given them from time to time to discuss. These are managed with delicacy and circumspection, that the timid may not be alarmed. In like manner, the political doctrines of the Order are inculcated with the utmost caution. After the mind of the pupil has been warmed by the pictures of universal happiness, and convinced that it is a possible thing to unite all the inhabitants of the earth in one great society, and after it has been made out, in some measure to the satisfaction of the pupil, that a great addition of happiness is gained by the abolition of national distinctions and animosities, it may frequently be no hard task to make him think that patriotism is a narrow-minded monopolising sentiment, and even incompatible with the more enlarged views of the Order, namely, the uniting the whole human race into one great and happy society. Princes are a chief feature of national distinction. Princes, therefore, may now be safely represented as unnecessary. If so, loyalty to Princes loses much of its sacred character; and the so frequent enforcing of it in our common political discussions may now be easily made to appear a selfish maxim of rulers, by which they may more easily enslave the people; and thus, it may at last appear, that religion, the love of our particular country, and loyalty to our Prince, should be resisted, if, by these partial or narrow views, we prevent the accomplishment of that Cosmo-political happiness which is continually held forth as the great object of the Order. It is in this point of view that the terms of devotion to the Order which are inserted in the oath of admission are now explained. The authority of the ruling powers is therefore represented as of inferior moral weight to that of the Order. "These powers are despots, when they do not conduct themselves by its principles; and it is therefore our duty to surround them with its members, so that the profane may have no access to them. Thus we are able most powerfully to promote its interests. If any person is more disposed to listen to Princes than to the Order, he is not fit for it, and must rise no higher. We must do our utmost to procure the advancement of Illuminati into all important civil offices."

Accordingly the Order laboured in this with great zeal and success. A correspondence was discovered, in which it is plain, that by their influence, one of the greatest ecclesiastical dignities was filled up in opposition to the right and authority of the Archbishop of Spire, who is there represented as a tyrannical and bigotted priest. They contrived to place their Members as tutors to the youth of distinction. One of them, Baron Leuchtsenring, took the charge of a young prince without any salary. They insinuated themselves into all public offices, and particularly into courts of justice. In like manner, the chairs in the University of Ingolstadt were (with only two exceptions) occupied by Illuminati. "Rulers who are members must be promoted through the ranks of the Order only in proportion as they acknowledge the goodness of its great object, and manner of procedure. Its object may be said to be the checking the tyranny of princes, nobles, and priests, and establishing an universal equality of condition and of religion." The pupil is now informed "that such a religion is contained in the Order, is the perfection of Christianity, and will be imparted to him in due time."

These and other principles and maxims of the Order are partly communicated by the verbal instruction of the Mentor, partly by writings, which must be punctually returned, and partly read by the pupil at the Mentor's house (but without taking extracts) in such portions as he shall direct. The rescripts by the pupil must contain discussions on these subjects, and of anecdotes and descriptions of living characters; and these must be zealously continued, as the chief mean of advancement. All this while the pupil knows only his Mentor, the Minervals, and a few others of his own rank. All mention of degrees, or other business of the Order, must be carefully avoided, even in the meetings with other Members: "For the Order wishes to be secret, and to work in silence; for thus it is better secured from the oppression of the ruling powers, and because this secrecy gives a greater zest to the whole."

This short account of the *Noviciate*, and of the lowest class of Illuminati, is all we can get from the authority of Mr. Weishaupt. The higher degrees were not published by him. Many circumstances appear suspicious, and are certainly susceptible of different turns, and may easily be pushed to very dangerous extremes. The accounts given by the four professors confirm these suspicions. They declare upon oath, that they make all these accusations in consequence of what they heard in the Meetings, and of what they knew of the Higher Orders.

But since the time of the suppression by the Elector, discoveries have been made which throw great light on the subject. A collection of original papers and correspondence was found by searching the house of one Zwack (a Member) in 1786. The following year a much larger collection was found at the house of Baron Bassus; and since that time Baron Knigge, the most active Member next to Weishaupt, published an account of some of the higher degrees, which had been formed by himself. A long while after this were published, *Neueste Arbeitung des Spartacus und Philo in der Illuminaten Orden,* and *Hohere Granden des Illum. Ordens.* These two works give an account of the whole secret constitution of the Order, its various degrees, the manner of conferring them, the instructions to the intrants, and an explanation of the connection of the Order with Free Masonry, and a critical history. We shall give some extracts from such of these as have been published.

Weishaupt was the founder in 1776. In 1778 the number of Members was considerably increased, and the Order was fully established. The Members took antique names. Thus Weishaupt took the name of Spartacus, the man who headed the insurrection of slaves, which in Pompey's time kept Rome in terror and uproar for three years. Zwack was called Cato. Knigge was Philo. Bassus was Hannibal. Hertel was Marius. Marquis Constanza was Diomedes. Nicholai, an eminent and learned bookseller in Berlin, and author of several works of reputation, took the name of Lucian, the great scoffer at all religion. Another was Mahomet, &c. It is remarkable, that except Cato and Socrates, we have not a name of any ancient who was eminent as a teacher and practiser of virtue. On the contrary, they seem to have affected the characters of the free-thinkers and turbulent spirits of antiquity. In the same manner they gave ancient names to the cities and countries of Europe. Munich was Athens, Vienna was Rome, &c.

### Spartacus to Cato, Feb. 6, 1778.

"*Mon but est de faire valoir la raison.* As a subordinate object I shall endeavour to gain security to ourselves, a backing in case of misfortunes, and assistance from without. I shall therefore press the cultivation of science, especially such sciences as may have an influence on our reception in the world, and may serve to remove obstacles out of the way. We have to struggle with pedantry, with intolerance, with divines and statesmen, and above all, princes and priests are in our way. Men are unfit as they are, and must be formed; each class must be the school of trial for the next. This will be tedious, because it is hazardous. In the last classes I propose academies under the direction of the Order. This will secure us the adherence of the Literati. Science shall here be the lure. Only those who are assuredly proper subjects shall be picked out from among the inferior classes for the higher mysteries, which contain the first principles and means of promoting a happy life. No religionist must, on any account, be admitted into these: For here we work at the discovery and extirpation of superstition and prejudices. The instructions shall be so conducted that each shall disclose what he thinks he conceals within his own breast, what are his ruling propensities and passions, and how far he has advanced in the command of himself. This will answer all the purposes of auricular confession. And in particular, every person shall be made a spy on another and on all around him. Nothing can escape our sight; by these means we shall readily discover who are contented, and receive with relish the peculiar state-doctrines and religious opinions that are laid before them; and, at last, the trust-worthy alone will be admitted to a participation of the whole maxims and political constitution of the Order. In a council composed of such members we shall labour at the contrivance of means to drive by degrees the enemies of reason and of humanity out of the world, and to establish a peculiar morality and religion fitted for the great Society of mankind.

"But this is a ticklish project, and requires the utmost circumspection. The squeamish will start at the sight of religious or political novelties; and they must be prepared for them. We must be particularly careful about the books which we recommend; I shall confine them at first to moralists and reasoning historians. This will prepare for a patient reception, in the higher classes, of works of a bolder flight, such as Robinet's *Systeme de la Nature—Politique Naturelle—Philosophie de la Nature—Systeme Social—*The writings of Mirabaud, &c. Helvetius is fit only for the strongest stomachs. If any one has a copy already, neither praise nor find fault with him. Say nothing on such subjects to intrants, for we don't know how they will be received—folks are not yet prepared. Marius, an excellent man, must be dealt with. His stomach, which cannot yet digest such strong food, must acquire a better tone. The allegory on which I am to found the mysteries of the Higher Orders is *the fire-worship of the Magi.* We must have some worship, and none is so apposite. LET THERE BE LIGHT, AND THERE SHALL BE LIGHT. This is my motto, and is my fundamental principle. The degrees will be *Feurer Orden, Parsen Orden;** all very practicable. In the course through these there will be no STA BENE (this is the answer given to one who solicits preferment, and is refused.) For I engage that none shall enter this class who has not laid aside his prejudices. No man is fit for our Order who is not a Brutus or a Catiline, and is not ready to go every length.—Tell me how you like this?"

### Spartacus to Cato, March 1778.

"To collect unpublished works, and information from the archives of States, will be a most useful service. We shall be able to show in a very ridiculous light the claims of our despots. Marius (keeper of the archives of the Electorate) has ferreted out a noble document, which we have got. He makes it, forsooth, a case of conscience—how silly that—since only that is *sin,* which is *ultimately* productive of mischief. In this case, where the advantage far exceeds the hurt, it is meritorious virtue. It will do more good in our hands than by remaining for 1000 years on the dusty shelf."

*This is evidently the *Mystere du Mithrus* mentioned by Barruel, in his History of Jacobinism, and had been carried into France by Bede and Busche.

There was found in the hand-writing of Zwack a project for a Sisterhood, in subserviency to the designs of the Illuminati. In it are the following passages:

"It will be of great service, and procure us both much information *and money,* and will suit charmingly the taste of many of our truest members, who are lovers of the sex. It should consist of two classes, the virtuous, and the freer hearted (i.e. those who fly out of the common tract of prudish manners); they must not know of each other, and must be under the direction of men, but without knowing it. Proper books must be put into their hands, and such (but secretly) as are flattering to their passions."

There are, in the same hand-writing, Description of a strong box, which, if forced open, shall blow up and destroy its contents—Several receipts for procuring abortion—A composition which blinds or kills when spurted in the face—A sheet, containing a receipt for sympathetic ink—Tea for procuring abortion—*Herbæ quæ habent qualitatem deleteriam*—A method for filling a bed-chamber with pestilential vapours—How to take off impressions of seals, so as to use them afterwards as seals—A collection of some hundreds of such impressions, with a list of their owners, princes, nobles, clergymen, merchants, &c.—A receipt *ad excitandum furorem uterinum*—A manuscript entitled, "Better than Horus." It was afterwards printed and distributed at Leipzig fair, and is an attack and bitter satire on all religion. This is in the hand-writing of Ajax. As also a dissertation on suicide. N. B. His sister-in-law threw herself from the top of a tower. There was also a set of portraits, or characters of eighty-five ladies in Munich; with recommendations of some of them for members of a Lodge of Sister Illuminatæ; also injunctions to all the Superiors to learn to write with both hands; and that they should use more than one cypher.

Immediately after the publication of these writings, many defences appeared. It was said that the dreadful medical apparatus were with propriety in the hands of Counsellor Zwack, who was a judge of a criminal court, and whose duty it was therefore to know such things. The same excuse was offered for the collection of seals; but how came these things to be put up with papers of the Illuminati, and to be in the hand writing of one of that Order? Weishaupt says, "These things were not carried into effect—only spoken of, and are justifiable when taken in proper connection." This however he has not pointed out; but he appeals to the account of the Order, which he had published at Regensburg, and in which neither these things are to be found, nor any possibility of a connection by which they may be justified. "All men, says he, are subject to errors, and the best man is he who best conceals them. I have never been guilty of any such vices or follies: for proof, I appeal to the whole tenor of my life, which my reputation, and my struggles with hostile cabals, had brought completely into public view long before the institution of this Order, without abating any thing of that flattering regard which was paid to me by the first persons of my country and its neighbourhood; a regard well evinced by their confidence in me as the best instructor of their children." In some of his private letters, we learn the means which he employed to acquire this influence among the youth, and they are such as could not fail. But we must not anticipate. "It is well known that I have made the chair which I occupied in the university of Ingolstadt, the resort of the first class of the German youth; whereas formerly it had only brought round it the low-born practitioners in the courts of law. I have gone through the whole circle of human enquiry. I have exorcised spirits—raised ghosts—discovered treasures—interrogated the Cabala—*hatte Loto gespielt*—I have never transmuted metals."—(A very pretty and respectable circle indeed, and what vulgar spirits would scarcely have included within the pale of their curiosity.) "The tenor of my life has been the opposite of every thing that is vile; and no man can lay any such thing to my charge. I have reason to rejoice that these writings have appeared; they are a vindication of the Order and of my conduct. I can, and must declare to God, and I do it now in the most solemn manner, that in my whole life I never saw or heard of the so much condemned secret writings; and in particular, respecting these abominable means; such as poisoning, abortion, &c. was it ever known to me in any case, that any of my friends or acquaintances ever even thought of them, advised them, or made any use of them. I was indeed always a schemer and projector, but never could engage much in detail. My general plan is good, though in the detail there may be faults. I had myself to form. In another situation, and in an active station in life, I should have been keenly occupied, and the founding an Order would never have come into my head. But I would have executed much greater things, had not government always opposed my exertions, and placed others in the situations which suited my talents. It was the full conviction of this, and of what could be done, if every man were placed in the office for which he was fitted by nature and a proper education, which first suggested to me the plan of illumination." Surely Mr. Weishaupt had a very serious charge, the education of youth; and his encouragement in that charge was the most flattering that an Illuminatus could wish for, because he had brought round him the youth whose influence in society was the greatest and who would most of all contribute to the diffusing good principles, and exciting to good conduct through the whole state. "I did not," says he, "bring deism into Bavaria more than into Rome. I found it here, in great vigour, more abounding than in any of the neighbouring Protestant states. I am proud to be known to the world as the founder of the Order of Illuminati; and I repeat my wish to have for my epitaph,

*"Hic situs est Phaethon, currûs auriga paterni,*
*"Quem si non tenuit, magnis tamen excidit ausis."*

The second discovery of secret correspondence at Sandersdorff, the feat of Baron Batz (Hannibal) contains still more interesting facts.

### Spartacus to Cato.

"What shall I do? I am deprived of all help. Socrates, who would insist on being a man of consequence among us, and is really a man of talents, and of a *right way of thinking,* is eternally besotted. Augustus is in the worst estimation imaginable. Alcibiades sits the day long with the vintner's pretty wife, and there he sighs and pines. A few days ago, at Corinth, Tiberius attempted to ravish the wife of Democides, and her husband came in upon them. Good heavens! what *Areopagitæ* I have got. When the worthy man Marcus Aurelius comes to Athens (Munich) what will he think? What a meeting with dissolute immoral wretches, whore-masters, liars, bankrupts, braggarts, and vain fools! When he sees all this, what will he think? He will be ashamed to enter into an Association," (observe, Reader, that Spartacus writes this in August 1783, in the very time that he was trying to murder Cato's sister) "where the chiefs raise the highest expectations, and exhibit such a wretched example; and all this from self-will, from sensuality. Am I not in the right—that this man—that any such worthy man—whose name alone would give us the selection of all Germany—will declare that the whole province of Grecia (Bavaria) innocent and guilty, must be excluded. I tell you, we may study; and write, and toil till death. We may sacrifice to the Order, our health, our fortune, and our reputation (alas the loss!) and these Lords, following their own pleasures, will whore, cheat, steal, and drive on like shameless rascals; and yet must be *Areopagitæ*, and interfere in every thing. Indeed, my dearest friend, we have only enslaved ourselves."

In another part of this fine correspondence, Diomedes has had the good fortune to intercept a Q. L. (*Quibus licet*) in which it is said, and supported by proofs, that Cato had received 250 florins as a bribe for his sentence in his capacity as a judge in a criminal court; (the end had surely sanctified the means.) In another, a Minerval complains of his Mentor for having by lies occasioned the dismission of a physician from a family, by which he obtained the custom of the house and free access, which favor he repaid by debauching the wife; and he prays to be informed whether he may not get another Mentor, saying, that although that man had always given him the most excellent instructions, and he doubted not would continue them, yet he felt a disgust at the hypocrisy, which would certainly diminish the impression of the most salutary truths. (Is it not distressing to think, that this promising youth will by and by laugh at his former simplicity, and follow the steps and not the instructions of his physician.) In another place, Spartacus writes to Marius (in confidence) that another worthy Brother, an *Areopagitæ*, had stolen a gold and a silver watch, and a ring, from Brutus *(Savioli)* and begs Marius, in another letter, to try, while it was yet possible, to get the things restored, because the culprit was a most *excellent man (Vortrefflich)* and of vast use to the Order, having the direction of an eminent seminary of young *gentlemen;* and because Savioli was much in good company, and did not much care for the Order, except in so far as it gave him an opportunity of knowing and leading some of them, and of steering his way at court.

I cannot help inserting here, though not the most proper place, a part of a provincial report from Knigge, the man of the whole *Areopagitæ* who shows any thing like urbanity or gentleness of mind.

"Of my whole colony (Westphalia) the most brilliant is Claudiopolis *(Neuwied.)* There they work, and direct, and do wonders."

If there ever was a spot upon earth where men may be happy in a state of cultivated society, it was the little principality of Neuwied. I saw it in 1770. The town was neat, and the palace handsome and in good taste; all was clean. But the country was beyond conception delightful; not a cottage that was out of repair, not a hedge out of order; it had been the hobby (pardon me the word) of the Prince, who made it his *daily* employment to go through his principality regularly, and assist every householder, of whatever condition, with his advice, and with his purse; and, when a freeholder could not of himself put things into a thriving condition, the Prince sent his workmen and did it for him. He endowed schools for the common people, and two academies for the gentry and the people of business. He gave little portions to the daughters, and prizes to the well-behaving sons of the labouring people. His own household was a pattern of elegance and economy; his sons were sent to Paris to learn elegance, and to England to learn science and agriculture. In short, the whole was like a romance (and was indeed romantic.) I heard it spoken of with a smile at the table of the Bishop of Treves, at Ehrenbretstein, and was induced to see it next day as a curiosity: And yet even here, the fanaticism of Knigge would distribute his poison, and tell the blinded people, that they were in a state of sin and misery, that their Prince was a despot, and that they would never be happy till he was made to fly, and till they were all made equal.

They got their wish; the swarm of French locusts sat down on Neuwied's beautiful fields in 1793, and entrenched themselves; and in three months, Prince and farmers houses, and cottages, and schools, and academies—all vanished; and all the subjects were made equal, and free (as they were expressly told by the French General) to weep.

*Discite justitiam moniti, et non temnere divos!*

To proceed:

### Spartacus to Cato.

"By this plan we shall direct all mankind. In this manner, and by the simplest means, we shall set all in motion and in flames. The occupations must be so allotted and contrived, that we may, in secret, influence all political transactions." N. B. This alludes to a part that is withheld from the public, because it contained the allotment of the most rebellious and profligate occupations to several persons whose common names could not be traced. "I have considered," says Spartacus, "every thing, and so prepared it, that if the Order should this day go to ruin, I shall in a year re-establish it more brilliant than ever." Accordingly it got up again in about this space of time, under the name of the GERMAN UNION, appearing in the form of READING SOCIETIES. One of these was set up in Zwack's house; and this raising a suspicion, a visitation was made at Landshut, and the first set of the private papers were found. The scheme was, however, zealously prosecuted in other parts of Germany, as we shall see by and by. "Nor," continues Spartacus, "will it signify though all should be betrayed and printed. I am so certain of success, in spite of all obstacles (for the springs are in every heart) that I am indifferent, though it should involve my life and my liberty. What! Have thousands thrown away their lives about *homoios* and *homoiousios,* and shall not this cause warm even the heart of a coward? But I have the art to draw advantage even from misfortune; and when you would think me sunk to the bottom, I shall rise with new vigour. Who would have thought, that a professor at Ingolstadt was to become the teacher of the professors of Gottingen, and of the greatest men in Germany?"

## Spartacus to Cato.

"Send me back my degree of *Illuminatus Minor;* it is the wonder of all men here (I may perhaps find time to give a translation of the discourse of reception, which contains all that can be said of this Association to the public;) as also the two last sheets of my degree, which is in the keeping of Marius, and Celsus, under 100 locks which contains my history of the lives of the Patriarchs." N. B. Nothing very particular has been discovered of these lives of the Patriarchs. He says, that there were above sixty sheets of it. To judge by the care taken of it, it must be a favorite work, very hazardous, and very catching.

In another letter to Cato, we have some hints of the higher degrees, and concerning a peculiar morality, and a popular religion, which the Order was one day to give the world. He says, "There must *(a la Jesuite)* not a single purpose ever come in sight that is ambiguous, and that may betray our aims against religion and the state. One must speak sometimes one way and sometimes another, but so as never to contradict ourselves, and so that, with respect to our true way of thinking, we may be impenetrable. When our strongest things chance to give offence, they must be explained as attempts to draw answers which discover to us the sentiments of the person we converse with." N. B. This did not always succeed with him.

Spartacus says, speaking of the priests degree, "One would almost imagine, that this degree, as I have managed it, is genuine Christianity, and that its end was to free the Jews from slavery. I say, that Free Masonry is concealed Christianity. My explanation of the hieroglyphics, at least, proceeds on this supposition; and as I explain things, no man need be ashamed of being a Christian. Indeed I afterwards throw away this name, and substitute *Reason.* But I assure you this is no small affair; a new religion, and a new state-government, which so happily explain one and all of these symbols, and combines them in one degree, You may think that this is my chief work; but I have three other degrees, all different, for my class of higher mysteries, in comparison with which this is but child's play; but these I keep for myself as General, to be bestowed by me only on the *Benemeritissimi*," (surely such as Cato, his dearest friend, and the possessor of such pretty secrets, as abortives, poisons, pestilential vapours, &c.) "The promoted may be Areopagites or not. Were you here I should give you this degree without hesitation. But it is too important to be intrusted to paper, or to be bestowed otherwise than from my own hand. It is the key to history, to religion, and to every state-government in the world."*

Spartacus proceeds, "There shall be but three copies for all Germany. You can't imagine what respect and curiosity my priest-degree has raised; and, which is wonderful, a famous Protestant divine, who is now of the Order, is persuaded that the religion contained in it is the true sense of Christianity. O MAN, MAN! TO WHAT MAY'ST THOU NOT BE PERSUADED. Who would imagine that I was to be the founder of a new religion."

In this scheme of Masonic Christianity, Spartacus and Philo laboured seriously together. Spartacus sent him the materials, and Philo worked them up. It will therefore illustrate this capital point of the constitution of the Order, if we take Philo's account of it.

### Philo to Cato.

"We must consider the ruling propensities of every age of the world. At present the cheats and tricks of the priests have roused all men against them, and against Christianity. But, at the same time superstition and fanaticism rule with unlimited dominion, and the understanding of man really seems to be going backwards. Our task, therefore, is doubled. We must give such an account of things, that fanatics shall not be alarmed, and that shall, notwithstanding, excite a spirit of free enquiry. We must not throw away the good with the bad, the child with the dirty water; but we must

---

*I observe, in other parts of his correspondence where he speaks of this, several singular phrases, which are to be found in two books; *Antiquité devoilée par ses Usages,* and *Origine du Despotisme Oriental.* These contain indeed much of the maxims inculcated in the reception discourse of the degree *Illuminatus Minor.* Indeed I have found, that Weishaupt is much less an inventor than he is generally thought.

make the secret doctrines of Christianity be received as the secrets of genuine Free Masonry. But farther, we have to deal with the despotism of Princes. This increases every day. But then, the spirit of freedom breathes and sighs in every corner; and, by the assistance of hidden schools of wisdom, Liberty and Equality, the natural and imprescriptible rights of man, warm and glow in every breast. We must therefore unite these extremes. We proceed in this manner.

"Jesus Christ established no new Religion; he would only set Religion and Reason in their ancient rights. For this purpose he would unite men in a common bond. He would fit them for this by spreading a just morality, by enlightening the understanding, and by assisting the mind to shake off all prejudices. He would teach all men, in the first place, to govern themselves. Rulers would then be needless, and equality and liberty would take place without any revolution, by the natural and gentle operation of reason and expediency. This great Teacher allows himself to explain every part of the Bible in conformity to these purposes; and he forbids all wrangling among his scholars, because every man may there find a reasonable application to his peculiar doctrines. Let this be true or false, it does not signify. This was a simple Religion, and it was so far inspired; but the minds of his hearers were not fitted for receiving these doctrines. I told you, says he, but you could not bear it. Many therefore were called, but few were chosen. To these elect were entrusted the most important secrets; and even among them there were degrees of information. There was a seventy, and a twelve. All this was in the natural order of things, and according to the habits of the Jews, and indeed of all antiquity. The Jewish Theosophy was a mystery; like the Eleusinian, or the Pythagorean, unfit for the vulgar, And thus the doctrines of Christianity were committed to the *Adepti*, in a *Disciplina Arcani*. By these they were maintained, like the Vestal Fire. They were kept up, only in hidden societies, who handed them down to posterity; and they are now possessed by the genuine Free Masons."

N. B. This explains the origin of many anonymous pamphlets which appeared about this time in Germany, showing that Free Masonry was Christianity. They have doubtless been the works of Spartacus and his partizans among the Eclectic Masons. Nicholai, the great apostle of infidelity, had given very favorable reviews of these performances, and having always shown himself an advocate of such writers as depreciated Christianity, it was natural for him to take this opportunity of bringing it still lower in the opinion of the people. Spartacus therefore conceived a high opinion of the importance of gaining Nicholai to the Order. He had before this gained Leuchtsenring, a hot-headed fanatic, who had spied Jesuits in every corner, and set Nicholai on his journey through Germany, to hunt them out. This man finding them equally hated by the Illuminati, was easily gained, and was most zealous in their cause. He engaged Nicholai, and Spartacus exults exceedingly in the acquisition, saying, "that he was an unwearied champion, *et quidem contentissimus.*" Of this man Philo says, "that he had spread this Christianity into every corner of Germany. I have put meaning," says Philo, "to all these dark symbols, and have prepared both degrees, introducing beautiful ceremonies, which I have selected from among those of the ancient communions, combined with those of the Rosaic Masonry; and now," says he, "it will appear that *we* are the only true Christians. We shall now be in a condition to say a few words to Priests and Princes. I have so contrived things, that I would admit even Popes and Kings, after the trials which I have prefixed; and they would be glad to be of the Order."

But how is all this to be reconciled with the plan of Illumination, which is to banish Christianity altogether. Philo himself in many places says, "that it is only a cloak, to prevent squeamish people from starting back." This is done pretty much in the same way that was practised in the French Masonry. In one of their degrees, the Master's degree is made typical of the death of Jesus Christ, the preacher of Brotherly love. But in the next step, the *Chevalier du Soleil*, it is Reason that has been destroyed and entombed, and the Master in this degree, the *Sublime Philosophe*, occasions the discovery of the place where the body is hid. Reason tries again, and superstition and tyranny disappear, and all becomes clear; man becomes free and happy.

Let us hear Spartacus again.

### Spartacus, in another place.

"We must, 1st. gradually explain away all our preparatory pious frauds. And when persons of discernment find fault, we must desire them to consider the end of all our labour. This sanctifies our means, which at any rate are harmless, and have been useful, even in this case, because they procured us a patient hearing, when otherwise men would have turned away from us like petted children. This will convince them of our sentiments in all the intervening points; and our ambiguous expressions will then be interpreted into an endeavour to draw answers of any kind, which may show us the minds of our pupils. 2d. We must unfold, from history and other writings, the origin and fabrication of all religious lies whatever; and then, 3d. We give a critical history of the Order. But I cannot but laugh, when I think of the ready reception which all this has met with from the grave and learned divines of Germany and of England; and I wonder how their William failed when he attempted to establish a Deistical Worship in London (what can this mean?*) for, I am certain, that it must have been most acceptable to that learned and free people. But they had not the enlightening of our days." I may here remark, that Weishaupt is presuming too much on the ignorance of his friend, for there was a great deal of this enlightening in England at the time he speaks of, and if I am not mistaken, even this celebrated Professor of Irreligion has borrowed most of his scheme from this kingdom. This to be sure is nothing in our praise. But the PANTHEISTICON of Toland resembles Weishaupt's Illumination in every thing but its rebellion and its villany. Toland's Socratic Lodge is an elegant pattern for Weishaupt, and his Triumph of Reason, his Philosophic Happiness, his God, or *Anima Mundi*, are all so like the harsh system of Spartacus, that I am convinced that he has copied them, stamping them with the roughness of his own character. But to go on; Spartacus says of the English: "Their poet Pope made his Essay on Man a system of pure naturalism, without knowing it, as Brother Chrysippus did with my Priest's Degree, and was equally astonished when this was

*It means an attempt made by *David Williams,* [Am: Ed]

pointed out to him. Chrysippus is religious, but not superstitious. Brother Lucian (Nicholai, of whom I have already said so much) says, that the grave Zolikofer now allows that it would be a very proper thing to establish a Deistical Worship at Berlin. I am not afraid but things will go on very well. But Philo, who was entrusted with framing the Priest's Degree, has destroyed it without any necessity; it would, forsooth, startle those who have a hankering for Religion. But I always told you that Philo is fanatical and prudish. I gave him fine materials, and he has stuffed it full of ceremonies and child's play, and as Minos says, *c'est jouer la religion*. But all this may be corrected in the revision by the *Areopagitœ*."

N. B. I have already mentioned Baron Knigge's conversion to Illuminatism by the M. de Constanza, whose name in the Order was Diomedes. Knigge (henceforth Philo) was, next to Spartacus, the most serviceable man in the Order, and procured the greatest number of members. It was chiefly by his exertions among the Masons in the Protestant countries, that the *Eclectic System* was introduced, and afterwards brought under the direction of the Illuminati. This conquest was owing entirely to his very extensive connections among the Masons. He travelled like a philosopher from city to city, from Lodge to Lodge, and even from house to house, before his Illumination, trying to unite the Masons, and he now went over the same ground to extend the *Eclectic System,* and to get the Lodges put under the direction of the Illuminati, by their choice of the Master and Wardens. By this the Order had an opportunity of noticing the conduct of individuals; and when they had found out their manner of thinking, and that they were fit for their purpose, they never quitted them till they had gained them over to their party. We have seen, that he was by no means void of religious impressions, and we often find him offended with the atheism of Spartacus. Knigge was at the same time a man of the world, and had kept good company. Weishaupt had passed his life in the habits of a college. Therefore he knew Knigge's value, and communicated to him all his projects, to be dressed up by him for the taste of society. Philo was of a much more affectionate disposition, with something of a devotional turn, and was shocked at the hard indifference of Spartacus. After labouring four years with great zeal, he was provoked with the disingenuous tricks of Spartacus, and he broke off all connection with the Society in 1784, and some time after published a declaration of all that he had done in it. This is a most excellent account of the plan and principles of the Order (at least as he conceived it, for Spartacus had much deeper views) and shows that the aim of it was to abolish Christianity, and all the state-governments in Europe, and to establish a great republic. But it is full of romantic notions and enthusiastic declamation, on the hackneyed topics of universal citizenship, and liberty and equality. Spartacus gave him line, and allowed him to work on, knowing that he could discard him when he chose. I shall after this give some extracts from Philo's letters, from which the reader will see the vile behaviour of Spartacus, and the nature of his ultimate views. In the mean time we may proceed with the account of the principles of the system.

### Spartacus to Cato.

"Nothing would be more profitable to us than a right history of mankind. Despotism has robbed them of their liberty. How can the weak obtain protection? Only by union; but this is rare. Nothing can bring this about but hidden societies. Hidden schools of wisdom are the means which will one day free men from their bonds. These have in all ages been the archives of nature, and of the rights of men; and by them shall human nature be raised from her fallen state. Princes and nations shall vanish from the earth. The human race will then become one family, and the world will be the dwelling of rational men.

"Morality alone can do this. The head of every family will be what Abraham was, the patriarch, the priest, and the unlettered lord of his family, and Reason will be the code of laws to all mankind. THIS," says Spartacus, "is our GREAT SECRET. True, there may be some disturbance; but by and by the unequal will become equal; and after the storm all will be calm. Can the unhappy consequences remain when the grounds of dissension are removed? Rouse yourselves therefore, O men! assert your rights; and then will Reason rule with unperceived sway; and ALL SHALL BE HAPPY.*

"Morality will perform all this; and morality is the fruit of Illumination; duties and rights are reciprocal. Where Octavius has no right, Cato owes him no duty. Illumination shews us our rights, and Morality follows; that Morality which teaches us to be *of age,* to be *out of wardenship,* to be *full grown,* and to *walk without the leading-strings of priests and princes.*

"Jesus of Nazareth, the Grand Master of our Order, appeared at a time when the world was in the utmost disorder, and among a people who for ages had groaned under the yoke of bondage. He taught them the lessons of reason. To be more effective, he took in the aid of Religion—of opinions which were current—and, in *a very clever manner,* he combined his secret doctrines with the popular religion, and with the customs which lay to his hand. In these he wrapped up his lessons—he taught by parables. Never did any prophet lead men so easily and so securely along the road of liberty. He concealed the precious meaning and consequences of his doctrines; but fully disclosed them to a chosen few. He speaks of a kingdom of the upright and faithful; his Father's kingdom, whose children we also are. Let us only take Liberty and Equality as the great aim of his doctrines, and Morality as the way to attain it, and every thing in the New Testament will be comprehensible; and Jesus will appear as the Redeemer of slaves. Man is fallen from the condition of Liberty and Equality, the STATE OF PURE NATURE. He is under subordination and civil bondage, arising from the vices of man. This is the FALL, and ORIGINAL SIN. The KINGDOM OF GRACE is that restoration which may be brought about by Illumination and a just Morality. This is the NEW BIRTH. When man lives under government, he is fallen, his worth is gone, and his nature tarnished. By subduing our passions, or limiting their cravings, we may recover a great deal of our original worth, and live in a state of grace. This is the redemption of men

*Happy France! Cradle of illumination, where the morning of Reason has dawned, dispelling the clouds of Monarchy and Christianity, where the babe has sucked the blood of the unenlightened, and Murder! Fire! Help! has been the lullaby to sing it to sleep.

—this is accomplished by Morality; and when this is spread over the world, we have THE KINGDOM OF THE JUST.

"But alas! the task of self-formation was too hard for the subjects of the Roman empire, corrupted by every species of profligacy. A chosen few received the doctrines in secret, and they have been handed down to us (but frequently almost buried under rubbish of man's invention) by the Free Masons. These three conditions of human society are expressed by the rough, the split and the polished stone. The rough stone, and the one that is split, express our condition under civil government; rough by every fretting inequality of condition; and split, since we are no longer one family; and are farther divided by differences of government, rank, property, and religion; but when reunited in one family, we are represented by the polished stone. G. is Grace; the Flaming Star is the Torch of Reason. Those who possess this knowledge are indeed ILLUMINATI. Hiram is our fictitious Grand Master, slain for the REDEMPTION OF SLAVES; the Nine Masters are the Founders of the Order. Free Masonry is a Royal Art, inasmuch as it teaches us to walk without trammels, and to govern ourselves."

Reader, are you not curious to learn something of this all-powerful morality, so operative on the heart of the truly illuminated—of this *disciplina arcani,* entrusted only to the chosen few, and handed down to Professor Weishaupt, to Spartacus, and his associates, who have cleared it of the rubbish heaped on it by the dim-sighted Masons, and now beaming in its native lustre on the minds of the *Areopagitæ?* The teachers of ordinary Christianity have been labouring for almost 2000 years, with the New Testament in their hands; many of them with great address, and many, I believe, with honest zeal. But alas! they cannot produce such wonderful and certain effects (for observe, that Weishaupt repeatedly assures us that his means are certain) probably for want of this *disciplina arcani,* of whose efficacy so much is said. Most fortunately, Spartacus has given us a brilliant specimen of the ethics which illuminated himself on a trying occasion, where an ordinary Christian would have been much perplexed, or would have taken a road widely different from that of this illustrious apostle of light. And seeing that several of the *Areopagitæ* co-operated in the transaction, and that it was carefully concealed from the profane and dim-sighted world, we can have no doubt but that it was conducted according to the *disciplina arcani* of Illumination. I shall give it in his own words.

### Spartacus to Marius, September 1783.

"I am now in the most embarrassing situation; it robs me of all rest, and makes me unfit for every thing. I am in danger of losing at once my honor and my reputation, by which I have long had such influence. What think you —my sister-in-law is with child. I have sent her to Eurriphon, and am endeavouring to procure a marriage-licence from Rome. How much depends on this uncertainty—and there is not a moment to lose. Should I fail, what is to be done? What a return do I make by this to a person to whom I am so much obliged! (we shall see the probable meaning of this exclamation by and by.) We have tried every method in our power to destroy the child; and I hope she is determined on every thing—even d—. (Can this mean death?) But alas! Euriphon is, I fear, too timid (alas! poor woman, thou art now under the *disciplina arcani*) and I see no other expedient. Could I be but assured of the silence of Celsus (a physician at Ingoldstadt) he *can* relieve me, and he *promised me as much* three years ago. Do speak to him, if you think he will be staunch. I would not let Cato (his dearest friend, and his chief or only confidant in the scheme of Illumination) know it yet, because the affair in other respects requires his whole friendship. (Cato had all the pretty receipts.) Could you but help me out of this distress, you would give me life, honor, and peace, *and strength to work again in the great cause*. If you cannot, be assured I will venture on the most desperate stroke (poor sister!) for it is fixed.—I will not lose my honor. I cannot conceive what devil has made me to go astray—*me who have always been so careful on such occasions*. As yet all is quiet, and none know of it but you and Euriphon. Were it but time to undertake any thing—but alas! it is the fourth month. These damned priests too—for the action is so criminally accounted by them, and scandalises the blood. This makes the utmost efforts and the most desperate measures absolutely necessary."

It will throw some light on this transaction if we read a letter from Spartacus to Cato about this time.

"One thing more, my dearest friend—Would it be agreeable to you to have me for a brother-in-law. If this should be agreeable, and if it can be brought about without prejudice to my honor, as I hope it may, I am not without hopes that the connection may take place. But in the mean time keep it a secret, and only give me permission to enter into correspondence on the subject with the good lady, to whom I beg you will offer my respectful compliments, and I will explain myself more fully to you by word of mouth, and tell you my whole situation. But I repeat it—the thing must be gone about with address and caution. I would not for all the world deceive a person who certainly has not deserved so of me."

What interpretation can be put on this? Cato seems to be brother to the poor woman—he was unwittingly to furnish the drugs, and he was to be dealt with about consenting to a marriage, which could not be altogether agreeable to him, since it required a dispensation, she being already the sister-in-law of Weishaupt, either the sister of his former wife, or the widow of a deceased brother. Or perhaps Spartacus really wishes to marry Cato's sister, a different person from the poor woman in the straw; and he conceals this adventure from his trusty friend Cato, till he sees what becomes of it. The child may perhaps be got rid of, and then Spartacus is a free man. There is a letter to Cato, thanking him for his friendship in the affair of the child—but it gives no light. I meet with another account, that the sister of Zwack threw herself from the top of a tower, and beat out her brains. But it is not said that it was an only sister; if it was, the probability is, that Spartacus had paid his addresses to her, and succeeded, and that the subsequent affair of his marriage with his sister-in-law or something worse, broke her heart. This seems the best account of the matter. For Hertel (Marius) writes to Zwack in November 1782: "Spartacus is this day gone home, but has left his sister-in-law pregnant behind (this is from Bassus Hoss.) About the new year he hopes to be made merry by a——; who will be before all kings and princes—a young Spartacus. The Pope also will respect him, and legitimate him before the time."

Now, vulgar Christian, compare this with the former declaration of Weishaupt, in page 80, where he appeals to the tenor of his former life, which had been so severely scrutinised, without diminishing his high reputation and great influence, and his ignorance and abhorrence of all those things found in Cato's repositories. You see this was a surprise—he had formerly proceeded cautiously.—He is the best man," says Spartacus, "who best conceals his faults."—He was disappointed by Celsus, *who had promised him his assistance on such occasions* three years ago, during which time he had been busy in "forming himself." How far he has advanced, the reader may judge.

One is curious to know what became of the poor woman: she was afterwards taken to the house of Baron Bassus; but here the foolish woman, for want of that courage which Illumination, and the bright prospect of eternal sleep should have produced, took fright at the *disciplina arcani,* left the house, and in the hidden society of a midwife and nurse brought forth a young Spartacus, who now lives to thank his father for his endeavours to murder him. A *"damned priest,"* the good Bishop of Freysingen, knowing the cogent reasons, procured the dispensation, and Spartacus was obliged, like another dim-sighted mortal, to marry her. The scandal was hushed, and would not have been discovered had it not been for these private writings.

But Spartacus says (page 84) "that when you think him sunk to the bottom, he will spring up with double vigour." In a subsequent work called *Short Amendment of my Plan,* he says, "If men were not habituated to wicked manners, his letters would be their own justification." He does not say that he is without fault; "but they are faults of the understanding—not of the heart. He had, first of all, to form himself; and this is a work of time." In the affair of his sister-in-law he admits the facts, and the attempts to destroy the child; "but this is far from proving any depravity of heart. In his condition, his honor at stake, what else was left him to do? His greatest enemies, the Jesuits, have taught that in such a case it is lawful to make away with the child," and he quotes authorities from their books. "In the introductory fault he has the example of the best of men. The second was its natural consequence, it was altogether involuntary, and, in the eye of a philosophical judge (I presume of the Gallic School) who does not square himself by the harsh letters of a *blood-thirsty lawgiver,* he has but a very trifling account to settle. He had become a public teacher, and was greatly followed; this example *might have ruined many young men.* The eyes of the Order also were fixed on him. The edifice rested on his credit; had he fallen, *he could no longer have been in a condition to treat the matters of virtue so as to make a lasting impression.* It was chiefly his anxiety to support the credit of the Order which determined him to take this step. It makes *for* him, but by no means *against* him; and the persons who are most in fault are the slavish inquisitors, who have published the transaction, in order to make his character more remarkable, and to hurt the Order through his person; and they have not scrupled, for this hellish purpose, to stir up a child against its father ! ! !"

I make no reflections on this very remarkable, and highly useful story, but content myself with saying, that this justification by Weishaupt (which I have been careful to give in his own words) is the greatest instance of effrontery and insult on the sentiments of mankind that I have ever met with. We are all supposed as completely corrupted as if we had lived under the full blaze of Illumination.

In other places of this curious correspondence we learn that Minos, and others of the *Areopagitæ,* wanted to introduce Atheism at once, and not go hedging in the manner they did; affirming it was easier to show at once that Atheism was friendly to society, than to explain all their Masonic Christianity, which they were afterwards to show to be a bundle of lies. Indeed this purpose, of not only abolishing Christianity, but all positive religion whatever, was Weishaupt's favorite scheme from the beginning. Before he canvassed for his Order, in 1774, he published a fictitious antique, which he called *Sidonii Apollinaris Fragmenta,* to prepare (as he expressly says in another place) mens minds for the doctrines of Reason, which contains all the detestable doctrines of Robinet's *Systeme de la Nature.* The publication of the second part was stopped. Weishaupt says, in his APOLOGY FOR THE ILLUMINATI, that before 1780 he had retracted his opinions about Materialism, and about the inexpediency of Princes. But this is false: Philo says expressly, that every thing remained on its original footing in the whole practice and dogmas of the Order when he quitted it in July 1784. All this was concealed, and even the abominable Masonry, in the account of the Order which Weishaupt published at Regensburg; and it required the constant efforts of Philo to prevent bare or flat Atheism from being uniformly taught in their degrees. He had told the council that Zeno would not be under a roof with a man who denied the immortality of the soul. He complains of Minos's cramming irreligion down their throats in every meeting, and says, that he frightened many from entering the Order. "Truth," says Philo, "is a clever, but a modest girl, who must be led by the hand like a gentlewoman, but not kicked about like a whore." Spartacus complains much of the squeamishness of Philo; yet Philo is not a great deal behind him in irreligion. When describing to Cato the Christianity of the Priest-degree, as he had manufactured it, he says, "It is all one whether it be true or false, we must have it, that we may tickle those who have a hankering for religion." All the odds seems to be, that he was of a gentler disposition, and had more deference even for the absurd prejudices of others. In one of his angry letters to Cato he says; "The vanity and self conceit of Spartacus would have got the better of all prudence, had I not checked him, and prevailed on the *Areopagitæ* but to defer the developement of the bold principles till we had firmly secured the man. I even wished to entice the candidate the more by giving him back all his former bonds of secrecy, and leaving him at liberty to walk out without fear; and I am certain that they were, by this time, so engaged that we should not have lost one man. But Spartacus had composed an exhibition of his last principles, for a discourse of reception, in which he painted his three favorite mysterious degrees, which were to be conferred by him alone, in colours which had fascinated his own fancy. But they were the colours of hell, and would have scared the most intrepid; and because I represented the danger of this, and by force obtained the omission of this picture, he became my implacable enemy. I abhor treachery and profligacy, and leave him to blow himself and his Order in the air."

Accordingly this happened. It was this which terrified one of the four professors, and made him impart his doubts to the rest. Yet Spartacus seems to have profited by the apprehensions of Philo; for in the last reception, he, for the first time, exacts a bond from the intrant, engaging himself for ever to the Order, and swearing that he will never draw back. Thus admitted, he becomes a sure card. The course of his life is in the hands of the Order, and his thoughts on a thousand dangerous points; his reports concerning his neighbours and friends; in short, his honor and his neck. The Deist, thus led on, has not far to go before he becomes a Naturalist or Atheist; and then the eternal sleep of death crowns all his humble hopes.

Before giving an account of the higher degrees, I shall just extract from one letter more on a singular subject.

### Minos to Sebastian, 1782.

"The proposal of Hercules to establish a Minerval school for girls is excellent, but requires much circumspection. Philo and I have long conversed on this subject. We cannot improve the world without improving women, who have such a mighty influence on the men. But how shall we get hold of them? How will their relations, particularly their mothers, immersed in prejudices, consent that others shall influence their education? We must begin with grown girls. Hercules proposes the wife of Ptolemy Magus. I have no objection; and I have four step-daughters, fine girls. The oldest in particular is excellent. She is twenty-four, has read much, is above all prejudices, and in religion she thinks as I do. They have much acquaintance among the young ladies their relations (N. B. we don't know the rank of Minos, but as he does not use the word *Damen*, but *Frauenzimmer*, it is probable that it is not high.) It may immediately be a very pretty Society, under the management of Ptolemy's wife, but really under *his* management. You must contrive pretty degrees, and dresses, and ornaments, and elegant and decent rituals. No man must be admitted. This will make them become more keen, and they will go much farther than if we were present, or than if they thought that we knew of their proceedings. Leave them to the scope of their own fancies, and they will soon invent mysteries which will put us to the blush, and create an enthusiasm which we can never equal. They will be our great apostles. Reflect on the respect, nay the awe and terror inspired by the female mystics of antiquity. (Think of the Danaids—think of the Theban *Bacchantes.*) Ptolemy's wife must direct them, and she will be instructed by Ptolemy, and my step-daughters will consult with me. We must always be at hand to prevent the introduction of any improper question. We must prepare themes for their discussion—thus we shall confess them, and inspire them with our sentiments. No man however must come near them. This will fire their roving fancies, and we may expect rare mysteries. But I am doubtful whether this Association will be durable. Women are fickle and impatient. Nothing will please them but hurrying from degree to degree, through a heap of insignificant ceremonies, which will soon lose their novelty and influence. To rest seriously in one rank, and to be still and silent when they have found out that the whole is a cheat (hear the words of an experienced Mason) is a task of which they are incapable. They have not our motives to persevere for years, allowing themselves to be led about, and even then to hold their tongues when they find that they have been deceived. Nay there is a risk that they may take it into their heads to give things an opposite turn, and then, by voluptuous allurements, heightened by affected modesty and decency, which give them an irresistible empire over the best men, they may turn our Order upside down, and in their turn will lead the new one."

Such is the information which may be got from the private correspondence. It is needless to make more extracts of every kind of vice and trick. I have taken such as show a little of the plan of the Order, as far as the degree of *Illuminatus Minor,* and the vile purposes which are concealed under all their specious declamation. A very minute account is given of the plan, the ritual, ceremonies, &c. and even the instructions and discourses, in a book called the *Achte Illuminat,* published at *Edessa* (Frankfort) in 1787. Philo says, "that this is quite accurate, but that he does not know the author." I proceed to give an account of their higher degrees, as they are to be seen in the book called *Neueste Arbeitung des Spartacus und Philo*. And the authenticity of the accounts is attested by Grollman, a private gentleman of independent fortune, who read them, signed and sealed by Spartacus and the *Areopagitæ*.

The series of ranks and progress of the pupil were arranged as follows:

| | | |
|---|---|---|
| NURSERY, | · · · · · · | Preparation, |
| | · · · · · · | Novice, |
| | · · · · · · | Minerval, |
| | · · · · · · | Illumin. Minor. |

| | | | |
|---|---|---|---|
| MASONRY, | *Symbolic* | · · · · | Apprentice, |
| | | · · · · | Fellow Craft, |
| | | · · · · | Master, |
| | *Scotch* | *Illum. Major,* | Scotch Novice, |
| | | *Illum. dirigens,* | Scotch Knight. |

| | | |
|---|---|---|
| MYSTERIES. | Lesser, | Presbyter, Priest, Prince, Regent, |
| | Greater, | *Magus,* *Rex.* |

The Reader must be almost sick of so much villany, and would be disgusted with the minute detail, in which the cant of the Order is ringing continually in his ears. I shall therefore only give such a short extract as may fix our notions of the object of the Order, and the morality of the means employed for attaining it. We need not go back to the lower degrees, and shall begin with the *ILLUMINATUS DIRIGENS*, or Scotch Knight.

After a short introduction, teaching us how the holy secret Chapter of Scotch Knights is assembled, we have, I. Fuller accounts and instructions relating to the whole. II. Instructions for the lower classes of Masonry. III. Instructions relating to Mason Lodges in general. IV. Account of a reception into this degree, with the bond which each subscribes before he can be admitted. V. Concerning the solemn Chapter for reception. VI. Opening of the Chapter. VII. Ritual of Reception, and the Oath. VIII. Shutting of the Chapter. IX. *Agapé,* or Love Feast. X. Ceremonies of the consecration of the Chapter. Appendix A, Explanation of the Symbols of Free Masonry. B, Catechism for the Scotch Knight. C, Secret Cypher.

In No. I. it is said that the "chief study of the Scotch Knight is to work on all men in such a way as is most insinuating. II. He must endeavour to acquire the possession of considerable property. III. In all Mason Lodges we must try secretly to get the upper hand. The Masons do not know what Free Masonry is, their high objects, nor their highest Superiors, and should be directed by those who will lead them along the right road. In preparing a candidate for the degree of Scotch Knighthood, we must bring him into dilemmas by catching questions.—We must endeavour to get the disposal of the money of the Lodges of the Free Masons, or at least take care that it be applied to purposes favorable to our Order—but this must be done in a way that shall not be remarked. Above all, we must push forward with all our skill, the plan of Eclectic Masonry, and for this purpose follow up the circular letter already sent to all the Lodges with every thing that can increase their present embarrassment." In the bond of No. IV. the candidate binds himself to "consider and treat the Illuminati as the Superiors of Free Masonry, and endeavour in all the Mason Lodges which he frequents, to have the Masonry of the Illuminated, and particularly the Scotch Noviciate, introduced into the Lodge." (This is not very different from the Masonry of the *Chevalier de l' Aigle* of the Rosaic Masonry, making the Master's degree a sort of commemoration of the passion, but without giving that character to Christianity which is peculiar to Illuminatism.) Jesus Christ is represented as the enemy of superstitious observances, and the assertor of the Empire of Reason and of Brotherly love, and his death and memory as dear to mankind. This evidently paves the way for Weishaupt's Christianity. The Scotch Knight also engages "to consider the Superiors of the Order as the unknown Superiors of Free Masonry, and to contribute all he can to their gradual union." In the Oath, No. VII. the candidate says, "I will never more be a flatterer of the great, I will never be a lowly servant of princes; but I will strive with spirit, and with address, for virtue, wisdom, and liberty. I will powerfully oppose superstition, slander, and despotism; so, that like a true son of the Order, I may serve the world. I will never sacrifice the general good, and the happiness of the world, to my private interest. I will boldly defend my Brother against slander, will follow out the traces of the pure and true Religion pointed out to me in my instructions, and in the doctrines of Masonry; and will faithfully report to my Superiors the progress I make therein."

When he gets the stroke which dubs him a Knight, the Preses says to him, "Now prove thyself, by thy ability, equal to Kings, and never from this time forward bow thy knee to one who is, like thyself, but a man."

No. IX is an account of the Love-Feast.

1st, There is a Table Lodge, opened as usual, but in virtue of the ancient Master-word. Then it is said, "Let moderation, fortitude, morality, and genuine love of the Brethren, with the overflowing of innocent and careless mirth reign here." (This is almost verbatim from Toland.)
2d, In the middle of a bye-table is a chalice, a pot of wine, an empty plate, and a plate of unleavened bread— All is covered with a green cloth.

3d, When the Table Lodge is ended, and the Prefect sees no obstacle, he strikes on this bye-table the stroke of Scotch Master, and his signal is repeated by the Senior Warden. All are still and silent. The Prefect lifts off the cloth.

4th, The Prefect asks, whether the Knights are in the disposition to partake of the Love-Feast in earnest, peace, and contentment. If none hesitates, or offers to retire, he takes the plate with the bread and says,

"J. of N. our Grand-Master, in the night in which he was betrayed by his friends, persecuted for his love for truth, imprisoned, and condemned to die, assembled his trusty Brethren, to celebrate his last Love-Feast—which is signified to us in many ways. He took bread (taking it) and broke it (breaking it) and blessed it, and gave it to his disciples, &c.—This shall be the mark of our Holy Union, &c. Let each of you examine his heart, whether love reigns in it, and whether he, in full imitation of our Grand-Master, is ready to lay down his life for his Brethren.

"Thanks be to our Grand-Master, who has appointed this feast as a memorial of his kindness, for the uniting of the hearts of those who love him.—Go in peace, and blessed be this new Association which we have formed.— Blessed be ye who remain loyal and strive for the good cause."

5th, The Prefect immediately closes the Chapter with the usual ceremonies of the *Loge de Table*.

6th, It is to be observed, that no priest of the Order must be present at this Love-Feast, and that even the Brother Servitor quits the Lodge.

I must observe here, that Philo, the manufacturer of this ritual, has done it very injudiciously; it has no resemblance whatever to the Love-Feast of the primitive Christians, and is merely a copy of a similar thing in one of the steps of French Masonry. Philo's reading in church-history was probably very scanty, or he trusted that the candidates would not be very nice in their examination of it, and he imagined that it would do well enough, and "tickle such as had a religious hankering." Spartacus disliked it exceedingly—it did not accord with his serious conceptions, and he justly calls it *Jouer la Religion*.

The discourse of reception is to be found also in the secret correspondence *(Nachtrag* II. *Abtheilung,* p. 44). But it is needless to insert it here. I have given the substance of this and of all the Cosmo-political declamations already in the panegyric introduction to the account of the process of education. And in Spartacus's letter, and in Philo's I have given an abstract of the introduction to the explanation given in this degree of the symbols of Free Masonry. With respect to the explanation itself, it is as slovenly and wretched as can be imagined, and shows that Spartacus trusted to much more operative principles in the human heart for the reception of his nonsense than the dictates of unbiased reason. None but promising subjects were admitted thus far—such as would not boggle; and their principles were already sufficiently apparent to assure him that they would be contented with any thing that made game of religion, and would be diverted by the seriousness which a chance devotee might exhibit during these silly caricatures of Christianity and Free Masonry. But there is considerable address in the way that Spartacus prepares his pupils for having all this mummery shown in its true colours, and overturned.

"Examine, read, think on these symbols. There are many things which one cannot find out without a guide nor even learn without instructions. They require study and zeal. Should you in any future period think that you have conceived a clearer notion of them, that you have found a paved road, declare your discoveries to your Superiors; it is thus that you improve your mind; they expect this of you; *they* know the true path—but will not point it out— enough if they assist you in every approach to it, and warn you when you recede from it. They have even put things in your way to try your powers of leading yourself through the difficult track of discovery. In this process the weak head finds only child's play—the initiated finds objects of thought which language cannot express, and the thinking mind finds food for his faculties." By such forewarnings as these Weishaupt leaves room for any deviation, for any sentiment or opinion of the individual that he may afterwards choose to encourage, and "to whisper in their ear (as he expresses it) many things which he did not find it prudent to insert in a printed compend."

But all the principles and aim of Spartacus and of his Order are most distinctly seen in the third or Mystery Class. I proceed therefore to give some account of it. By the Table it appears to have two degrees, the Lesser and the Greater Mysteries, each of which have two departments, one relating chiefly to Religion and the other to Politics.

The Priest's degree contains, 1. An Introduction. 2. Further Accounts of the Reception into this degree. 3. What is called Instruction in the Third Chamber, which the candidate must read over. 4. The Ritual of Reception. 5. Instruction for the First Degree of the Priest's Class, called

*Instructio in Scientificis.* 6. Account of the Consecration of a Dean, the Superior of this Lower Order of Priests.

The Regent degree contains, 1. Directions to the Provincial concerning the dispensation of this degree. 2. Ritual of Reception. 3. System of Direction for the whole Order. 4. Instruction for the whole Regent degree. 5. Instruction for the Prefects or Local Superiors. 6. Instruction for the Provincials.

The most remarkable thing in the Priest's degree is the Instruction in the Third Chamber. It is to be found in the private correspondence. *(Nachtrage Original Schriften* 1787, 2nd *Abtheilung,* page 44.) There it has the title *Discourse to the Illuminati Dirigentes,* or Scotch Knights. In the critical history, which is annexed to the *Neueste Arbeitung,* there is an account given of the reason for this denomination; and notice is taken of some differences between the instructions here contained and that discourse.

This instruction begins with sore complaints of the low condition of the human race; and the causes are deduced from religion and state-government. "Men originally led a patriarchal life, in which every father of a family was the sole lord of his house and his property, while he himself possessed general freedom and equlity. But they suffered themselves to be oppressed—gave themselves up to civil societies, and formed states. Even by this they fell; and this is the fall of man, by which they were thrust into unspeakable misery. To get out of this state, to be freed and born again, there is no other mean than the use of pure Reason, by which a general morality may be established, which will put man in a condition to govern himself, regain his original worth, and dispense with all political supports, and particularly with rulers. This can be done in no other way but by secret associations, which will by degrees, and in silence, possess themselves of the government of the States, and make use of those means for this purpose which the wicked use for attaining their base ends. Princes and Priests are in particular, and *kat' exochen,* the wicked, whose hands must tie up by means of these associations, if we cannot root them out altogether.

"Kings are parents. The paternal power ceases with the incapacity of the child; and the father injures his child, if he pretends to retain his right beyond this period. When a nation comes of age, their state of wardship is at an end."

Here follows a long declamation against patriotism, as a narrow-minded principle when compared with true Cosmo-politism. Nobles are represented as "a race of men that serve not the nation but the Prince, whom a hint from the Sovereign stirs up against the nation, who are retained servants and ministers of despotism, and the mean for oppressing national liberty. Kings are accused of a tacit convention, under the flattering appellation of the balance of power, to keep nations in subjection.

"The mean to regain Reason her rights—to raise liberty from its ashes—to restore to man his original rights—to produce the previous revolution in the mind of man—to obtain an eternal victory over oppressors—and to work the redemption of mankind, is secret schools of wisdom. When the worthy have strengthened their association by numbers, they are secure, and then they begin to become powerful, and terrible to the wicked, of whom many will, for safety, amend themselves—many will come over to our party, and we shall bind the hands of the rest, and finally conquer them. Whoever spreads general illumination augments mutual security; illumination and security make princes unnessary; illumination performs this by creating an effective Morality, and Morality makes a nation of full age fit to govern itself; and since it is not impossible to produce a just Morality, it is possible to regain freedom for the world."

"We must therefore strengthen our band, and establish a legion, which shall restore the rights of man, original liberty and independence.

"Jesus Christ"—but I am sick of all this. The following questions are put to the candidate:

1. "Are our civil conditions in the world the destinations that seem to be the end of our nature, or the purposes for which man was placed on this earth, or are they not? Do

states, civil obligations, popular religion, fulfill the intentions of men who established them? Do secret associations promote instruction and true human happiness, or are they the children of necessity, of the multifarious wants, of unnatural conditions, or the inventions of vain and cunning men?"

2. "What civil association, what science do you think to the purpose, and what are not?"

3. "Has there ever been any other in the world, is there no other more simple condition, and what do you think of it?"

4. "Does it appear possible, after having gone through all the nonentities of our civil constitutions, to recover for once our first simplicity, and get back to this honorable uniformity?"

5. "How can one begin this noble attempt; by means of open support, by forcible revolution, or by what other way?"

6. "Does Christianity give us any hint to this purpose? does it not recognize such a blessed condition as once the lot of man, and as still recoverable?"

7. "But is this holy religion the religion that is now professed by any sect on earth, or is it a better?"

8. "Can we learn this religion—can the world, as it is, bear the light? Do you think that it would be of service, before numerous obstacles are removed, if we taught men this purified religion, sublime philosophy, and the art of governing themselves? Or would not this hurt, by rousing the interested passions of men habituated to prejudices, who would oppose this as wicked?"

9. "May it not be more advisable to do away these corruptions bit by bit, in silence, and for this purpose to propagate these salutary and heart-consoling doctrines in secret?"

10. "Do we not perceive traces of such a secret doctrine in the ancient schools of philosophy, in the doctrines and instructions of the Bible, which Christ, the Redeemer and Liberator of the human race, gave to his trusty disciples? Do you not observe an education, proceeding by steps of this kind, handed down to us from his time till the present?"

In the ceremonial of Reception, crowns and sceptres are represented as tokens of human degradation. "The plan of operation, by which our higher degrees act, must work powerfully on the world, and must give another turn to all our present constitutions."

Many other questions are put to the pupil during his preparation, and his answers are given in writing. Some of these rescripts are to be found in the secret correspondence. Thus, "How far is the position true, that all those means may be used for a good purpose which the wicked have employed for a bad?" And along with this question there is an injunction to take counsel from the opinions and conduct of the learned and worthy out of the society. In one of the answers, the example of a great philosopher and Cosmo-polite is adduced, who betrayed a private correspondence entrusted to him, for the service of freedom; the case was Dr. Franklin's. In another, the power of the Order was extended to the putting the individual to death; and the reason given, was, that "this power was allowed to all Sovereignties, for the good of the State, and therefore belonged to the Order, which was to govern the world." ——"N. B. We must acquire the direction of education— of church-management—of the professorial chair, and of the pulpit. We must bring our opinions into fashion by every art—spread them among the people by the help of young writers. We must preach the warmest concern for humanity, and make people indifferent to all other relations. We must take care that our writers be well puffed, and that the Reviewers do not depreciate them; therefore we must endeavour by every mean to gain over the Reviewers and Journalists; and we must also try to gain the booksellers, who in time will see that it is their interest to side with us."

I conclude this account of the degree of Presbyter with remarking, that there were two copies of it employed occasionally. In one of them all the most offensive things in respect of church and state were left out.

In the Regent degree, the proceedings and instructions are conducted in the same manner. Here, it is said, "We must as much as possible select for this degree persons who are free, independent of all princes; particularly such as have frequently declared themselves discontented with the usual institutions, and their wishes to see a better government established."

Catching questions are put to the candidate for this degree; such as,

1. "Would the Society be objectionable which should (till the greater revolution of nature should be ripe) put monarchs and rulers out of the condition to do harm; which in silence prevents the abuse of power, by surrounding the great with its members, and thus not only prevents their doing mischief, but even makes them do good?"

2. "Is not the objection unjust, That such a Society may abuse its power. Do not our rulers frequently abuse their power, though we are silent? This power is not so secure as in the hands of our Members, whom we train up with so much care, and place about princes after mature deliberation and choice. If any government can be harmless which is erected by man, surely it must be ours, which is founded on morality, fore-sight, talents, liberty, and virtue," &c.

The candidate is presented for reception in the character of a slave; and it is demanded of him what has brought him into this most miserable of all conditions. He answers—Society—the State—Submissiveness—False Religion. A skeleton is pointed out to him, at the feet of which are laid a Crown and a Sword. He is asked, whether that is the skeleton of a King, a Nobleman, or a Beggar? As he cannot decide, the President of the meeting says to him, "the character of being a Man is the only one that is of importance."

In a long declamation on the hackneyed topics, we have

here and there some thoughts which have not yet come before us.

"We must allow the underlings to imagine (but without telling them the truth) that we direct all the Free Mason Lodges, and even all other Orders, and that the greatest monarchs are under our guidance, which indeed is here and there the case.

"There is no way of influencing men so powerfully as by means of the women. These should therefore be our chief study; we should insinuate ourselves into their good opinion, give them hints of emancipation from the tyranny of public opinion, and of standing up for themselves; it will be an immense relief to their enslaved minds to be freed from any one bond of restraint, and it will fire them the more, and cause them to work for us with zeal, without knowing that they do so; for they will only be indulging their own desire of personal admiration.

"We must win the common people in every corner. This will be obtained chiefly by means of the schools, and by open, hearty behaviour, show, condescension, popularity, and toleration of their prejudices, which we shall at leisure root out and dispel.

"If a writer publishes any thing that attracts notice, and is in itself just, but does not accord with our plan, we must endeavour to win him over, or decry him.

"A chief object of our care must be to keep down that slavish veneration for princes which so much disgraces all nations. Even in the *soi-disant* free England, the silly Monarch says, We are graciously pleased, and the more simple people say, Amen. These men, commonly very weak heads, are only the farther corrupted by this servile flattery. But let us at once give an example of our spirit by our behaviour with Princes; we must avoid all familiarity—never entrust ourselves to them—behave with precision, but with civility, as to other men—speak of them on an equal footing—this will in time teach them that they are by nature men, if they have sense and spirit, and that only by convention they are Lords. We must assiduously collect anecdotes, and the honorable and mean actions, both of the least and the greatest, and when their names occur in any records which are read in our meetings, let them ever be accompanied by these marks of their real worth.

"The great strength of our Order lies in its concealment; let it never appear in any place in its own name, but always covered by another name, and another occupation. *None is fitter than the three lower degrees of Free Masonry; the public is accustomed to it, expects little from it, and therefore takes little notice of it.* Next to this, the form of a learned or literary society is best suited to our purpose, and had Free Masonry not existed, this cover would have been employed; and it may be much more than a cover, *it may be a powerful engine in our hands. By establishing reading societies, and subscription libraries, and taking these under our direction, and supplying them through our labours, we may turn the public mind which way we will.*

In like manner we must try to obtain an influence in the military academies (this may be of mighty consequence) the printing-houses, booksellers shops, chapters, and in short in all offices which have any effect, either in forming, or in managing, or even in directing the mind of man: painting and engraving are highly worth our care."*

"Could our Prefect (observe it is to the *Illuminati Regentes* he is speaking, whose officers are *Prefecti*) fill the judicatories of a state with our worthy members, he does all that man can do for the Order. It is better than to gain the Prince himself. Princes should never get beyond the Scotch knighthood. They either never prosecute any thing, or they twist every thing to their own advantage.

"A Literary Society is the most proper form for the introduction of our Order into any state where we are yet strangers." (Mark this!)

* (They were strongly suspected of having published some scandalous caricatures, and some very immoral prints.) They scrupled at no mean, however base, for corrupting the nation. Mirabeau had done the same thing at Berlin. By political caricatures and filthy prints, they corrupt even such as cannot read.

"The power of the Order must surely be turned to the advantage of its Members. All must be assisted. They must be preferred to all persons otherwise of equal merit. Money, services, honor, goods, and blood, must be expended for the fully proved Brethren, and the unfortunate must be relieved by the funds of the Society."

As evidence that this was not only their instructions, but also their assiduous practice, take the following report from the overseer of Greece (Bavaria.)

**In Cato's hand-writing.**

"The number (about 600) of Members relates to Bavaria alone.

"In Munich there is a well-constituted meeting of *Illuminati Mejores*, a meeting of excellent *Illuminati Minores,* a respectable Grand Lodge, and two Minerval Assemblies. There is a Minerval Assembly at Freyssing, at Landsberg, at Burghausen, at Strasburg, at Ingolstadt, and at last at Regensburg.*

"At Munich we have bought a house, and by clever measures have brought things so far, that the citizens take no notice of it, and even speak of us with esteem. We can openly go to the house every day, and carry on the business of the Lodge. This is a great deal for this city. In the house is a good museum of natural history, and apparatus for experiments; also a library which daily increases. The garden is well occupied by botanic specimens, and the whole has the appearance of a society of zealous naturalists.

"We get all the literary journals. We take care, by well-timed pieces, to make the citizens and the Princes a little more noticed for certain little slips. We oppose the monks with all our might, and with great success.

"The Lodge is constituted entirely according to our system, and has broken off entirely from Berlin, and we have

*In this small *turbulent* city there were eleven secret societies of Masons, Rosycrucians, Clair-voyants," &c.

nearly finished our transactions with the Lodges of Poland, and shall have them under our direction.

"By the activity of our Brethren, the Jesuits have been kept out of all the professorial chairs at Ingolstadt, and our friends prevail."

"The Widow Duchess has set up her academy entirely according to our plan, and we have all the Professors in the Order. Five of them are excellent, and the pupils will be prepared for us.

"We have got Pylades put at the head of the Fisc, and he has the church-money at his disposal. By properly using this money, we have been enabled to put our Brother——'s household in good order; which he had destroyed by going to the Jews. We have supported more Brethren under similar misfortunes.

"Our Ghostly Brethren have been very fortunate this last year, for we have procured for them several good benefices, parishes, tutorships, &c.

"Through our means Arminius and Cortez have gotten Professorships, and many of our younger Brethren have obtained Bursaries by our help.

"We have been very successful against the Jesuits, and brought things to such a bearing, that their revenues, such as the Mission, the Golden Alms, the Exercises, and the Conversion Box, are now under the management of our friends. So are also their concerns in the university and the German school foundations. The application of all will be determined presently, and we have six members and four friends in the Court. This has cost our senate some nights want of sleep.

"Two of our best youths have got journies from the Court, and they will go to Vienna, where they will do us great service.

"All the German Schools, and the Benevolent Society, are at last under our direction.

"We have got several zealous members in the courts of justice, and we are able to afford them pay, and other good additions.

"Lately, we have got possession of the Bartholomew Institution for young clergymen, having secured all its supporters. Through this we shall be able to supply Bavaria with fit priests.

"By a letter from Philo we learn, that one of the highest dignities in the church was obtained for a zealous Illuminatus, in opposition even to the authority and right of the Bishop of Spire, who is represented as a bigotted and tyrannical priest."

Such were the lesser mysteries of the Illuminati. But there remain the higher mysteries. The system of these has not been printed, and the degrees were conferred only by Spartacus himself, from papers which he never entrusted to any person. They were only read to the candidate, but no copy was taken. The publisher of the *Neueste Arbeitung* says that he has read them (so says Grollman.) He says, "that in the first degree of MAGUS or PHILOSOPHUS, the doctrines are the same with those of Spinoza, where all is material, God and the world are the same thing, and all religion whatever is without foundation, and the contrivance of ambitious men." The second degree, or REX, teaches, "that every peasant, citizen, and householder is a sovereign, as in the Patriarchal state, and that nations must be brought back to that state, by whatever means are conducible—peaceably, if it can be done; but, if not, then by force—for all subordination must vanish from the face of the earth."

The author says further, that the German Union was, to his certain knowledge, the work of the Illuminati.

The private correspondence that has been published is by no means the whole of what was discovered at Landshut and Bassus Hoff, and government got a great deal of useful information, which was concealed, both out of regard to the families of the persons concerned, and also that the rest might not know the utmost extent of the discovery, and be less on their guard. A third collection was found under the foundation of the house in which the Lodge *Theodor von guten Rath* had been held. But none of this has appeared. Enough surely has been discovered to give the public a very just idea of the designs of the Society and its connections.

Lodges were discovered, and are mentioned in the private papers already published, in the following places.

| | |
|---|---|
| Munich | Hesse (many) |
| Ingolstadt | Buchenwerter |
| Frankfort | Monpeliard |
| Echstadt | Stutgard (3) |
| Hanover | Carlsruhe |
| Brunswick | Anspach |
| Calbe | Neuwied (2) |
| Magdenburgh | Mentz (2) |
| Cassel | Poland (many) |
| Osnabruck | Turin |
| Weimar | England (8) |
| Upper Saxony (several) | Scotland (2) |
| Austria (14) | Warsaw (2) |
| Westphalia (several) | Deuxponts |
| Heidelberg | Cousel |
| Mannheim | Treves (2) |
| Strasburgh (5) | Aix-la-Chappelle (2) |
| Spire | Bartschied |
| Worms | Hahrenberg |
| Dusseldorff | Switzerland (many) |
| Cologne | Rome |
| Bonn (4) | Naples |
| Livonia (many) | Ancona |
| Courland (many) | Florence |
| Frankendahl | France |
| Alsace (many) | Halland (many) |
| Vienna (4) | Dresden (4) |

America (several). N. B. This was before 1786.

I have picked up the names of the following members.

| | |
|---|---|
| Spartacus | Weishaupt, Professor. |
| Philo, | Knigge, Freyherr, i. e. Gentleman. |
| Amelius, | Bode, F. H. |
| Bayard, | Busche, F. H. |
| Diomedes, | Constanza, Marq. |
| Cato, | Zwack, Lawyer. |
| | Torring, Count. |
| | Kreitmaier, Prince. |
| | Utschneider, Professor. |
| | Cossandey, Professor. |
| | Renner, Professor. |
| | Grunberger, Professor. |
| | Balderbusch, F. H. |
| | Lippert, Counsellor. |
| | Kundl, ditto. |
| | Bart, ditto. |
| | Leiberhauer, Priest. |
| | Kundler, Professor. |
| | Lowling, Professor. |
| | Vachency, Councellor. |
| | Morausky, Count. |
| | Hoffstetter, Surveyor of Roads. |
| | Strobl, Bookseller. |
| Pythagoras, | Westenrieder, Professor. |
| | Babo, Professor. |
| | Baader, Professor. |
| | Burzes, Priest. |
| | Pfruntz, Priest. |
| Hannibal, | Bassus, Baron. |
| Brutus, | Savioli, Count. |
| Lucian, | Nicholai, Bookseller. |
| | Bahrdt, Clergyman. |
| Zoroaster, Confucius, | Baierhamer. |
| Hermes Trismegistus, | Socher, School Inspector. |
| | Dillis, Abbé. |
| Sulla, | Meggenhoff, Paymaster. |
| | Danzer, Canon. |
| | Braun, ditto. |
| | Fischer, Magistrate. |

|                      |                          |
|----------------------|--------------------------|
|                      | Frauenberger, Baron.     |
|                      | Kaltner, Lieutenant.     |
| Pythagoras,          | Drexl, Librarian.        |
| Marius,              | Hertel, Canon.           |
|                      | Dachsel.                 |
|                      | Dilling, Counsellor.     |
|                      | Seefeld, Count.          |
|                      | Gunsheim, ditto.         |
|                      | Morgellan, ditto.        |
| Saladin,             | Ecker, ditto.            |
|                      | Ow, Major.               |
|                      | Werner, Counsellor.      |
| Cornelius Scipio,    | Berger, ditto.           |
|                      | Wortz, Apothecary.       |
|                      | Mauvillon, Colonel.      |
|                      | Mirabeau, Count.         |
|                      | Orleans, Duke.           |
|                      | Hochinaer.               |
| Tycho Brahe,         | Gaspar, Merchant.        |
| Thales,              | Kapfinger.               |
| Attila,              | Sauer.                   |
| Ludovicus Bavarus,   | Losi.                    |
| Shaftesbury,         | Steger.                  |
| Coriolanus,          | Tropponero, Zuschwartz.  |
| Timon,               | Michel.                  |
| Tamerlane,           | Lange.                   |
| Livius,              | Badorffer.               |
| Cicero,              | Pfelt.                   |
| Ajax,                | Massenhausen, Count.     |

I have not been able to find who personated Minos, Euriphon, Celsius, Mahomet, Hercules, Socrates, Philippo Strozzi, Euclides, and some others who have been uncommonly active in carrying forward the great cause.

The chief publications for giving us regular accounts of the whole (besides the original writings) are,

1. *Grosse Absicht des Illuminaten Ordens.*
2. ——*Nachtrages (3.) an denselben.*
3. *Weishaupt's improved System.*
4. *System des Illum. Ordens aus dem Original-Schriften gezogen.*

I may now be permitted to make a few reflections on the accounts already given of this Order, which has so distinctly concentrated the casual and scattered efforts of its prompters, the *Chevaliers Bienfaisants*, the *Philalethes*, and *Amis Reunis* of France, and carried on the system of enlightening and reforming the world.

The great aim professed by the Order is *to make men happy;* and the means professed to be employed, as the only and surely effective, is *making them good;* and this is to be brought about by *enlightening the mind*, and *freeing it from the dominion of superstition and prejudices*. This purpose is effected by its *producing a just and steady morality*. This done, and becoming universal, there can be little doubt but that the peace of society will be the consequence—that government, subordination, and all the disagreeable coercions of civil governments will be unnecessary—and that society may go on peaceably in a state of perfect liberty and equality.

But surely it requires no angel from heaven to tell us that if every man is virtuous, there will be no vice; and that there will be peace on earth, and good will between man and man, whatever be the differences of rank and fortune; so that Liberty and Equality seem not to be the necessary consequences of this just Morality, nor necessary requisites for this national happiness. We may question, therefore, whether the Illumination which makes this a necessary condition is a clear and a pure light. It may be a false glare, showing the object only on one side, tinged with partial colours thrown on it by neighbouring objects. We see so much wisdom in the general plans of nature, that we are apt to think that there is the same in what relates to the human mind, and that the God of nature accomplishes his plans in this as well as in other instances. We are even disposed to think that human nature would suffer by it. The rational nature of man is not contented with meat and drink, and raiment, and shelter, but is also pleased with exerting many powers and faculties, and with gratifying many tastes, which could hardly have any existence in a society where all are equal. We say that there can be no doubt that the pleasure arising from the contemplation of the works of art—the pleasure of intellectual cultivation, the pleasure of mere ornament, are rational, distinguish man from a brute, and are so general, that there is hardly a mind so rude as not to feel them. Of all these, and of all the difficult sciences, all most rational, and in themselves most innocent, and most delightful to a cultivated mind, we should be deprived in a society where all are equal. No individual could give employment to the talents necessary for creating and improving these ornamental comforts of life. We are absolutely certain that, even in the most favorable situations on the face of the earth, the most untainted virtue in every breast could not raise man to that degree of cultivation that is possessed by citizens very low in any of the states of Europe; and in the situation of most countries we are acquainted with, the state of man would be much lower: for, at our very setting out, we must grant that the liberty and equality here spoken of must be complete; for there must not be such a thing as a farmer and his cottager. This would be as unjust, as much the cause of discontent, as the gentleman and the farmer.

This scheme therefore seems contrary to the designs of our Creator, who has every where placed us in these situations of inequality that are here so much scouted, and has given us strong propensities by which we relish these enjoyments. We also find that they may be enjoyed in peace and innocence. And lastly, We imagine that the villain, who, in the station of a professor, would plunder a Prince, would also plunder the farmer if he were his cottager. The illumination therefore that appears to have the best chance of making mankind happy, is that which will teach us the Morality which will respect the comforts of cultivated Society, and teach us to protect the possessors in the innocent enjoyment of them; that will enable us to perceive and admire the taste and elegance of Architecture and Gardening, without any wish to sweep the gardens and their owner from off the earth, merely because he is their owner.

We are therefore suspicious of this Illumination, and apt to ascribe this violent antipathy to Princes and subordination to the very cause that makes true Illumination, and just Morality proceeding from it, so necessary to public happiness, namely, the vice and injustice of those who cannot innocently have the command of those offensive elegancies of human life. Luxurious tastes, keen desires, and unbridled passions, would prompt to all this, and this Illumination is, as we see, equivalent to them in effect. The aim of the Order is not to enlighten the mind of man, and show him his moral obligations, and by the practice of his duties to make society peaceable, possession secure, and coercion unnecessary, so that all may be at rest and happy, even though all *were* equal; but to get rid of the coercion which must be employed in place of Morality, that the innocent rich may be robbed with impunity by the idle and profligate poor. But to do this, an unjust casuistry must be employed in place of a just Morality; and this must be defended or suggested, by misrepresenting the true state of man, and of his relation to the universe, and by removing the restrictions of religion, and giving a superlative value to all those constituents of human enjoyment, which true Illumination shows us to be but very small concerns of a rational and virtuous mind. The more closely we examine the principles and practice of the Illuminati, the more clearly do we perceive that this is the case. Their first and immediate aim is to get the possession of riches, power, and influence, without industry; and, to accomplish this, they want to abolish Christianity; and then dissolute manners and universal profligacy will procure them the adherence of all the wicked, and enable them to overturn all the civil governments of Europe; after which they will think of farther conquests, and extend their operations to the other quarters of the globe, till they have reduced mankind to the state of one undistinguishable chaotic mass.

But this is too chimerical to be thought their real aim. Their Founder, I dare say, never entertained such hopes, nor troubled himself with the fate of distant lands. But it comes in his way when he puts on the mask of humanity and benevolence: it must embrace all mankind, only because it must be stronger than patriotism and loyalty, which stand in his way. Observe that Weishaupt took a name expressive of his principles. Spartacus was a gladiator, who headed an insurrection of Roman slaves, and for three years kept the city in terror. Weishaupt says in one of his letters, "I never was fond of empty titles; but surely that man has a childish soul who would not as readily chuse the name

of Spartacus as that of Octavius Augustus." The names
which he gives to several of his gang express their differences of sentiments. Philo, Lucian, and others, are very
significantly given to Knigge, Nicholai, &c. He was vain
of the name Spartacus, because he considered himself as
employed somewhat in the same way, leading slaves to
freedom. Princes and Priests are mentioned by him on all
occasions in terms of abhorrence.

Spartacus employs powerful means. In the style of the
Jesuits (as he says) he considers every mean as consecrated
by the end for which it is employed, and he says with
great truth,

> *"Flectere si nequeo superos, Acheronta movebo."*

To save his reputation, he scruples not to murder his
innocent child, and the woman whom he had held in his
arms with emotions of fondness and affection. But lest this
should appear too selfish a motive, he says, "had I fallen,
my precious Order would have fallen with me; the Order
which is to bless mankind. I should not again have been
able to speak of virtue so as to make any lasting impression.
My example might have ruined many young men." This
he thinks will excuse, nay sanctify any thing. "My letters
are my greatest vindication." He employs the Christian Religion, which he thinks a falsehood, and which he is afterwards to explode, as the mean for inviting Christians of
every denomination, and gradually cajoling them, by clearing up their Christian doubts in succession, till he lands
them in Deism; or, if he finds them unfit, and too religious,
he gives them a *Sta bene,* and then laughs at the fears, or
perhaps madness, in which he leaves them. Having got
them this length, they are declared to be fit, and he receives them into the higher mysteries. But lest they should
still shrink back, dazzled by the Pandemonian glare of
Illumination which will now burst upon them, he exacts
from them, for the first time, a bond of perseverance. But,
as Philo says, there is little chance of tergiversation. The
life and honor of most of the candidates are by this time
in his hand. They have been long occupied in the vile and
corrupting office of spies on all around them, and they
are found fit for their present honors, because they have

discharged this office to his satisfaction, by the reports which they have given in, containing stories of their neighbours, nay even of their own gang. They may be ruined in the world by disclosing these, either privately or publicly. A man who had once brought himself into this perilous situation durst not go back. He might have been left indeed in any degree of Illumination; and, if Religion has not been quite eradicated from his mind, he must be in that condition of painful anxiety and doubt that makes him desperate, fit for the full operation of fanaticism, and he may be engaged *in the cause of God,* "to commit all kind of wickedness with greediness." In this state of mind, a man shuts his eyes, and rushes on. Had Spartacus supposed that he was dealing with good men, his conduct would have been the reverse of all this. There is no occasion for this bond from a person convinced of the excellency of the Order. But he knew them to be unprincipled, and that the higher mysteries were so daring, that even some of such men would start at them. But they must not blab.

Having thus got rid of Religion, Spartacus could with more safety bring into view the great aim of all his efforts— to rule the world by means of his Order. As the immediate mean for attaining this, he holds out the prospect of freedom from civil subordination. Perfect Liberty and Equality are interwoven with every thing; and the flattering thought is continually kept up, that "by the wise contrivance of this Order, the most complete knowledge is obtained of the real worth of every person; the Order will, *for its own sake,* and therefore *certainly,* place every man in that situation in which he can be most effective. The pupils are convinced that the Order *will* rule the world. Every member therefore becomes a ruler." We all think ourselves qualified to rule. The difficult task is to obey with propriety; but we are honestly generous in our prospects of future command. It is therefore an alluring thought, both to good and bad men. By this lure the Order will spread. If they are active in insinuating their members into offices, and in keeping out others (which the private correspondence shows to have been the case) they may have had frequent experience of their success in gaining an influence on the world. This must whet their zeal. If Weishaupt was a sincere Cosmopolite, he had the pleasure of seeing "his work prospering in his hands."

It surely needs little argument now to prove, that the Order of Illuminati had for its immediate object the abolishing of Christianity (at least this was the intention of the Founder) with the sole view of overturning the civil government, by introducing universal dissoluteness and profligacy of manners, and then getting the assistance of the corrupted subjects to overset the throne. The whole conduct in the preparation and instruction of the Presbyter and *Regens* is directed to this point. Philo says, "I have been at unwearied pains to remove the fears of some who imagine that our Superiors want to abolish Christianity; but by and by their prejudices will wear off, and they will be more at their ease. Were I to let them know that our General holds all Religion to be a lie, and uses even Deism, only to lead men by the nose.—Were I to connect myself again with the Free Masons, and tell them our designs to ruin their Fraternity by this circular letter (a letter to the Lodge in Courland)—Were I but to give the least hint to any of the Princes of Greece (Bavaria)—No, my anger shall not carry me so far.—An Order forsooth, which in this manner abuses human nature—which will subject men to a bondage more intolerable than Jesuitism.—I could put it on a respectable footing, and the world would be ours. Should I mention our fundamental principles (even after all the pains I have been at to mitigate them) so unquestionably dangerous to the world, who would remain? What signifies the innocent ceremonies of the Priest's degree, as I have composed it, in comparison with your maxim, that we may use for a good end those means which the wicked employ for a base purpose?"

Brutus writes, "Numenius now acquiesces in the mortality of the soul; but, I fear we shall lose Ludovicus Bavarus. He told Spartacus, that he was mistaken when he thought that he had swallowed his stupid Masonry. No, he saw the trick, and did not admire the end that required it. I don't know what to do; a *Sta bene* would make him mad, and he will blow us all up.

"The Order must possess the power of life and death

in consequence of our Oath; and with propriety, for the same reason, and by the same right, that any government in the world possesses it: For the Order comes in their place, making them unnecessary. When things cannot be otherwise, and ruin would ensue if the Association did not employ this mean, the Order must, as well as public rulers, employ it for the good of mankind; therefore for its own preservation. (N. B. Observe here the casuistry.) Nor will the political constitutions suffer by this, for there are always thousands equally ready and able to supply the place."

We need not wonder that Diomedes told the Professors, "that death, inevitable death, from which no potentate could protect them, awaited every traitor of the Order;" nor that the French Convention proposed to take off the German Princes and Generals by sword or poison, &c.

Spartacus might tickle the fancy of his Order with the notion of ruling the world; but I imagine that his darling aim was ruling the Order. The happiness of mankind was, like Weishaupt's Christianity, a mere tool, a tool which the *Regentes* made a joke of. But Spartacus would rule the *Regentes;* this he could not so easily accomplish. His despotism was insupportable to most of them, and finally brought all to light. When he could not persuade them by his own firmness, and indeed by his superior wisdom and disinterestedness in other respects, and his unwearied activity, he employed jesuitical tricks, causing them to fall out with each other, setting them as spies on each other, and separating any two that he saw attached to each other, by making the one a Master of the other; and, in short, he left nothing undone that could secure his uncontrouled command. This caused Philo to quit the Order, and made *Bassus, Von Torring, Kreitmaier,* and several other gentlemen, cease attending the meetings; and it was their mutual dissentions which made them speak too freely in public, and call on themselves so much notice. At the time of the discovery, the party of Weishaupt consisted chiefly of very mean people, devoted to him, and willing to execute his orders, that by being his servants, they might have the pleasure of commanding others.

The objects, the undoubted objects of this Association,

are surely dangerous and detestable; viz. to overturn the present constitutions of the European States, in order to introduce a chimera which the history of mankind shows to be contrary to the nature of man.

*Naturam expellas furcâ, tamen usque recurret.*

Suppose it possible, and done in peace, it could not stand, unless every principle of activity in the human mind be enthralled, all incitement to exertion and industry removed, and man brought into a condition incapable of improvement; and this at the expence of every thing that is valued by the best of men—by misery and devastation—by loosening all the bands of society. To talk of morality and virtue in conjunction with such schemes, is an insult to common sense; dissoluteness of manners alone can bring men to think of it.

Is it not astonishing therefore, to hear people in this country express any regard for this institution? Is it not grieving to the heart to think that there are Lodges of Illuminated among us? I think that nothing bids fairer for weaning our inconsiderate countrymen from having any connection with them, than the faithful account here given. I hope that there are few, very few of our countrymen, and none whom we call friend, who can think that an Order which practised such things can be any thing else than a ruinous Association, a gang of profligates. All their professions of the love of mankind are vain; nay, their Illumination must be a bewildering blaze, and totally ineffectual for its purpose, for it has had no such influence on the leaders of the band; yet it seems quite adequate to the effects it has produced; for such are the characters of those who forget God.

If we in the next place attend to their mode of education, and examine it by those rulers of common sense that we apply in other cases of conduct, we shall find it equally unpromising. The system of Illuminatism is one of the explanations of Free Masonry; and it has gained many partisans. These explanations rest their credit and their preference on their own merits. There is something in themselves, or in one of them as distinguished from another, which procures it the preference for its own sake. Therefore, to give this Order any dependence on Free Masonry, is to degrade the Order. To introduce a Masonic Ritual into a manly institution is to degrade it to a frivolous amusement for great children. Men really exerting themselves to reform the world, and qualified for the task, must have been disgusted with such occupations. They betray a frivolous conception of the talk in which they are really engaged. To imagine that men engaged in the struggle and rivalship of life, under the influence of selfish, or mean, or impetuous passions, are to be wheedled into candid sentiments, or a generous conduct, as a froward child may sometimes be made gentle and tractable by a rattle or a humming-top, betrays a great ignorance of human nature, and an arrogant self-conceit in those who can imagine that all but themselves are babies. The further we proceed, the more do we see of this *want of wisdom*. The whole procedure of their instruction supposes such a complete surrender of freedom of thought, of common sense, and of common caution, that it seems impossible that it should not have alarmed every sensible mind. This indeed happened before the Order was seven years old. It was wise indeed to keep their *Areopagitæ* out of sight; but who can be so silly as to believe that their unknown superiors were all and always faultless men. But had they been the men they were represented to be—if I have any knowledge of my own heart, or any capacity of drawing just inferences from the conduct of others, I am persuaded that the knowing his superiors would have animated the pupil to exertion, that he might exhibit a pleasing spectacle to such intelligent and worthy judges. Did not the Stoics profess themselves to be encouraged in the scheme of life, by the thought that the immortal Gods were looking on and passing their judgments on their manner of acting the part assigned them? But what abject spirit will be contented with working, zealously working, for years, after a plan of which he is *never* to learn the full meaning. In short, the only knowledge that he can perceive is knowledge in its worst form, *Cunning*. This must appear in the contrivances by which he will soon find that he is kept in complete subjection. If he is a true and zealous Brother, he has put himself in the power of his Superiors by his rescripts, which they required of him on pretence of their learning his own character, and of his learning how to know the characters of other men. In these rescripts they have got his thoughts on many delicate points, and on the conduct of others. His Directors may ruin him by betraying him: and this without being seen in it. I should think that wise men would know that none but weak or bad men would subject themselves to such a task. They exclude the good, the manly, the only fit persons for assisting them in their endeavours to inform and to rule the world. Indeed I may say that this exclusion is almost made already by connecting the Order with Free Masonry. Lodges are not the resorts of such men. They may sometimes be found there for an hour's relaxation. But these places are the haunts of the young, the thoughtless, the idle, the weak, the vain, or of designing Literati; and accordingly this is the condition of three-fourths of the Illuminati whose names are known to the public. I own that the reasons given to the pupil for prescribing these tasks are clever, and well adapted to produce their effect. During the flurry of reception, and the glow of expectation, the danger may not be suspected; but I hardly imagine that it will remain unperceived when the pupil sits down to write his first lesson. Mason Lodges, however, were the most likely places for finding and enlisting members. Young men, warmed by declamations teeming with the flimsy moral cant of Cosmo-politism, are in the proper frame of mind for this Illumination. It now appears also, that the dissentions in Free Masonry must have had great influence in promoting this scheme of Weishaupt's, which was, in many particulars, so unpromising, because it presupposes such a degradation of the mind. But when the schismatics in Masonry disputed with warmth, trifles came to acquire unspeakable importance. The hankering after wonder was not in the least abated by all the tricks which had been detected, and the impossibility of the wished-for discovery had never been demonstrated to persons prepossessed in its favor. They still *chose* to believe that the symbols contained some important secret; and happy will be the man who finds it out. The more frivolous the symbols, the more does the heart cling to the mystery; and, to a mind in this anxious state, Weishaupt's proffer was enticing. He laid before them a scheme which was somewhat feasible, was magnificent, surpassing our conceptions, but at the same time such as permitted us to expatiate on the subject, and even to amplify it at pleasure in our imaginations without absurdity.

It does not appear to me wonderful, therefore, that so many were fascinated till they became at last regardless of the absurdity and inconsistency of the means by which this splendid object was to be attained. Hear what Spartacus himself says of hidden mysteries. "Of all the means I know to lead men, the most effectual is a concealed mystery. The hankering of the mind is irresistible; and if once a man has taken it into his head that there is a mystery in a thing, it is impossible to get it out, either by argument or experience. And then, we can so change notions by merely changing a word. What more contemptible than *fanaticism;* but call it *enthusiasm;* then add the little word *noble,* and you may lead him over the world. Nor are we, in these bright days, a bit better than our fathers, who found the pardon of their sins mysteriously contained in a much greater sin, viz. leaving their family, and going barefooted to Rome."

Such being the employment, and such the disciples, should we expect the fruits to be very precious? No. The doctrines which were gradually unfolded were such as suited those who continued in the *Cursus Academicus.* Those who did not, because they did not like them, got a *Sta bene;* they were not fit for advancements. The numbers however were great; Spartacus boasted of 600 in Bavaria alone in 1783. We don't know many of them; few of those we know were in the upper ranks of life; and I can see that it required much wheedling, and many letters of long worded German compliments from the proud Spartacus, to win even a young Baron or a Graf just come of age Men in an easy situation in life could not brook the employment of a spy, which is base, cowardly, and corrupting, and has in all ages and countries degraded the person who engages in it. Can the person be called wise who thus enslaves himself? Such persons give up the right of private judgment, and rely on their unknown Superiors with the blindest and most abject confidence. For their sakes, and to rivet still faster their own fetters, they engage in the most corrupting of all employments—and for what?—To learn something more of an order, of which every degree explodes the doctrine of a former one. Would it have hurt the young *Illuminatus* to have it explained to him all at once? Would not this fire his mind—when he sees with the same glance the great object, and the fitness of the means for attaining it? Would not the exalted characters of the Superior, so much excelling himself in talents, and virtue, and happiness (otherwise the Order is good for nothing) warm his heart, and fill him with emulation, since he sees in them, that what is so strongly preached to him is an attainable thing? No, no—it is all a trick; he must be kept like a child, amused with rattles, and stars, and ribands —and all the satisfaction he obtains is, like the Masons, the fun of seeing others running the same gauntlet.

Weishaupt acknowledges that the great influence of the Order may be abused. Surely, in no way so easily or so fatally as by corrupting or seductive lessons in the beginning. The mistake or error of the pupil is undiscoverable by himself (according to the genuine principles of Illumination) for the pupil must believe his Mentor to be infallible—with him alone he is connected—his lessons only must he learn. Who can tell him that he has gone wrong—or who can set him right? yet he certainly may be misled.

Here, therefore, there is confusion and deficiency. There must be some standard to which appeal can be made; but this is inaccessible to all within the pale of the Order; it is therefore without this pale, and independent of the Order —and it is attainable only by abandoning the Order. The QUIBUS LICET, the PRIMO, the SOLI, can procure no light to the person who does not know that he has been led out of the right road to virtue and happiness. The Superiors indeed draw much useful information from these reports, though they affect to stand in no need of it, and they make a cruel return.

All this is so much out of the natural road of instruction, that, on this account alone, we may presume that it is wrong. We are generally safe when we follow nature's plans. A child learns in his father's house, by seeing, and by imitating, and in common domestic education, he gets much useful knowledge, and the chief habits which are afterwards to regulate his conduct. Example does almost every thing; and, with respect to what may be called living, as distinguishable from profession, speculation and argumentative instruction are seldom employed, or of any use. The indispensableness of mutual forbearance and obedience, for domestic peace and happiness, forms most of these habits; and the child, under good parents, is kept in a situation that makes virtue easier than vice, and he becomes wise and good without any express study about the matter.

But this Illumination plan is darkness over all—it is too artificial—and the topics, from which counsel is to be drawn, cannot be taken from the peculiar views of the Order—for these are yet a secret for the pupil—and must ever be a secret for him while under tuition. They must therefore be drawn from common sources, and the Order is of no use; all that can naturally be effectuated by this Association is the forming, and assiduously fostering a narrow, Jewish, corporation spirit, totally opposite to the benevolent pretensions of the Order. The pupil can see nothing but this, that there is a set of men, whom he does not know, who may acquire incontroulable power, and may perhaps make use of him, but for what purpose, and in what way, he does not know; how can he know that his endeavours are to make man happier, any other way than as he might have known it without having put this collar round his own neck?

These reflections address themselves to all men who profess to conduct themselves by the principles and dictates of common sense and prudence, and who have the ordinary share of candour and good will to others. It requires no singular sensibility of heart, nor great generosity, to make such people think the doctrines and views of the Illuminati false, absurd, foolish, and ruinous. But I hope that I address them to thousands of my countrymen and friends, who have much higher notions of human nature, and who cherish with care the affections and the hopes that are suited to a rational, a benevolent, and a high-minded being, capable of endless improvement.

To those who enjoy the cheering confidence in the superintendance and providence of God, who consider themselves as creatures whom he has made, and whom he cares for, as the subjects of his moral government, this Order must appear with every character of falsehood and absurdity on its countenance. What CAN BE MORE IMPROBABLE than this, that He, whom we look up to as the contriver, the maker, and director, of this goodly frame of things, should have so far mistaken his own plans, that this world of rational creatures should have subsisted for thousands of years, before a way could be found out, by which his intention of making men good and happy could be accomplished; and that this method did not occur to the great Artist himself, nor even to the wisest, and happiest, and best men upon earth; but to a few persons at Munich in Bavaria, who had been trying to raise ghosts, to change lead into gold, to tell fortunes, or discover treasures, but had failed in all their attempts; men who had been engaged for years in every whim which characterises a weak, a greedy, or a gloomy mind. Finding all these beyond their reach, they combined their powers, and, at once, found out this infinitely more important SECRET—for secret it must still be, otherwise not only the Deity, but even those philosophers, will still be disappointed.

Yet this is the doctrine that must be swallowed by the Minervals and the *Illuminati Minores,* to whom it is not yet safe to disclose the grand secret, *that there is no such superintendance of Deity.* At last, however, when the pupil has conceived such exalted notions of the knowledge of his teachers, and such low notions of the blundering projector of this world, it may be no difficult matter to persuade him that all his former notions were only old wives tales. By this time he must have heard much about superstition, and how mens minds have been dazzled by this splendid picture of a Providence and a moral government of the universe. It now appears incompatible with the great object of the Order, the principles of universal liberty and equality—it is therefore rejected without farther examination, for this reason alone. This was precisely the argument used in France for rejecting revealed religion. It was incompatible with their Rights of Man.

It is richly worth observing how this principle can warp the judgment, and give quite another appearance to the same object. The reader will not be displeased with a most remarkable instance of it, which I beg leave to give at length.

Our immortal Newton, whom the philosophers of Europe

look up to as the honor of our species, whom even Mr. Bailly, the President of the National Assembly of France, and Mayor of Paris, cannot find words sufficiently energetic to praise; this patient, sagacious, and successful observer of nature, after having exhibited to the wondering world the characteristic property of that principle of material nature by which all the bodies of the solar system are made to form a connected and permanent universe; and after having shown that this law of action alone was adapted to this end, and that if gravity had deviated but one thousandth part from the inverse duplicate ratio of the distances, the system must, in the course of a very few revolutions, have gone into confusion and ruin—he sits down, and views the goodly scene—and then closes his Principles of Natural Philosophy with this reflection (his *Scholium generale.*)

"This most elegant frame of things could not have arisen, unless by the contrivance and the direction of a wise and powerful Being; and if the fixed stars are the centres of systems, these systems must be similar; and all these, constructed according to the same plan, are subject to the government of *one* Being. All these he governs, not as the soul of the world, but as the Lord of all; therefore, on account of his government, he is called the Lord God— *Pantokrator;* for God is a relative term, and refers to subjects. Deity is God's government, not of his own body, as those think who consider him as the soul of the world, but of his servants. The supreme God is a Being eternal, infinite, absolutely perfect. But a being, however perfect, without government, is not God; for we say, *my* God, *your* God, the God of Israel. We cannot say *my* eternal, *my* infinite. We may have some notions indeed of his attributes, but can have none of his nature. With respect to bodies, we see only shapes and colour—hear only sounds—touch only surfaces. These are attributes of bodies; but of their essence we know nothing. As a blind man can form no notion of colours, we can form none of the manner in which God perceives, and understands, and influences every thing.

"Therefore we know God only by his attributes. What are these? The wise and excellent contrivance, structure, and final aim of all things. In these his perfections we admire him, and we wonder. In his direction or government, we venerate and worship him—we worship him as his servants; and God, without dominion, without providence, and final aims, is Fate—not the object either of reverence, of hope, of love, or of fear."

But mark the emotions which affected the mind of another excellent observer of Nature, the admirer of Newton, and the person who has put the finishing stroke to the Newtonian philosophy, by showing that the acceleration of the moon's mean motion, is the genuine result of a gravitation decreasing in the precise duplicate ratio of the distance inversely; I mean Mr. Delaplace, one of the most brilliant ornaments of the French academy of sciences. He has lately published the *Systeme du Monde* a most beautiful compend of astronomy and of the Newtonian philosophy. Having finished his work with the same observation, "That a gravitation inversely proportional to the squares of the distances was the only principle which could unite material Nature into a permanent system;" *he* also sits down—surveys the scene—points out the parts which he had brought within our ken—and then makes this reflection: "Beheld in its totality, astronomy is the noblest monument of the human mind, its chief title to intelligence. But, seduced by the illusions of sense, and by self conceit, we have long considered ourselves as the centre of these motions; and our pride has been punished by the groundless fears which we have created to ourselves. We imagine, forsooth, that all this is for us, and that the stars influence our destinies! But the labours of ages have convinced us of our error, and we find ourselves on an insignificant planet, almost imperceptible in the immensity of space. But the sublime discoveries we have made richly repay this humble situation. Let us cherish these with care, as the delight of thinking beings—they have destroyed our mistakes as to our relation to the rest of the universe; errors which were the more fatal, because the social Order depends on justice and truth alone. Far be from us the dangerous maxim, that it is sometimes useful to depart from these, and to deceive men, in order to insure their happiness; but cruel experience has shewn us that these laws are never totally extinct."

There can be no doubt as to the meaning of these last words—they cannot relate to astrology—this was entirely out of date. The "attempts to deceive men, in order to insure their happiness," can only be those by which we are made to think too highly of ourselves. "Inhabitants of this pepper-corn, we think ourselves the peculiar favorites of Heaven, nay, the chief objects of care to a Being, the Maker of all; and then we imagine that, after this life, we are to be happy or miserable, according as we accede or not to this subjugation to opinions which enslave us. But truth and justice have broken these bonds."—But where is the force of the argument which entitles this perfecter of the Newtonian philosophy to exult so much? It all rests on this, That this earth is but as a grain of mustard-seed. Man would be more worth attention had he inhabited Jupiter or the Sun. Thus may a Frenchman look down on the noble creatures who inhabit Orolong or Pelew. But whence arises the absurdity of the intellectual inhabitants of this pepper-corn being a proper object of attention? it is because our shallow comprehensions cannot, at the same glance, see an extensive scene, and perceive its most minute detail.

David, a King, and a soldier had some notions of this kind. The heavens, it is true, pointed out to him a Maker and Ruler, which is more than they seem to have done to the Gallic philosopher; but David was afraid that he would be forgotten in the crowd, and cries out, "Lord! what is man, that thou art mindful of *him?*" But David gets rid of his fears, not by becoming a philosopher, and discovering all this to be absurd—he would still be forgotten—he at once thinks of what he is—a noble creature—high in the scale of nature. "But," says he, "I had forgotten myself. Thou hast made man but a little lower than the angels—thou hast crowned him with glory and honor—thou hast put all things under his feet." Here are exalted sentiments, fit for the creature whose ken pierces through the immensity of the visible universe, and who sees his relation to the universe, being nearly allied to its Sovereign, and capable of rising continually in his rank, by cultivating those talents which distinguish and adorn it.

Thousands, I trust, there are, who think that this life is but a preparation for another, in which the mind of man will have the whole wonders of creation and of providence laid open to its enraptured view, where it will see and comprehend with one glance what Newton, the most patient and successful of all the observers of nature, took years of meditation to find out—where it will attain that pitch of wisdom, goodness, and enjoyment, of which our consciences tell us we are capable, tho' it far surpasses that of the wisest, the best, and the happiest of men. Such persons will consider this Order as degrading and detestable, and as in direct opposition to their most confident expectations: For it pretends to what is impossible, to perfect peace and happiness in this life. They believe, and they feel, that man must be made perfect through sufferings, which shall call into action powers of mind that otherwise would never have unfolded themselves—powers which are frequently sources of the purest and most soothing pleasures, and naturally make us rest our eyes and hopes on that state where every tear shall be wiped away, and where the kind affections shall become the never-failing sources of pure and unfading delight. Such persons see the palpable absurdity of a preparation which is equally necessary for all, and yet must be confined to the minds of a few, who have the low and indelicate appetite for frivolous play-things, and for gross sensual pleasures. Such minds will turn away from this boasted treat with loathing and abhorrence.

I am well aware that some of my readers may smile at this, and think it an enthusiastical working up of the imagination, similar to what I reprobate in the case of Utopian happiness in a state of universal Liberty and Equality. It is like, they will say, to the declamation in a sermon by persons of the trade, who are trained up to finesse, by which they allure and tickle weak minds.

I acknowledge, that in the present case, I do not address myself to the cold hearts, who contentedly

*"Sink and slumber in their cells of clay;"*

——Peace to all such;——but to the *felices animæ, quibus hæc cognoscere cura;"*—to those who *have enjoyed* the pleasures of science, who have been successful—who have made discoveries—who have really illuminated the world—

to the Bacons, the Newtons, the Lockes.—Allow me to mention one, Daniel Bernoulli, the most elegant mathematician, the only philosopher, and the most worthy man, of that celebrated family. He said to a gentleman (Dr. Staehling) who repeated it to me, that "when reading some of those wonderful guesses of Sir Isaac Newton, the subsequent demonstration of which has been the chief source of fame to his most celebrated commentators—his mind has sometimes been so overpowered by thrilling emotions, that he has wished that moment to be his last; and that it was this which gave him the clearest conception of the happiness of heaven." If such delightful emotions could be excited by the perception of mere truth, what must they be when each of these truths is an instance of wisdom, and when we recollect, that what we call wisdom in the works of nature, is always the nice adaptation of means for producing *beneficent* ends; and that each of these affecting qualities is susceptible of degrees which are boundless, and exceed our highest conceptions. What can this complex emotion or feeling be but rapture? But Bernoulli is a Doctor of Theology—and therefore a suspicious person, perhaps one of the combination hired by despots to enslave us. I will take another man, a gentleman of rank and family, a soldier, who often signalised himself as a naval commander—who at one time forced his way through a powerful fleet of the Venetians with a small squadron, and brought relief to a distressed garrison. I would desire the reader to peruse the conclusion of Sir Kenhelm Digby's *Treatises on Body and Mind;* and after having reflected on the state of science at the time this author wrote, let him coolly weigh the incitements to manly conduct which this soldier finds in the differences observed between body and mind; and then let him say, on his conscience, whether they are more feeble than those which he can draw from the eternal sleep of death. If he thinks that they are—he is in the proper frame for initiation into Spartacus's higher mysteries. He may be either Magus or Rex.

Were this a proper place for considering the question as a question of science or truth, I would say, that every man who has been a *successful* student of nature, and who will rest his conclusions on the same maxims of probable reasoning that have procured him success in his past researches, will consider it as next to certain that there is another state of existence for rational man. For he must own, that if this be not the case, there is a most singular exception to a proposition which the whole course of his experience has made him consider as a truth founded on universal induction, viz. that *nature accomplishes all her plans,* and that every class of beings attains all the improvement of which it is capable. Let him but turn his thoughts inward, he will feel that his intellect is capable of improvement, in comparison with which Newton is but a child. I could pursue this argument very far, and (I think) warm the heart of every man whom I should wish to call my friend.

What opinion will be formed of this Association by the modest, the lowly-minded, the candid, who acknowledge that they too often feel the superior force of present and sensible pleasures, by which their minds are drawn off from the contemplation of what their consciences tell them to be right—to be their dutiful and filial sentiments and emotions respecting their great and good Parent—to be their dutiful and neighbourly affections, and their proper conduct to all around them—and which diminish their veneration for that purity of thought and moderation of appetite which becomes their noble natures. What must *they* think of this Order? Conscious of frequent faults, which would offend themselves if committed by their dearest children, they look up to their Maker with anxiety—are sorry for having so far forgotten their duty, and fearful that they may again forget it. Their painful experience tells them that their reason is often too weak, their information too scanty, or its light is obstructed by passion and prejudices, which distort and discolour every thing; or it is unheeded during their attention to present objects. Happy should they be, if it should please their kind Parent to remind them of their duty from time to time, or to influence their mind in any way that would compensate for their own ignorance, their own weakness, or even their indolence and neglect. They dare not expect such a favor, which their modesty tells them they do not deserve, and which they fear may be unfit to be granted; but when such a comfort is held out to them, with eager hearts they receive it—they bless the kindness that granted it, and the hand that brings it.——
Such amiable characters have appeared in all ages, and in

all situations of mankind. They have not in all instances been wise—often have they been precipitate, and have too readily catched at any thing which pretended to give them the so much wished-for assistances; and, unfortunately, there have been enthusiasts, or villains, who have taken advantage of this universal wish of anxious man; and the world has been darkened by cheats, who have misrepresented God to mankind, have filled us with vain terrors, and have then quieted our fears by fines, and sacrifices, and mortifications, and services, which they said made more than amends for all our faults. Thus was our duty to our neighbour, to our own dignity, and to our Maker and Parent, kept out of sight, and religion no longer came in aid to our sense of right and wrong; but, on the contrary, by these superstitions it opened the doors of heaven to the worthless and the wicked.——But I wish not to speak of these men, but of the good, the candid, the MODEST, the HUMBLE who know their failings, who love their duties, but wish to know, to perceive, and to love them still more. These are they who think and believe that "the Gospel has brought life and immortality to light," that is, within their reach. They think it worthy of the Father of mankind, and they receive it with thankful hearts, admiring above all things the simplicity of its morality, comprehended in one sentence, "Do to another what you can reasonably wish that another should do to you," and THAT PURITY OF THOUGHT AND MANNERS WHICH DISTINGUISHES IT FROM ALL THE SYSTEMS OF MORAL INSTRUCTION THAT HAVE EVER BEEN OFFERED TO MEN. Here they find a ground of resignation under the troubles of life, and a support in the hour of death, quite suited to the diffidence of their character. Such men are ready to grant that the Stoics were persons of noble and exalted minds, and that they had worthy conceptions of the rank of man in the scale of God's works; but they confess that they themselves do not feel all that support from Stoical principles which man too frequently needs; and they say that they are not singular in their opinions, but that the bulk of mankind are prevented, by their want of heroic fortitude, by their situation, or their want of the opportunities of cultivating their native strength of mind, from ever attaining this hearty submission to the will of Deity.——They maintain, that the Stoics were but a few, a very few, from among many millions—and therefore *their* being satisfied was but a trifle amidst the general discontent, and fretting, and despair.—Such men will most certainly start back from this Illumination with horror and fright—from a Society which gives the lie to their fondest hopes, makes a sport of their grounds of hope, and of their deliverer; and which, after laughing at their credulity, bids them shake off all religion whatever, and denies the existence of that Supreme Mind, the pattern of all excellence, who till now had filled their thoughts with admiration and love—from an Order which pretends to free them from spiritual bondage, and then lays on their necks a load ten times more oppressive and intolerable, from which they have no power of ever escaping. Men of sense and virtue will spurn at such a proposal; and even the profligate, who trade with Deity, must be sensible that they will be better off with their priests, whom they know, and among whom they may make a selection of such as will with patience and gentleness clear up their doubts, calm their fears, and encourage their hopes.

And all good men, all lovers of peace and of justice, will abhor and reject the thought of overturning the present constitution of things, faulty as it may be, merely in the endeavour to establish another, which the vices of mankind may subvert again in a twelvemonth. They must see, that in order to gain their point, the proposers have found it necessary to destroy the grounds of morality, by permitting the most wicked means for accomplishing any end that our fancy, warped by passion or interest, may represent to us as of great importance. They see, that instead of morality, vice must prevail, and that therefore there is no security for the continuance of this Utopian felicity; and, in the mean time, desolation and misery must lay the world waste during the struggle, and half of those for whom we are striving will be swept from the face of the earth. We have but to look to France, where in eight years there have been more executions and spoilations and distresses of every kind by the *pouvoir revolutionnaire,* than can be found in the long records of that despotic monarchy.

There is nothing in the whole constitution of the Illuminati that strikes me with more horror than the proposals of Hercules and Minos to enlist the women in this shocking warfare with all that "is good, and pure, and lovely, and of good report." They could not have fallen on any expedient that will be more effectual and fatal. If any of my countrywomen shall honor these pages with a reading, I would call on them, in the most earnest manner, to consider this as an affair of the utmost importance to themselves. I would conjure them by the regard they have for their own dignity, and for their rank in society, to join against these enemies of human nature, and profligate degraders of the sex; and I would assure them that the present state of things almost puts it in their power to be the saviours of the world. But if they are remiss, and yield to the seduction, they will fall from that high state to which they have arisen in Christian Europe, and again sink into that insignificancy or slavery in which the sex is found in all ages and countries out of the hearing of Christianity.

I hope that my countrywomen will consider this solemn address to them as a proof of the high esteem in which I hold them. They will not be offended then if, in this season of alarm and anxiety, when I wish to impress their minds with a serious truth, I shall wave ceremony which is always designing, and speak of them in honest but decent plainness.

Man is immersed in luxury. Our accommodations are now so numerous that every thing is pleasure. Even in very sober situations in this highly cultivated Society, there is hardly a thing that remains in the form of a necessary of life, or even of a mere conveniency—every thing is ornamented—it must not appear of use—it must appear as giving some sensible pleasure. I do not say this by way of blaming—it is nature—man is a refining creature, and our most boasted acquirements are but refinements on our necessary wants. Our hut becomes a palace, our blanket a fine dress, and our arts become sciences. This discontent with the natural condition of things, and this disposition to refinement, is a characteristic of our species, and is the great employment of our lives. The direction which this propensity chances to take in any age or nation, marks its character in the most conspicuous and interesting manner. All have it in some degree, and it is very conceivable that, in some, it may constitute the chief object of attention. If this be the case in any nations, it is surely most likely to be so in those where the accommodations of life are the most numerous—therefore in a rich and luxurious nation. I may surely, without exaggeration or reproach, give that appellation to our own nation at this moment. If you do not go to the very lowest class of people, who must labour all day, is it not the chief object of all to procure *perceptible pleasure* in one way or another? The sober and busy struggle in the thoughts and hopes of getting the means of enjoying the *comforts* of life without farther labour—and many have no other object than pleasure.

Then let us reflect that it is woman that is to *grace* the whole—It is in nature, it is the very constitution of man, that woman, and every thing connected with woman, must appear as the ornament of life. That this mixes with every other social sentiment, appears from the conduct of our species in all ages and in every situation. This I presume would be the case, even though there were no qualities or talents in the sex to justify it. This sentiment respecting the sex is necessary, in order to rear so helpless, so nice, and so improveable a creature as man; without it, the long abiding task could not be performed:—and I think that I may venture to say that it is performed in the different states of society nearly in proportion as this preparatory and indispensable sentiment is in force.

On the other hand, I think it no less evident that it is the desire of the women to be agreeable to the men, and that they will model themselves according to what they think will please. Without this adjustment of sentiments by nature, nothing would go on. We never observe any such want of symmetry in the works of God. If, therefore, those who take the lead, and give the fashion in society, were wise and virtuous, I have no doubt but that the women would set the brightest pattern of every thing that is excellent. But if the men are nice and fastidious sensualists, the women will be refined and elegant voluptuaries.

There is no deficiency in the female mind, either in talents or in dispositions; nor can we say with certainty that there is any subject of intellectual or moral discussion in which women have not excelled. If the delicacy of their constitution, and other physical causes, allow the female sex a smaller share of some mental powers, they possess others in a superior degree, which are no less respectable in their own nature, and of as great importance to society. Instead of descanting at large on their powers of mind, and supporting my assertions by the instances of a Hypatia, a Schurman, a Zenobia, an Elisabeth, &c. I may repeat the account given of the sex by a person of uncommon experience, who saw them without disguise, or any motive that could lead them to play a feigned part.—Mr. Ledyard, who traversed the greatest part of the world, for the mere indulgence of his taste for observation of human nature; generally in want, and often in extreme misery.

"I have (says he) always remarked that women, in all countries, are civil, obliging, tender, and humane; that they are ever inclined to be gay and cheerful, timorous and modest; and that they do not hesitate, like man, to perform a kind or generous action.—Not haughty, not arrogant, not supercilious, they are full of courtesy, and fond of society— more liable in general to err than man, but in general, also, more virtuous, and performing more good actions than he. To a woman, whether civilized or savage, I never addressed myself in the language of decency and friendship, without receiving a decent and friendly answer—with man it has often been otherwise.

"In wandering over the barren plains of inhospitable Denmark, through honest Sweden, and frozen Lapland, rude and churlish Finland, unprincipled Russia, and the wide spread regions of the wandering Tartar—if hungry, dry, cold, wet, or sick, the women have ever been friendly to me, and uniformly so; and to add to this virtue (so worthy of the appellation of benevolence) these actions have been performed in so free and so kind a manner, that if I was thirsty, I drank the sweetest draught, and if hungry, I ate the coarse meal with a double relish."

And these are they whom Weishaupt would corrupt! One of these, whom he had embraced with fondness, would he have murdered, to save his honor, and qualify himself to preach virtue! But let us not be too severe on Weishaupt —let us wash ourselves clear of all stain before we think of reprobating him. Are we not guilty in some degree, when we do not cultivate in the women those powers of mind, and those dispositions of heart, which would equally dignify them in every station as in those humble ranks in which Mr. Ledyard most frequently saw them? I cannot think that we do this. They are not only to *grace* the whole of cultivated society, but it is in their faithful and affectionate personal attachment that we are to find the sweetest pleasures that life can give. Yet in all the situations where the manner in which they are treated is not dictated by the stern laws of necessity, are they not trained up for mere amusement—are not serious occupations considered as a task which hurts their loveliness? What is this but selfishness, or as if they had no virtues worth cultivating? Their *business* is supposed to be the ornamenting themselves, as if nature did not dictate this to them already, with at least as much force as is necessary. Every thing is prescribed to them *because it makes them more lovely*— even their moral lessons are enforced by this argument, and Miss Woolstoncroft is perfectly right when she says that the fine lessons given to young women by Fordyce or Rousseau are nothing but selfish and refined voluptuousness. This advocate of her sex puts her sisters in the proper point of view, when she tells them that they are, like man, the subjects of God's moral government—like man, preparing themselves for boundless improvement in a better state of existence. Had she adhered to this view of the matter, and kept it constantly in sight, her book (which doubtless contains many excellent things, highly deserving of their serious consideration) would have been a most valuable work. She justly observes, that the virtues of the sex are great and respectable, but that in our mad chace of pleasure, only pleasure, they are little thought of or attended to. Man trusts to his own uncontroulable power, or to the general goodness of the sex, that their virtues will appear when we have occasion for them;—"but we will send for these some other time;"—Many noble displays do they make of the most difficult attainments. Such is the patient bearing up under misfortunes, which has no brilliancy to support it in the effort. This is more difficult than braving danger in an active and conspicuous situation. How often is a woman left with a family and the shattered remains of a fortune, lost perhaps by dissipation or by indolence—

and how seldom, how very seldom, do we see woman shrink from the task, or discharge it with negligence? Is it not therefore folly next to madness, not to be careful of this our greatest blessing—of things which so nearly concern our peace—nor guard ourselves, and these our best companions and friends, from the effects of this fatal Illumination? It has indeed brought to light what dreadful lengths men will go, when under the fanatical and dazzling glare of happiness in a state of liberty and equality, and spurred on by insatiable luxury, and not held in check by moral feelings and the restraints of religion—and mark, reader, that the women have here also taken the complexion of the men, and have even gone beyond them. If we have seen a son present himself to the National Assembly of France, professing his satisfaction with the execution of his father three days before, and declaring himself a true citizen, who prefers the nation to all other considerations; we have also seen, on the same day, wives denouncing their husbands, and (O shocking to human nature!) mothers denouncing their sons, as bad citizens and traitors. Mark too what return the women have met with for all their horrid services, where, to express their sentiments of civism and abhorrence of royalty, they threw away the character of their sex, and bit the amputated limbs of their murdered countrymen.* Surely these patriotic women merited that the rights of their sex should be considered in full council, and they were well entitled to a seat; but there is not a single act of their government in which the sex is considered as having any rights whatever, or that they are things to be cared for.

Are not the accursed fruits of Illumination to be seen in the present humiliating condition of woman in France? pampered in every thing that can reduce them to the mere instrument of animal pleasure. In their present state of national moderation (as they call it) and security, see Madame Talien come into the public theatre, accompanied by other *beautiful* women (I was about to have misnamed

*I say this on the authority of a young gentleman, an emigrant, who saw it, and who said, that they were women, not of the dregs of the Palais Royal, not of infamous character, but well dressed.—I am sorry to add, that the relation, accompanied with looks of horror and disgust, only provoked a contemptuous smile from an illuminated British Fair one.

them Ladies) laying aside all modesty, and presenting themselves to the public view, with bared limbs, *à la Sauvage,* as the alluring objects of desire. I make no doubt but that this is a serious matter, encouraged, nay, prompted by government. To keep the minds of the Parisians in the present fever of dissolute gaiety, they are at more expence from the national treasury for the support of the sixty theatres, than all the pensions and honorary offices in Britain, three times told, amount to. Was not their abominable farce in the church of Notre Dame a bait of the same kind, in the true spirit of Weishaupt's *Eroterion?* I was pleased to see among the priests of that solemnity Mr. Brigonzi, an old acquaintance, formerly *Machiniste* (and excellent in his profession) to the opera at the palace in St. Petersburg. He was a most zealous Mason, and Chevalier de l'Orient; and I know that he went to Paris in the same capacity of *Machiniste de l'Opera;* so that I am next to certain that this is the very man. But what will be the end of all this? The fondlings of the wealthy will be pampered in all the indulgences which fastidious voluptuousness finds necessary for varying or enhancing its pleasures; but they will either be slighted as toys, or they will be immured; and the companions of the poor will be drudges and slaves.

I am fully persuaded that it was the enthusiastic admiration of Grecian democracy that recommended to the French nation the dress *à la Grecque,* which exhibits, not the elegant, ornamented beauty, but the beautiful female, fully as well as Madame Talien's dress *à la Sauvage.* It was no doubt with the same adherence to *serious principle,* that Mademoiselle Therouanne was most beautifully dressed *à l'Amazonne* on the 5th of October 1789, when she turned the heads of so many young officers of the regiments at Versailles. The Cytherea, the *hominum divumque voluptas,* at the cathedral of Notre Dame, was also dressed *à la Grecque;* and in this, and in much of the solemnities of that day, I recognized the taste and invention of my old acquaintance Brigonzi. I recollected the dresses of our *premiere & seconde Surveillantes* in the *Loge de la Fidelité.* There is a most evident and characteristic change in the whole system of female dress in France. The *Filles de l'Opera* always gave the *ton,* and were surely withheld by no rigid principle. They sometimes produced very extravagant and fantastic forms, but these were almost always in the style of the highest ornament, and they trusted, for the rest of the impression which they wished to make, to the fascinating expression of elegant movements. This indeed was wonderful, and hardly conceivable by any who have not seen a grand ballet performed by good actors. I have shed tears of the most sincere and tender sorrow during the exhibition of Antigone, set to music by Traetta, and performed by Madame Meilcour and S$^{re}$ Torelli, and Zantini. I can easily conceive the impression to be still stronger, though perhaps of another kind, when the former superb dresses are changed for the expressive simplicity of the Grecian. I cannot help thinking that the female ornaments in the rest of Europe, and even among ourselves, have less elegance since we lost the *imprimatur* of the French court. But see how all this will terminate, when we shall have brought the sex so low, and will not even wait for a Mahometan paradise. What can we expect but such a dissoluteness of manners, that the endearing ties of relation and family, and mutual confidence within doors, will be slighted, and will cease; and every man must stand up for himself, single and alone, in perfect equality, and full liberty to do whatever his own arm (but that alone) is able to accomplish. This is not the suggestion of prudish fear, I think it is the natural course of things, and that France is at this moment giving to the world the fullest proof of Weishaupt's sagacity, and the judgment with which he has formed his plans. Can it tend to the improvement of our morals or manners to have our ladies frequent the gymnastic theatres, and see them decide, like the Roman matrons, on the merits of a naked gladiator or wrestler? Have we not enough of this already with our vaulters and posture-masters, and should we admire any lady who had a rage for such spectacles? Will it improve our taste to have our rooms ornamented with such paintings and sculptures as filled the cenaculum, and the study of the refined and elegant moralist Horace, who had the art—*ridendo dicere verum?* Shall we be improved when such indulgences are thought compatible with such lessons as he generally gives for the conduct of life? The pure Morality of Illuminatism is now employed in stripping Italy of all those precious remains of ancient art and voluptuousness; and Paris will ere long be the deposit and the resort of artists from all nations, there to study the works of ancient masters, and to return from thence pandars of public corruption. The plan is masterly, and the low-born Statesmen and Generals of France may in this respect be set on a level with a Colbert or a Condé. But the consequences of this Gallic dominion over the minds of fallen man will be as dreadful as their dominion over their lives and fortunes.

Recollect in what manner Spartacus proposed to corrupt his sisters (for we need not speak of the manner in which he expected that this would promote his plan—this is abundantly plain.) It was by destroying their moral sentiments, and their sentiments of religion.—Recollect what is the recommendation that the Atheist Minos gives of his step-daughters, when he speaks of them as proper persons for the Lodge of Sisters. "They have got over all prejudices, and, in matters of religion, they think as I do." These profligates judged rightly that this affair required much caution, and that the utmost attention to decency, and even delicacy, must be observed in their rituals and ceremonies, otherwise they would be *disgusted*. This was judging fairly of the feelings of a female mind. But they judged falsely, and only according to their own coarse experience, when they attributed their disgust and their fears to coyness. Coyness is indeed the instinctive attribute of the female. In woman it is very great, and it is perhaps the genuine source of the *disgust* of which the Illuminati were suspicious. But they have been dim-sighted indeed, or very unfortunate in their acquaintance, if they never observed any other source of repugnance in the mind of woman to what is immoral or immodest—if they did not see dislike—moral disapprobation. Do they mean to insinuate, that in that regard which modest women express in all their words and actions, for what every one understands by the terms decency, modesty, filthiness, obscenity, they only show female coyness? Then are they very blind instructors. But they are not so blind. The account given of the initiation of a young Sister at Frankfort, under the feigned name *Psycharion,* shows the most scrupulous attention to the moral feelings of the sex; and the confusion and disturbance which it occasioned among the ladies, after all their care, shows, that when they thought all right and delicate, they had been but coarse judges. Minos damns the ladies there, because they are too free, too rich, too republican, and too wise, for being led about by the nose (this is his own expression). But Philo certainly thought more correctly of the sex in general, when he says, Truth is a modest girl: She may be handed about like a lady, by good sense and good manners, but must not be bullied and driven about like a strumpet. I would give the discourses or addresses which were made on that occasion to the different classes of the assembly, girls, young ladies, wives, young men, and strangers, which are really well composed and pretty, were they not such as would offend my fair countrywomen.

The religious sentiments by which mortals are to be assisted, even in the discharge of their moral duties, and still more, the sentiments which are purely religious, and have no reference to any thing here, are precisely those which are most easily excited in the mind of woman. Affection, admiration, filial reverence, are, if I mistake not exceedingly, those in which the women far surpass the men; and it is on this account that we generally find them so much disposed to devotion, which is nothing but a sort of fond indulgence of these affections without limit to the imagination. The enraptured devotee pours out her soul in expressions of these feelings, just as a fond mother mixes the caresses given to her child with the most extravagant expressions of love. The devotee even endeavours to excite higher degrees of these affections, by expatiating on such circumstances in the divine conduct with respect to man as naturally awaken them; and he does this without any fear of exceeding; because Infinite Wisdom and Goodness will always justify the sentiment, and free the expression of it from all charge of hyperbole or extravagance.

I am convinced, therefore, that the female mind is well adapted to cultivation by means of religion, and that their native softness and kindness of heart will always be sufficient for procuring it a favorable reception from them. It is therefore with double regret that I see any of them join in the arrogant pretensions of our Illuminated philosophers, who see no need of such assistances for the knowledge and discharge of their duties. There is nothing so unlike that general modesty of thought, and that diffidence, which we are disposed to think the character of the female mind. I am inclined to think, that such deviations from the general conduct of the sex are marks of a harsher character, of a heart that has less sensibility, and is on the whole less amiable than that of others; yet it must be owned that there are some such among us. Much, if not the whole of this perversion, has, I am persuaded, been owing to the contagion of bad example in the men. They are made familiar with such expressions—their first horror is gone, and (would to heaven that I were mistaken!) some of them have already wounded their consciences to such a degree, that they have some reason to wish that religion may be without foundation.

But I would call upon all; and *these* women in particular, to consider this matter in another light—as it may affect themselves in this life; as it may affect their rank and treatment in ordinary society. I would say to them, that if the world shall once adopt the belief that this life is our all, then, the true maxim of rational conduct will be, to "eat and to drink, since to-morrow we are to die;" and that when they have nothing to trust to but the fondness of the men, they will soon find themselves reduced to slavery. The crown which they now wear will fall from their heads, and they will no longer be the arbiters of what is lovely in human life. The empire of beauty is but short; and even in republican France, it will not be many years that Madame Talien can fascinate the Parisian Theatre by the exhibition of her charms. Man is fastidious and changeable, and he is stronger than they, and can always take his own will with respect to woman. At present he is with-held by respect for her moral worth—and many are with-held by religion— and many more are with-held by public laws, which laws were framed at a time when religious truths influenced the minds and the conduct of men. When the sentiments of men change, they will not be so foolish as to keep in force laws which cramp their strongest desires. Then will the rich have their Harems, and the poor their drudges.

Nay, it is not merely the circumstance of woman's being considered as the moral companion of man that gives the sex its empire among us. There is something of this to be observed in all nations. Of all the distinctions which set our species above the other sentient inhabitants of this globe, making us as unlike to the best of them as they are to a piece of inanimate matter, there is none more remarkable than the differences observable in the appearances of those desires by which the race is continued. As I observed already, such a distinction is indispensably necessary. There must be a *moral* connection, in order that the human species may be a race of rational creatures, improveable, not only by the encreasing experience of the individual, but also by the heritable experience of the successive generations. It may be observed between the solitary pairs in Labrador, where human nature starves, like the stunted oak in the crevice of a baron rock; and it is seen in the cultivated societies of Europe, where our nature in a series of ages becomes a majestic tree. But, alas! with what differences of boughs and foliage! Whatever may be the native powers of mind in the poor but gentle Esquimaux, she can do nothing for the species but nurse a young one, who cannot run his race of life without incessant and hard labour to keep soul and body together—here therefore her station in society can hardly have a name, because there can hardly be said that there is an association, except what is necessary for repelling the hostile attacks of Indians, who seem to hunt them without provocation as the dog does the hare. In other parts of the world, we see that the consideration in which the sex is held, nearly follows the proportions of that aggregate of many different particulars, which we consider as constituting the cultivation of a society. We may perhaps err, and we probably do err, in our estimation of these degrees, because we are not perfectly acquainted with what is the real excellence of man. But as far as we *can* judge of it, I believe that my assertion is acknowledged. On this authority, I might presume to say, that it is in Christian Europe that man *has* attained his highest degree of cultivation—and it is undoubtedly here that the women have attained the highest rank. I may even add, that it is in that part of Europe where the essential and distinguishing doctrines of Christian morality are most generally acknowledged and attended to by the laws of the country, that woman acts the highest part in general society. But here we must be very careful how we form our notion, either of the society, or of the female rank—it is surely not from the two or three dozens who fill the highest ranks in the state. Their number is too small, and their situation is too particular, to afford the proper average. Besides, the situation of the individuals of this class in all countries is very much the same—and in all it is very artificial—accordingly their character is fantastical. Nor are we to take it from that class that is the most numerous of all, the lowest class of society, for these are the labouring poor, whose conduct and occupations are so much dictated to them by the hard circumstances of their situation, that scarcely any thing is left to their choice. The situation of women of this class must be nearly the same in all nations. But this class is still susceptible of some variety—and we see it—and I think that even here there is a perceptible superiority of the female rank in those countries where the purest Christianity prevails. We must however take our measures or proportions from a numerous class, but also a class in somewhat of easy circumstances, where moral sentiments call some attention, and persons have some choice in their conduct. And here, although I cannot pretend to have had many opportunities of observation, yet I have had some. I can venture to say that it is not in Russia, nor in Spain, that woman is, on the whole, the most important as a member of the community. I would say, that in Britain her important rights are more generally respected than any where else. No where is a man's character so much hurt by infidelity—no where is it so difficult to rub off the stigma of bastardy, or to procure a decent reception or society for an improper connection; and I believe it will readily be granted, that their share in successions, their authority in all matters of domestic trust, and even their opinions in what concerns life and manners, are fully more respected here than in any country.

I have been of the opinion (and every observation that I have been able to make since I first formed it confirms me in it) that woman is indebted to Christianity alone for the high rank she holds in society. Look into the writings of antiquity—into the works of the Greek and Latin poets —into the numberless panegyrics of the sex, to be found both in prose and verse—I can find little, very little indeed, where woman is treated with respect—there is no want of love, that is, of fondness, of beauty, of charms, of graces. But of woman as the equal of man, as a moral companion,

travelling with him the road to felicity—as his adviser—
his solace in misfortune—as a pattern from which he may
sometimes copy with advantage;—of all this there is
hardly a trace. Woman is always mentioned as an object of
passion. Chastity, modesty, sober-mindedness, are all considered in relation to this single point; or sometimes as of
importance in respect of œconomy or domestic quiet. Recollect the famous speech of Metellus Numidicus to the Roman
people, when, as Censor, he was recommending marriage.

"Si fine uxore possemus Quirites esse, omnes eâ mo-
lestiâ careremus. Sed quoniam ita natura tradidit, ut nec
cum illis commode, nec fine illis ullo modo vivi posset,
saluti perpetuæ potius quam brevi voluptati consulendum."
*Aul. Gell. Noct. Att. I. 6.*

What does Ovid, the great panegyrist of the sex, say for
his beloved daughter, whom he had praised for her attrac-
tions in various places of his Tristia and other compositions? He is writing her Epitaph—and the only thing he
can say of her as a rational creature is, that she is—
*Domifida*—not a Gadabout.—Search Apuleius, where you
will find many female characters *in abstracto*—You will
find that his little Photis was nearest to his heart, after all
his philosophy. Nay, in his pretty story of Cupid and
Psyche, which the very wise will tell you is a fine lesson
of moral philosophy, and a representation of the operations
of the intellectual and moral faculties of the human soul,
a story which gave him the finest opportunity, nay, almost
made it necessary for him, to insert whatever can ornament
the female character; what is his Psyche but a beautiful,
fond, and silly girl; and what are the whole fruits of any
acquaintance with the sex?—Pleasure. But why take more
pains in the search?—Look at their immortal goddesses—
is there one among them whom a wise man would select
for a wife or a friend?—I grant that a Lucretia is praised
—a Portia, an Arria, a Zenobia—but these are individual
characters—not representatives of the sex. The only Grecian ladies who made a figure by intellectual talents, were
your Aspasias, Sapphos, Phrynes, and other nymphs of this
cast, who had emerged from the general insignificance of
the sex, by throwing away what we are accustomed to call
its greatest ornament.

I think that the first piece in which woman is pictured as a respectable character, is the oldest novel that I am acquainted with, written by a Christian Bishop, Heliodorus— I mean the Adventures of Theagenes and Chariclea. I think that the Heroine is a greater character than you will meet with in all the annals of antiquity. And it is worth while to observe what was the effect of this painting. The poor Bishop had been deposed, and even excommunicated, for doctrinal errors, and for drawing such a picture of a heathen. The magistrates of Antioch, the most voluptuous and corrupted city of the East, wrote to the Emperor, telling him that this book had reformed the ladies of their city, where Julian the Emperor and his Sophists had formerly preached in vain, and they therefore prayed that the good Bishop might not be deprived of his mitre.—It is true, we read of Hypatia, daughter of Theon, the mathematician at Alexandria, who was a prodigy of excellence, and taught philosophy, *i. e.* the art of leading a good and happy life, with great applause in the famous Alexandrian school.— But she also was in the times of Christianity, and was the intimate friend of Syncellus and other Christian Bishops.

It is undoubtedly Christianity that has set woman on her throne, making her in every respect the equal of man, bound to the same duties, and candidate for the same happiness. Mark how woman is described by a Christian poet,

> ———"Yet when I approach
> Her loveliness, so absolute she seems,
> And in herself complete, so well to know
> Her own, that what she wills to do or say
> Seems *wisest, virtuousest, discreetest, best.*
>
> Neither her outside, form'd so fair,———
> So much delights me, as *those graceful acts,*
> *Those thousand decencies* that daily flow
> From all her words and actions, mix'd with love
> And sweet compliance, which declare unfeign'd
> *Union of mind, or in us both one soul.*
>
> ———And, to consummate all,
> *Greatness of mind,* and *nobleness,* their feat
> Build in her loveliest, *and create an awe*
> *About her, as a guard angelic plac'd."*

MILTON.

This is really moral painting, without any abatement of female charms.

This is the natural consequence of that purity of heart, which is so much insisted on in the Christian morality. In the instructions of the heathen philosophers, it is either not mentioned at all, or at most, it is recommended coldly, as a thing proper, and worthy of a mind attentive to great things.——But, in Christianity, it is insisted on as an indispensable duty, and enforced by many arguments peculiar to itself.

It is worthy of observation, that the most prominent superstitions which have dishonored the Christian churches, have been the excessive refinements which the enthusiastic admiration of heroic purity has allowed the holy trade to introduce into the manufacture of our spiritual fetters. Without this enthusiasm, cold expediency would not have been able to make the Monastic vow so general, nor have given us such numbers of convents. These were generally founded by such enthusiasts——the rulers indeed of the church *encouraged* this to the utmost, as the best levy for the spiritual power——but they could not *enjoin* such foundations. From the same source we may derive the chief influence of auricular confession. When these were firmly established, and were venerated, almost all the other corruptions of Christianity followed of course. I may almost add, that though it is here that Christianity has suffered the most violent attacks, it is here that the place is most tenable. ——Nothing tends so much to knit all the ties of society as the endearing connections of family, and whatever tends to lessen our veneration for the marriage contract, weakens them in the most effectual manner. Purity of manners is its most effectual support, and pure thoughts are the only sources from which pure manners can flow. I readily grant that this veneration for personal purity was carried to an extravagant height, and that several very ridiculous fancies and customs arose from this. Romantic love, and chivalry, are strong instances of the strange vagaries of our imagination, when carried along by this enthusiastic admiration of female purity; and so unnatural and forced, that they could only be temporary fashions. But I believe that, with all their ridicule, it would be a happy nation where this was the general creed and practice. Nor can I help thinking a nation on its decline, when the domestic connections cease to be venerated, and the illegitimate offspring of a nabob or a nobleman are received with ease into good company.

Nothing is more clear than that the design of the Illuminati was to abolish Christianity—and we now see how effectual this would be for the corruption of the fair sex, a purpose which they eagerly wished to gain, that they might corrupt the men. But if the women would retain the rank they now hold, they will be careful to preserve in full force on their minds this religion so congenial to their dispositions, which nature has made affectionate and kind.

And with respect to the men, is it not egregious folly to encourage any thing that can tend to blast our sweetest enjoyments? Shall we not do this most effectually if we attempt to corrupt what nature will always make us consider as the highest elegance of life? The divinity of the Stoics was, *"Mens sana in corpore sano"*—but it is equally true,

*"Gratior est pulchro veniens e corpore virtus."*

If therefore, instead of professedly tainting what is of itself beautiful, we could really work it up to

> "That fair form, which, wove in fancy's loom,
> "Floats in light visions round the poet's head,"

and make woman a pattern of perfection, we should undoubtedly add more to the heartfelt happiness of life than by all the discoveries of the Illuminati. See what was the effect of Theagenes and Chariclea.

And we should remember that with the fate of woman that of man is indissolubly knit. The voice of nature spoke through our immortal bard, when he made Adam say,

> ————————"From thy state
> Mine never shall be parted, bliss or woe."

Should we suffer the contagion to touch our fair partner, all is gone, and too late shall we say,

> "O fairest of creation! last and best
> Of all God's works, creature in whom excell'd
> Whatever can to fight or thought be form'd,
> *Holy, divine, good, amiable, or sweet!*
> How art thou lost—and now to death devote?—
> And me with thee hast ruin'd: for with thee
> Certain my resolution is to die."

# CHAP. III.

## The German Union.

WHEN SUCH a fermentation has been excited in the public mind, it cannot be supposed that the formal suppression of the Order of the Illuminati in Bavaria, and in the Duchy of Wirtemberg, by the reigning Princes, would bring all to rest again. By no means. The minds of men were predisposed for a change by the restless spirit of speculation in every kind of enquiry, and the leaven had been carefully and skilfully disseminated in every quarter of the empire, and even in foreign countries. Weishaupt said, on good grounds, that "if the Order should be discovered and suppressed, he would restore it with tenfold energy in a twelvemonth." Even in those states where it was formally abolished, nothing could hinder the enlisting new members, and carrying on all the purposes of the Order. The *Areopagitæ* might indeed be changed, and the feat of the direction transferred to some other place; but the Minerval and his Mentor could meet as formerly, and a ride of a few miles into another State, would bring him to a Lodge, where the young would be amused, and the more advanced would be engaged in serious mischief. Weishaupt never liked childrens play. He indulged Philo in it, because he saw him taken with such rattles; but his own projects were dark and solemn, and it was a relief to him now to be freed from that mummery. He soon found the bent of the person's mind on whom he had set his talons, and he says, that "no man ever escaped him whom he thought it worth while to secure." He had already filled the lists with enough of the young and gay, and when the present condition of the Order required sly and experienced heads, he no longer courted them by play-things. He communicated the ranks and the instructions by a letter, without any ceremony. The correspondence with Philo at the time of the breach with him shows the superiority of Spartacus. Philo is in a rage,

157

provoked to find a pitiful professor discontented with the immense services which he had received from a gentleman of his rank, and treating him with authority, and with disingenuity.—He tells Spartacus what still greater services he can do the Order, and that he can also ruin it with a breath.—But in the midst of this rage, he proposes a thousand modes of reconcilement. The smallest concession would make him hug Spartacus in his arms. But Spartacus is deaf to all his threats, and firm as a rock. Though he is conscious of his own vile conduct, he abates not in the smallest point his absolute authority—requires the most implicit submission, which he says "is due, not to him, but to the Order, and without which the Order must immediately go to ruin."—He does not even deign to challenge Philo to do his worst, but allows him to go out of the Order without one angry word. This shows his confidence in the energy of that spirit of restless discontent, and that hankering after reform which he had so successfully spread abroad.

This had indeed arisen to an unparalleled height, unexpected even by the seditious themselves. This appeared in a remarkable manner by the reception given to the infamous letters on the constitution of the Prussian States.

The general opinion was, that Mirabeau was the author of the letters themselves, and it was perfectly understood by every person, that the translation into French was a joint contrivance of Mirabeau and Nicholai. I was assured of this by the British Minister at that Court. There are some blunders in respect of names, which an inhabitant of the country could hardly be guilty of, but are very consistent with the self-conceit and precipitancy of this Frenchman.— There are several instances of the same kind in two pieces, which are known for certain to be his, viz. the *Chronique scandaleuse* and the *Histoire secrette de la Ceur àe Berlin*. These letters were in every hand, and were mentioned in every conversation, even in the Prussian dominions—and in other places of the Empire they were quoted, and praised, and commented on, although some of their contents were nothing short of rebellion.

Mirabeau had a large portion of that self-conceit which distinguishes his countrymen. He thought himself qualified not only for any high office in administration, but even for managing the whole affairs of the new King. He therefore endeavoured to obtain some post of honor. But he was disappointed, and, in revenge, did every thing in his power to make those in administration the objects of public ridicule and reproach. His licentious and profligate manners were such as excluded him from the society of the people of the first classes, whom it behoved to pay some attention to personal dignity. His opinions were in the highest degree corrupted, and he openly professed Atheism. This made him peculiarly obnoxious to the King, who was determined to correct the disturbances and disquiets which had arisen in the Prussian states from the indifference of his predecessor in these matters. Mirabeau therefore attached himself to a junto of writers and scribblers, who had united in order to disseminate licentious principles, both in respect of religion and of government. His wit and fancy were great, and he had not perhaps his equal for eloquent and biting satire. He was therefore caressed by these writers as a most valuable acquisition to their Society. He took all this deference as his just due; and was so confident in his powers, and so foolish as to advise, and even to admonish, the King. Highly obnoxious by such conduct, he was excluded from any chance of preferment, and was exceedingly out of humour. In this state of mind he was in a fit frame for Illumination. Spartacus had been eyeing him for some time, and at last communicated this honor to him through the intermedium of Mauvillon, another Frenchman, Lieutenant-Colonel in the service of the Duke of Brunswick. This person had been most active during the formal existence of the Order, and had contributed much to its reception in the Protestant states—he remained long concealed. Indeed his Illumination was not known till the invasion of Holland by the French rebels. Mauvillon then stepped forth, avowed his principles, and recommended the example of the French to the Germans. This encouragement brought even Philo again on the stage, notwithstanding his resentment against Spartacus, and his solemn declaration of having abjured all such societies—These, and a thousand such facts, show that the seeds of licentious Cosmo-politism had taken deep root, and that cutting down the crop had by no means destroyed the baneful plant—But this is not all—a new method of cultivation had been invented, and immediately adopted, and it was now growing over all Europe in another form.

I have already taken notice of the general perversion of the public mind which co-operated with the schisms of Free Masonry in procuring a listening ear to Spartacus and his associates. It will not be doubted but that the machinations of the Illuminati encreased this, even among those who did not enter into the Order. It was easier to diminish the respect for civil establishments in Germany than in almost any other country. The frivolity of the ranks and court offices in the different confederated petty states, made it impossible to combine dignity with the habits of a scanty income.—It was still easier to expose to ridicule and reproach those numberless abuses which the folly and the vices of men had introduced into religion. The influence on the public mind which naturally attaches to the venerable office of a moral instructor, was prodigiously diminished by the continual disputes of the Catholics and Protestants, which were carried on with great heat in every little principality. The freedom of enquiry, which was supported by the state in Protestant Germany, was terribly abused (for what will the folly of man not abuse) and degenerated into a wanton licentiousness of thought, and a rage for speculation and scepticism on every subject whatever. The struggle, which was originally between the Catholics and the Protestants, had changed, during the gradual progress of luxury and immorality, into a contest between reason and superstition. And in this contest the denomination of superstition had been gradually extended to every doctrine which professed to be of divine revelation, and reason was declared to be, for certain, the only way in which the Deity can inform the human mind.

Some respectable Catholics had published works filled with liberal sentiments. These were represented as villanous machinations to inveigle Protestants. On the other hand, some Protestant divines had proposed to imitate this liberality by making concessions which might enable a good Catholic to live more at ease among the Protestants, and might even accelerate an union of faiths. This was hooted beyond measure, as Jesuitical, and big with danger. While the sceptical junto, headed by the editors of the *Deutsche Bibliothek* and the *Berlin Monatschrift,* were recommending every performance that was hostile to the established faith of the country, Leuchtsenring was equally busy, finding Jesuits in every corner, and went about with all the inquietude of a madman, picking up anecdotes. Zimmerman, the respectable physician of Frederick King of Prussia, gives a diverting account of a visit which he had by Leuchtsenring at Hanover, all trembling with fears of Jesuits, and wishing to persuade him that his life was in danger from them. Nicholai was now on the hunt, and during this crusade Philo laid hands on him, being introduced to his acquaintance by Leuchtsenring, who was, by this time, cured of his zeal for Protestantism, and had become a disciple of Illuminatism. Philo had gained his good opinion by the violent attack which he had published on the Jesuits and Rosycrucians by the orders of Spartacus.—He had not far to go in gaining over Nicholai, who was at this time making a tour through the Lodges. The sparks of Illumination which he perceived in many of them pleased him exceedingly, and he very cheerfully received the precious secret from Philo.

This acquisition to the Order was made in January 1782. Spartacus was delighted with it, considered Nicholai as a most excellent champion, and gave him the name of *Lucian,* the great scoffer at all religion, as aptly expressing his character.

Nicholai, on his return to Berlin, published many volumes of his discoveries. One would imagine that not a Jesuit had escaped him. He mentions many strange schismatics, both in religion and in Masonry—but he never once mentions an *Illuminatus.*—When they were first checked, and before the discovery of the secret correspondence, he defended them, and strongly reprobated the proceedings of the Elector of Bavaria, calling it vile persecution—Nay, after the discovery of the letters found in Zwack's house, he persisted in his defence, vindicated the possession of the abominable receipts, and highly extolled the character of Weishaupt.—But when the discovery of papers in the house of Batz informed the public that he himself had long been an *Illuminatus,* he was sadly put to

it to reconcile his defence with any petentions to religion.*
—Weishaupt saved him from disgrace, as he thought, by his
publication of the system of Illuminatism—Nicholai then
boldly said that he knew no more of the Order than was
contained in that book, that is, only the two first degrees.

But before this, Nicholai had made to himself a most
formidable enemy. The history of this contest is curious
in itself, and gives us a very instructive picture of the machinations of that *conjuration des philosophes,* or gang of
scribblers who were leagued against the peace of the world.
The reader will therefore find it to our purpose. On the
authority of a lady in Courland, a Countess von der Recke,
Nicholai had accused Dr. Stark of Darmstadt (who made
such a figure in Free Masonry) of Jesuitism, and of having
even submitted to the *tonsure.* Stark was a most restless
spirit—had gone through every mystery in Germany, Illuminatism excepted, and had ferreted out many of Nicholai's
hidden transactions. He was also an unwearied book-maker,
and dealt out these discoveries by degrees, keeping the eye
of the public continually upon Nicholai. He had suspected
his Illumination for some time past, and when the secret
came out, by Spartacus's letter, where he boasts of his acquisition, calling Nicholai a most sturdy combatant, and
saying that he was *contentissimus,* Stark left no stone unturned, till he discovered that Nicholai had been initiated
in all the horrid and most profligate mysteries of Illuminatism, and that Spartacus had at the very first entrusted
him with his most darling secrets, and advised with him on
many occasions.†

*He impudently pretended that the papers containing the system
and doctrines of Illumination, came to him at Berlin, from an unknown hand. But no one believed him—it was inconsistent with what
is said of him in the secret correspondence. He had said the same
thing concerning the French translation of the Letters on the Constitution of the Prussian States. Fifty copies were found in his ware-
house. He said that they had been sent from Strasburg, and that he
had never sold one of them.—Supposing both these assertions to be
true, it appears that Nicholai was considered as a very proper hand
for dispersing such poison.

†Of this we have complete proof in the private correspondence.
Philo, speaking in one of his letters of the gradual change which
was to be produced in the minds of their pupils from Christianity to
Deism, says, "Nicholai informs me, that even the pious Zollikofer has
now been convinced that it would be proper to set up a deistical
church in Berlin." It is in vain that Nicholai says that his knowledge

This complete blasting of his moral character could not be patiently borne, and Nicholai was in his turn the bitter enemy of Stark, and, in the paroxysms of his anger, published every idle tale, although he was often obliged to contradict them in the next Review. In the course of this attack and defence, Dr. Stark discovered the revival of the Illuminati, or at least a society which carried on the same great work in a somewhat different way.

Dr. Stark had written a defence against one of Nicholai's accusations, and wished to have it printed at Leipzig. He therefore sent the manuscript to a friend, who resided there. This friend immediately proposed it to a most improper person, Mr. Pott, who had written an anonymous commentary on the King of Prussia's edict for the uniformity of religious worship in his dominions. This is one of the most shameless attacks on the established faith of the nation, and the authority and conduct of the Prince, that can be imagined. Stark's friend was ignorant of this, and spoke to Pott, as the partner of the great publisher Walther. They, without hesitation, undertook the publishing; but when six weeks had passed over, Stark's friend found that it was not begun. Some exceptionable passages, which treated with disrespect the religion of Reason, were given as the cause of delay; and he was told that the author had been written to about them, but had not yet returned an answer. This was afterwards found to be false. Then a passage in the preface was objected to, as treating roughly a lady in Courland, which Walther could

of the Order was only of what Weishaupt had published; for Philo says that that corrected system had not been introduced into it when he quitted it in 1784. But Nicholai deserves no credit—he is one of the most scandalous examples of the operation of the principles of Weishaupt. He procured admission into the Lodges of Free Masons and Rosycrucians, merely to act the dishonorable part of a spy, and he betrayed their secrets as far as he could. In the appendix to the 7th volume of his journey, he declaims against the Templar Masons, Rosycrucians, and Jesuits, for their blind submission to unknown superiors, their superstitions, their priesthoods, and their base principles —and yet had been five years in a society in which all these were carried to the greatest height. He remains true to the Illuminati alone, because they had the same object in view with himself and his atheistical associates. His defence of Protestantism is all a cheat; and perhaps he may be considered as an enemy equally formidable with Weishaupt himself. This is the reason why he occupies so many of these pages.

not print, because he had connections with that court. The author must be entreated to change his expressions. After another delay, paper was wanting. The MS. was withdrawn. Walther now said that he would print it immediately, and again got it into his hands, promising to send the sheets as they came from the press. These not appearing for a long time, the agent made enquiry, and found that it was sent to Michaelis at Halle, to be printed there. The agent immediately went thither, and found that it was printing with great alterations, another title, and a guide or key, in which the work was perverted and turned into ridicule by a Dr. Bahrdt, who resided in that neighbourhood. An action of recovery and damages was immediately commenced at Leipzig, and after much contest, an interdict was put on Michaelis's edition, and a proper edition was ordered immediately from Walther, with security that it should appear before Bahrdt's key. Yet when it was produced at the next fair, the booksellers had been already supplied with the spurious edition; and as this was accompanied by the key, it was much more saleable ware, and completely supplanted the other.

This is surely a strong instance of the machinations by which the Illuminati have attempted to destroy the Liberty of the Press, and the power they have to discourage or suppress any thing that is not agreeable to the taste of the literary junto. It was in the course of this transaction that Dr. Stark's agent found people talking in the coffee-houses of Leipzig and Halle of the advantages of public libraries, and of libraries by subscription, in every town, where persons could, at a small expence, see what was passing in the learned world. As he could not but acquiesce in these points, they who held this language began to talk of a general Association, which should act in concert over all Germany, and make a full communication of its numerous literary productions, by forming societies for reading and instruction, which should be regularly supplied with every publication. Flying sheets and pamphlets were afterwards put into his hands, stating the great use of such an Association, and the effect which it would speedily produce by enlightening the nation. By and by he learned that such an Association did really exist, and that it was called the GERMAN

UNION, for ROOTING OUT SUPERSTITION AND PREJUDICES,
AND ADVANCING TRUE CHRISTIANITY. On enquiry, however,
he found that this was to be a Secret Society, because it
had to combat prejudices which were supported by the great
of this world, and because its aim was to promote that general information which priests and despots dreaded above
all things. This Association was accessible only through the
reading societies, and oaths of secrecy and fidelity were required. In short, it appeared to be the old song of the Illuminati.

This discovery was immediately announced to the public, in an anonymous publication in defence of Dr. Stark.
It is supposed to be his own performance. It discloses a
scene of complicated villany and folly, in which the Lady
in Courland makes a very strange figure. She appears to
be a wild fanatic, deeply engaged in magic and ghost-raising, and leagued with Nicholai, Gedicke, and Biester,
against Dr. Stark. He is very completely cleared of the facts
alledged against him; and his three male opponents appear
void of all principle and enemies of all religion. Stark however would, in Britain, be a very singular character, considered as a clergyman. The frivolous secrets of Masonry
have either engrossed his whole mind, or he has laboured
in them as a lucrative trade, by which he took advantage
of the folly of others. The contest between Stark and the
Triumvirate at Berlin engaged the public attention much
more than we should imagine that a thing of so private a
nature would do. But the characters were very notorious;
and it turned the attention of the public to those clandestine
attacks which were made in every quarter on the civil and
religious establishments. It was obvious to every person,
that these reading societies had all on a sudden become
very numerous; and the characters of those who patronised
them only increased the suspicions which were now raised.

The first work that speaks expressly of the German
Union, is a very sensible performance *"On the Right of
Princes to direct the Religion of their subjects."* The next
is a curious work, a sort of narrative *Dialogue on the Characters of Nicholai, Gedicke, and Biester*. It is chiefly occupied with the contest with Dr. Stark, but in the 5th part,
it treats particularly of the German Union.

About the same time appeared some farther account, in a book called *Archives of Fanaticism and Illuminatism*. But all these accounts are very slight and unsatisfactory. The fullest account is to be had in a work published at Leipzig by Goschen the bookseller. It is entitled *"More Notes than Text, or the German Union of XXII, a new Secret Society for the Good of Mankind,"* Leipzig, 1789. The publisher says, that it was sent him by an unknown hand, and that he published it with all speed, on account of the many mischiefs which this Society (of which he had before heard several reports) might do to the world, and to the trade, if allowed to go on working in secret. From this work, therefore, we may form a notion of this redoubtable Society, and judge how far it is practicable to prevent such secret machinations against the peace and happiness of mankind.

There is another work, *"Further Information concerning the German Union* (Nähere Beleuchtung der Deutsche Union) *also showing how, for a moderate price, one may become a Scotch Free Mason."* Frankfort and Leipzig, 1789. The author says that he had all the papers in his hands; whereas the author of *More Notes than Text* acknowledges the want of some. But very little additional light is thrown on the subject by this work, and the first is still the most instructive, and will chiefly be followed in the account which is now to be laid before the reader.

The book *More Notes than Text* contains plans and letters, which the Twenty-two United Brethren have allowed to be given out, and of which the greatest part were printed, but were entrusted only to assured members.

No. I. is the first plan, printed on a single quarto page, and is addressed, *To all the Friends of Reason, of Truth, and of Virtue*. It is pretty well written, and states among other things, that "because a great number of persons are labouring, with united effort, to bring Reason under the yoke, and to prevent all instruction, it is therefore necessary that there be a combination which shall work in opposition to them, so that mankind may not sink anew into irrecoverable barbarism, when Reason and Virtue shall have been completely subdued, overpowered by the re-

straints which are put on our opinions."——"For this noble purpose a company of twenty-two persons, public instructors, and men in private stations, have united themselves, according to a plan which they have had under consideration for more than a year and a half, and which, in
their opinion, contains a method that is fair, and irresist-
able by any human power, for promoting the enlightening
and forming of mankind, and that will gradually remove all
the obstacles which superstition supported by force has
hitherto put in the way."

This address is intended for an enlisting advertisement,
and, after a few insignificant remarks on the Association, a
rix-dahler is required along with the subscription of acquiescence in the plan, as a compensation for the expences
attending this mode of intimation and consent.

Whoever pays the rix-dahler, and declares his wish to
join the Association, receives in a few days No. II. which
is a form of the Oath of secrecy, also printed on a single
4to page. Having subscribed this, and given a full designa-
tion of himself, he returns it agreeably to a certain address;
and soon after, he gets No. III printed on a 4to sheet. This
number contains what is called the Second Plan, to which
all the subsequent plans and circular letters refer. A copy
therefore of this will give us a pretty full and just notion
of the Order, and its mode of operation. It is entitled,

### The Plan of the Twenty-Two,

And begins with this declaration. "We have united, in
order to accomplish the aim of the exalted Founder of
Christianity, viz. the enlightening of mankind, and the dethronement of superstition and fanaticism, by means of a
secret fraternization of all who love the work of God.

"Our first exertion, which has already been very extensive, consists in this, that, by means of confidential persons we allow ourselves to be announced every where as
a Society united for the above-mentioned purpose; and we
invite and admit into brotherhood with ourselves every person who has a sense of the importance of this matter, and
wishes to apply to us and see our plans.

"We labour first of all to draw into our Association all good and learned writers. This we imagine will be the easier obtained, as they must derive an evident advantage from it. Next to such men, we seek to gain the masters and secretaries of the Post-offices, in order to facilitate our correspondence.

"Besides these, we receive persons of every condition and station, excepting princes and their ministers. Their favorites, however, may be admitted, and may be useful by their influence in behalf of Truth and Virtue.

"When any person writes to us, we send him an oath, by which he must abjure all treachery or discovery of the Association, till circumstances shall make it proper for us to come forward and show ourselves to the world. When he subscribes the oath, he receives the plan, and if he finds this to be what satisfies his mind as a thing good and honorable, he becomes our friend only in so far as he endeavours to gain over his friends and acquaintances. Thus we learn who are really our zealous friends, and our numbers increase in a double proportion.

"This procedure is to continue till Providence shall so far bless our endeavours, that we acquire an active Brother and coadjutor in every place of note, where there is any literary profession; and for this purpose we have a secretary and proper office in the centre of the Association, where every thing is expedited, and all reports received. When this happy epoch arrives, we begin our second operation," That is to say,

"We intimate to all the Brotherhood in every quarter, on a certain day, *that* THE GERMAN UNION *has now acquired a consistence*, and we now divide the fraternised part of the nation into ten or twelve *Provinces* or *Dioceses*, each directed by its *Diocesan* at his office: and these are so arranged in due subordination, that all business comes into the UNION-HOUSE as into the centre of the whole.

"Agreeably to this manner of proceeding there are two classes of the Brotherhood, the *Ordinary,* and the *Managing* Brethren. The latter alone know the aim of the Association, and all the means for attaining it; and they alone constitute the UNION, the name, and the connection of which is not intended to be at all conspicuous in the world.

"To this end the business takes a new external form. The Brethren, to wit, speak not of the Union in the places where they reside, nor of a Society, nor of enlightening the people; but they assemble, and act together in every quarter, merely as a LITERARY SOCIETY, bring into it all the lovers of reading and of useful knowledge; and such in fact are the *Ordinary Brethren,* who only know that an Association exists in their place of residence, for the encouragement of literary men, but by no means that it has any connection with any other similar Society, and that they all constitute one whole. But these Societies will naturally point out to the intelligent Brethren such persons as are proper to be selected for carrying forward the great work. For persons of a serious turn of mind are not mere loungers in such company, but show in their conversation the interest they take in real instruction. And the cast of their reading, which must not be checked in the beginning in the smallest degree, although it may be gradually directed to proper subjects of information, will point out in the most unequivocal manner their peculiar ways of thinking on the important subjects connected with our great object. Here, therefore, the active Brethren will observe in secret, and will select those whom they think valuable acquisitions to the sacred Union. They will invite such persons to unite with themselves in their endeavours to enlighten the rest of mankind, by calling their attention to profitable subjects of reading, and to proper books. Reading Societies, therefore, are to be formed in every quarter, and to be furnished with proper books. In this provision attention must be paid to two things. The taste of the public must be complied with, that the Society may have any effect at all in bringing men together who are born for somewhat more than just to look about them. But the general taste may, and must also be carefully and skilfully directed to subjects that will enlarge the comprehension, will fortify the heart, and, by habituating the mind to novelty, and to successful discovery, both in physics and in morals, will hinder the timid from being startled at doctrines and maxims which are singular, or perhaps opposite to those which are current in ordinary society. Commonly a man speaks as if he thought he was uttering his own sentiments, while he is only echoing the general sound. Our minds are dressed in a prevailing fashion as much as our bodies, and with stuff as little congenial to sentiment, as a piece of woollen cloth is to the human skin. So careless and indolent are men, even in what they call serious conversation. Till reflection becomes a habit, what is really a thought startles, however simple, and, if really uncommon, it astonishes and confounds. Nothing, therefore, can so powerfully tend to the improvement of the human character, as well managed Reading Societies.

"When these have been established in different places, we must endeavour to accomplish the following intermediate plans: 1. To introduce a general literary Gazette or Review, which, by uniting all the learned Brethren, and combining with judgment and address all their talents, and steadily proceeding according to a distinct and precise plan, may in time supplant every other Gazette, a thing which its intrinsic merit and comprehensive plan will easily accomplish. 2. To select a secretary for our Society, who shall have it in charge to commission the books which they shall select in conformity to the great aim of the Association, and who shall undertake to commission all other books for the curious in his neighbourhood. If there be a bookseller in the place, who can be gained over and sworn into the Society, it will be proper to choose him for this office, since, as will be made more plain afterwards, the trade will gradually come into the plan, and fall into the hands of the Union.

"And now, every eye can perceive the progressive moral influence which the Union will acquire on the nation. Let us only conceive what superstition will lose, and what instruction must gain by this; when, 1. In every Reading Society the books are selected by our Fraternity. 2. When we have confidential persons in every quarter, who will make it their serious concern to spread such performances as promote the enlightening of mankind, and to introduce them even into every cottage. 3. When we have the loud voice of the public on our side, and since we are able, either to scout into the shade all the fanatical writings which appear in the reviews that are commonly read, or to warn the public against them; and, on the other hand, to bring into notice and recommend those performances alone which give light to the human mind. 4. When we by degrees bring the whole trade of bookselling into our hands (as the good writers will bring all their performances into the market through our means) we shall bring it about, that at last the writers who labour in the cause of superstition and restraint, will have neither a publisher nor readers. 5. When, lastly, by the spreading of our Fraternity, all good hearts and sensible men will adhere to us, and by our means will be put in a condition that enables them to work in silence upon all courts, families, and individuals in every quarter, and acquire an influence in the appointment of court-officers, stewards, secretaries, parish-priests, public teachers, and private tutors.

"Remark, That we shall speedily get the trade into our hands (which was formerly the aim of the association called the *Gelehrtenbuchhandlung*) is conceivable by this, that every writer who unites with us immediately acquires a triple number of readers, and finds friends in every place who promote the sale of his performance; so that his gain is increased manifold, and consequently all will quit the booksellers, and accede to us by degrees. Had the above-named association been constructed in this manner, it would, long ere now, have been the only shop in Germany."

The book called *Fuller Information*, &c. gives a more particular account of the advantages held forth to the literary manufacturers of Germany by this Union *for God's work*. The class of literary Brothers, or writers by trade, was divided into *Mesopolites, Aldermen, Men,* and *Cadets.*

The MESOPOLITES, or Metropolitans, are to be attached to the archive-office, and to be taken care of in the Union-House, when in straits through age or misfortune. They will be occupied in the department of the sciences or arts, which this Association professes principally to cherish. They are also Brethren of the third degree of Scotch Free Masonry, a qualification to be explained afterwards. The Union-House is a building which the ostensible Founder of the Union professed to have acquired, or speedily to acquire at————, through the favor and protection of a German Prince, who is not named.

ALDERMEN are persons who hold public offices, and are engaged to exercise their genius and talents in the sciences. These also are Brothers of the third rank of Scotch Free Masonry, and out of their number are the Diocesans and the Directors of the Reading Societies selected.

The members who are designed simply MEN, are Brothers of the second rank of Masonry, and have also a definite scientific occupation assigned them.

The CADETS are writers who have not yet merited any particular honors, but have exhibited sufficient dispositions and talents for different kinds of literary manufacture.

Every member is bound to bring the productions of his genius to market through the Union. An Alderman receives for an original work 80 per cent. of the returns, and 70 for a translation. The member of the next class receives 60, and the Cadet 50. As to the expence of printing, the Alderman pays nothing, even though the work should lie on hand unsold; but the *Man* and the *Cadet* must pay one half. Three months after publication at the fairs an account is brought in, and after this, yearly, when and in what manner the author shall desire.

In every diocese will be established at least one Reading Society, of which near 800 are proposed. To each of these will a copy of an *Alderman's* work be sent. The same favor will be shown to a dissertation by a *Man,* or by a *Cadet,* provided that the manuscript is documented by an Alderman, or formally approved by him upon serious perusal. This *imprimatur,* which must be considered as a powerful recommendation of the work, is to be published in the *General Review* or *Gazette.* This is to be a vehicle of political as well as of literary news; and it is hoped that, by its intrinsic worth, and the recommendation of the members, it will soon supplant all others. (With respect to affairs of the Union, a sort of cypher was to be employed in it. Each Diocesan was there designed by a letter, of a size that marked his rank, and each member by a number. It was to appear weekly, at the very small price of five-and-twenty shillings.)—But let us return to the plan.

When every thing has been established in the manner set forth above, the Union will assume the following republican form (the reader always recollecting that this is not to appear to the world, and to be known only to the *managing* Brethren.)

Here, however, there is a great blank. The above-named sketch of this Constitution did not come to the hands of the person who furnished the bookseller with the rest of the information. But we have other documents which give sufficient information for our purpose. In the mean time, let us just take the papers as they stand.

No. IV. Contains a list of the German Union, which the sender received in manuscript. Here we find many names which we should not have expected, and miss many that were much more likely to have been partners in this patriotic scheme. There are several hundred names, but very few designations; so that it is difficult to point out the individuals to the public. Some however are designed, and the writer observes that names are found, which, when applied to some individuals whom he knows, accord surprisingly with the anecdotes that are to be seen in the private correspondence of the Illuminati, and in the romance called Materials for the History of Socratism (Illuminatism.*) It is but a disagreeable remark, that the list of the Union contains the names of many public teachers, both from the pulpit, and from the academic chair in all its degrees; and among these are several whose cyphers show that they have been active hands. Some of these have in their writings given evident proofs of their misconception of the simple

---

*This, by the by, is a very curious and entertaining work, and, had the whole affair been better known in this country, would have been a much better antidote against the baneful effects of that Association than any thing that I can give to the public, being written with much acuteness and knowledge of the human mind, and agreeably diversified with anecdote and ironical exhibition of the affected wisdom and philanthropy of the knavish Founder and his coadjutors. If the present imperfect and desultory account shall be found to interest the public, I doubt not but that a translation of this novel, and some other fanciful performances on the subjects will be read with entertainment and profit.

truths, whether dogmatical or historical, of revealed religion, or of their inclination to twist and manufacture them
so as to chime in with the religion and morality of the Sages
of France. But it is more distressing to meet with unequivocal names of some who profess in their writings to consider
these subjects as an honest man should consider them, that
is, according to the plain and common sense of the words;
whereas we have demonstrative proofs that the German
Union had the diametrically opposite purpose in view. The
only female in the list is the *Grafin von der Recke,* the lady
who gave Dr. Stark of Darmstadt so much trouble about
his *Tonsure.* This Lady, as we have already seen, could not
occupy herself with the frivolities of dress, flirtation, or domestic cares. *"Femina fronte patet, vir pectore."* She was
not pleased however at finding her name in such a Plebein
list, and gave oath, along with Biester at the centre, that she
was not of the Association. I see that the public was not
satisfied with this denial. The Lady has published some
more scandal against Stark since that time, and takes no
notice of it; and there have appeared many accounts of
very serious literary connections between these two persons
and the man who was afterwards discovered to be the chief
agent of the Union.

No. V. is an important document. It is a letter addressed
to the sworn members of the Union, reminding the beloved
fellow-workers that "the bygone management of the business has been expensive, and that the XXII. do not mean
to make any particular charge for their own compensation.
But that it was necessary that all and each of the members
should know precisely the object of the association, and the
way which mature consideration had pointed out as the
most effectual method of attaining this object. Then, and
not till then, could the worthy members act by one plan,
and consequently with united force. To accomplish this
purpose, one of their number had composed a Treatise *on
Instruction, and the means of promoting it."** This work
has been revised by the whole number, and may be considered as the result of their deepest reflection. They

---

*Ucber AUFFKLARUNG *und deren Beförderungs-Mittel.* The only
proper translation of this word would be, *clearing up,* or *enlightening. Instruction* seems the single word that comes nearest to the precise meaning of *Auffklarung,* but is not synonymous.

say, that it would be a signal misfortune should this Association, this undertaking, so important for the happiness of mankind, be cramped in the very beginning of its brilliant progress. They therefore propose to print this work, this Holy Scripture of their faith and practice, by subscription. (They here give a short account of the work.) And they request the members to encourage the work by subscribing and by exerting more than their usual activity in procuring subscriptions, and in recommending the performance in the newspapers. Four persons are named as Diocesans, who are to receive the money, which they beg may be speedily advanced in order to purchase paper, that the work may be ready for the first fair (Easter 1788.)

No. VI. is a printed paper (as is No. V.) without date, farther recommending the Essay on Instruction. No. VII. is in manuscript, without date. It is addressed to "a worthy man," intimating that the like are sent to others, to whom will also speedily be forwarded an improved plan, with a request to cancel or destroy the former contained in No. III. It is added, that the Union now contains, among many others, more than two hundred of the most respectable persons in Germany, of every rank and condition, and that in the course of the year (1788) a general list will be sent, with a request that the receiver will point out such as he does not think worthy of perfect confidence. It concludes with another recommendation of the book *on Instruction*, on the returns from which first work of the German Union the support of the secretary's office is to depend.

Accordingly No. VIII. contains this plan, but it is not entitled *The Improved Plan*. Such a denomination would have called in doubt the infallibility of the XXII. It is therefore called the *Progressive* (Vorlaufig) plan, a title which leaves room for every subsequent change. It differs from the former only in some unimportant circumstances. Some expressions, which had given offence or raised suspicions, are softened or cancelled. Two copies of this, which we may call A and B, are given, differing also in some circumstances.

"The great aim of the German Union, is the good of mankind, which is to be attained only by means of mental Illumination *(Aufklarung)* and the dethroning of fanaticism and moral despotism." Neither paper has the expression which immediately followed in the former plan, "that this had been the aim of the exalted Founder of Christianity." The paper A refers, on the present subject, to a dissertation printed in 1787 without a name, *On the Freedom of the Press, and its Limitation.* This is one of the most licentious pieces that has been published on the subject, not only enforcing the most unqualified liberty of publishing every thing a man pleases, but exemplifying it in the most scandalous manner; libelling characters of every sort, and persons of every condition, and this frequently in the most abusive language, and expressions so coarse, as shewed the author to be either habituated to the coarsest company, or determined to try boldly once for all, what the public eye can bear. The piece goes on: "The Union considers it as a chief part of its secret plan of operation, to include the trade of bookselling in their circle. By getting hold of this, they have it in their power to encrease the number of writings which promote instruction, and to lessen that of those which mar it, since the authors of the latter will by degrees lose both their publishers and their readers. That the present booksellers may do them no harm, they will by degrees draw in the greater part of them to unite with them."— The literary newspaper is here strongly insisted on, and, in addition to what was said in the former plan, it is said, "that they will include political news, as of mighty influence on the public mind, and as a subject that merits the closest attention of the moral instructor." For what Illumination is that mind susceptible of, that is so blinded by the prejudice created and nursed by the habits of civil subordination, that it worships stupidity or wickedness under a coronet, and neglects talents and virtue under the bearskin cap of the boor. We must therefore represent political transactions, and public occurrences, not as they affect that artificial and fanatical creature of imagination that we see every where around us, wheeled about in a chariot, but as it affects a MAN, rational, active, freeborn man. By thus stripping the transaction of all foreign circumstances, we see it as it affects, or ought to affect ourselves. Be assured that this new form of political intelligence will be highly interesting, and that the Gazette of the Union will soon supersede all others, and, of itself, will defray all our necessary expences."

This is followed by some allusions to a secret correspondence that is quick, unsusceptible of all discovery or treachery, and attended with no expence, by which the business of the secret plan *(different from either of those communicated to the sworn Brethren at large)* is carried on, and which puts the members in a condition to learn every thing that goes on in the world, for or against their cause, and also teaches them to know mankind, to gain an influence over all, and enables them effectually to promote their best subjects into all offices, &c. and finally, from which every member, whether statesmen, merchant, or writer, can draw his own advantages. Some passages, here and in another place, make me imagine that the Union hoped to get the command of the post-offices, by having their Brethren in the direction.

It is then said, that "it is supposed that the levy will be sufficiently numerous in the spring of the ensuing year. When this takes place, a general synod will be held, in which the *plan of secret operations* will be finally adjusted, and accommodated to local circumstances, so as to be digested into a law that will need no farther alteration. A proper person will set off from this synod, with full powers, to visit every quarter where there are sworn Brethren, and he will there establish a Lodge after the ancient simple ritual, and will communicate verbally the *plan of secret operation*, and certain instructions. These Lodges will then establish a managing fund or box. Each Lodge will also establish a Reading Society, under the management of a bookseller residing in the place, or of some person acquainted with the mechanical conduct of things of this nature. There must also be a collector and agent *(Expediteur)* so that in a moment the Union will have its offices or *comptoirs* in every quarter, through which it carries on the trade of bookselling, and guides the ebb and flow of its correspondence. And thus the whole machine will be set in motion, and its activity is all directed from the centre."

I remark, that here we have not that exclusion of Princes and ministers that was in the former plan; they are not even mentioned. The exclusion in express terms could not but surprise people, and appear somewhat suspicious.

No. IX. is a printed circular letter to the sworn Brethren, and is subscribed "by their truly associated Brother Barthels, *Oberamtsman* (first bailiff) for the King of Prussia, at Halle on the Saal."

In this letter the Brethren are informed that "the XXII. were wont to meet sometimes at Halle, and sometimes at Berlin. But unavoidable circumstances oblige them not only to remain concealed for some time, but even to give up their relation to the Union, and withdraw themselves from any share in its proceedings. These circumstances are but temporary, and will be completely explained in due time. They trust, however, that this necessary step on their part will not abate the zeal and activity of men of noble minds, engaged in the cause by the conviction of their own hearts. They have therefore communicated to their worthy Brother BARTHELS all necessary informations, and have unanimously conferred on him the direction of the secretary's office, and have provided him with every document and mean of carrying on the correspondence. He has devoted himself to the honorable office, giving up all other employments. They observe that by this change in the manner of proceeding, the Association is freed from an objection made with justice to all other secret societies, namely, that the members subject themselves to blind and unqualified submission to unknown superiors."—"The Society is now in the hands of its own avowed members. Every thing will soon be arranged according to a constitution purely republican; a Diocesan will be chosen, and will direct in every province, and report to the centre every second month, and instructions and other informations will issue in like manner from the centre.

"If this plan shall be approved of by the Associated, H. Barthels will transmit to all the Dioceses general lists of the Union, and the PLAN OF SECRET OPERATION, the result of deep meditation of the XXII. and admirably calculated for carrying on with irresistible effect their noble and patriotic plan. To stop all cabal, and put an end to all slander and suspicion, H. Barthels thinks it proper that the Union shall step forward, and declare itself to the world, and openly name some of its most respectable members. The public must however be informed only with respect to the *exterior* of the Society, for which purpose he had written a sheet

to be annexed as an appendix to the work, ON INSTRUC-
TION, declaring that to be the work of the Society, and a
sufficient indication of its most honorable aim. He desires
such members as choose to share the honor with him, to
send him their names and proper designations, that they
may appear in that appendix. And, lastly, he requests them
to instruct him, and co-operate with him, according to the
concerted rules of the Union, in promoting the cause of
God and the happiness of mankind."

The Appendix now alluded to makes No. X. of the
packet sent to the Bookseller Goschen of Leipzig, and is
dated December 1788. It is also found in the book *On Instruction,* &c. printed at Leipzig in 1789, by Walther. Here,
however, the Appendix is dated January 1789. This edition
agrees in the main with that in the book from which I have
made such copious extracts, but differs in some particulars
that are not unworthy of remark.

In the packet it is written, *"The undersigned, as Member
and Agent of the German Union,* in order to rectify several
mistakes and injurious slanders and accusations, thinks it
necessary that the public itself should judge of their object
and conduct."—Towards the end it is said, "and all who
have any doubts may apply to those named below, and are
invited to write to them." No names however are sub-
joined.—In the appendix to the book it is only said, "the
agent of the German Union, &c. and "persons who wish
to be better informed may write to the agent, under the
address, *To the German Union*—under cover to the shop
of Walther, bookseller in Leipzig."—Here too there are
no names, and it does not appear that any person has
chosen to come from behind the curtain.*

There has already been so much said about *Enlightening,* that the reader must be almost tired of it. He is assured
in this performance that the Illumination proposed by the

*Walther is an eminent bookseller, and carries on the business of
publishing to a great extent, both at Leipzig and other places. He was
the publisher of the most virulent attacks on the King of Prussia's
Edict on Religion, and was brought into much trouble about the
Commentary by Pott which is mentioned above. He also publishes
many of the sceptical and licentious writings which have so much
disturbed the peace of Germany.

Union is not that of the *Wolfenbuttle Fragments,* nor that of HORUS, nor that of *Bahrdt.* The *Fragments* and *Horus* are books which aim directly, and without any concealment, to destroy the authority of our Scriptures, either as historical narrations or as revelations of the intentions of providence and of the future prospects of man. The Theological writings of *Bahrdt* are gross perversions, both of the sense of the text, and of the moral instructions contained in it, and are perhaps the most exceptionable performances on the subject. They are stigmatised as absurd, and coarse, and indecent, even by the writers on the same side; yet the work recommended so often, as containing the elements of that Illumination which the world has to expect from the Union, not only coincides in its general principles with these performances, but is almost an abstract of some of them, particularly of his *Popular Religion,* his *Paraphrase on the Sermon on the Mount,* and his MORALITY OF RELIGION. We have also seen that the book on the Liberty of the Press is quoted and recommended as an elementary book. Nay, both the work on Instruction and that on the Liberty of the Press are now known to be Bahrdt's.

But these principles, exceptionable as they may be, are probably not the worst of the institution. We see that the *outside* alone of the Union is to be shewn to the public. Barthels felicitates the public that there is no subordination and blind obedience to unknown superiors; yet, in the same paragraph, he tells us that there is a secret plan of operations, that is known only to the Centre and the Confidential Brethren. The author of *Fuller Information* says that he has this plan, and would print it, were he not restrained by a promise.* He gives us enough however to show us that the higher mysteries of the Union are precisely the same with those of the Illuminati. Christianity is expressly said to have been a Mystical Association, and its founder the Grand Master of a Lodge. The Apostles, Peter, James, John, and Andrew, were the ELECT, and Brethren of the Third Degree, and initiated into all the mysteries. The remaining Apostles were only of the Second Degree; and the Seventy-Two were of the First Degree. Into this degree ordinary Christians may be admitted, and prepared

---

*This I find to be false, and the book a common job.

for further advancement. The great mystery is, that J——
C——was a NATURALIST, and taught the doctrine of a
Supreme Mind, the Spectator, but not the Governor of the
World, pretty nearly in the sense of the Stoics. The Initiated
Brethren were to be instructed by reading proper books.
Those particularly recommended are *Basedow's Practical
Knowledge, Eberhard's Apology for Socrates, Bahrdt's
Apology for Reason, Steinbardt's System of Moral Educa-
tion, Meiner's Ancient Mysteries, Bahrdt's Letters on the
Bible,* and *Bahrdt's Completion of the Plan and Aim of
J—— C——.* These books are of the most Antichristian
character, and some of them aim at shaking off all moral
obligation whatever.

Along with these religious doctrines, are inculcated the
most dangerous maxims of civil conduct. The despotism
that is aimed at over the minds of men, and the machinations and intrigues for obtaining possession of places of
trust and influence, are equally alarming, but being perfectly similar to those of the Illuminati, it is needless to
mention them.

The chief intelligence that we get from this author is that
the CENTRE of the Union is at a house in the neighbourhood of Halle. It is a sort of tavern, in a vineyard immediately without the city. This was bought by DOCTOR KARL
FRIEDERICH BAHRDT, and fitted up for the amusement of
the University Students. He calls it BAHRDT'S RUHE
(Bahrdt's Repose.) The author thinks that this must have
been the work of the Association, because Bahrdt had not
a farthing, and was totally unable for such an undertaking.
He may however have been the contriver of the institution.
He has never affirmed or denied this in explicit terms, nor
has he ever said who are the XXII coadjutors. Wucherer, an
eminent bookseller at Vienna, seems to have been one of
the most active hands, and in one year admitted near 200
members, among whom is his own shoemaker. He has published some of the most profligate pamphlets which have
yet appeared in Germany.

The publication of the list of members alarmed the nation;
persons were astonished to find themselves in every quarter
in the midst of villains who were plotting against the peace

and happiness of the country, and destroying every sentiment of religion, morality, or loyalty. Many persons published in the newspapers and literary journals affirmations
and proofs of the false insertion of their names. Some acknowledged that curiosity had made them enter the Association, and even continue their correspondence with the
Centre, in order to learn something of what the Fraternity
had in view, but declared that they had never taken any
part in its proceedings. But, at the same time, it is certain
that many Reading Societies had been set up, during these
transactions, in every quarter of Germany, and that the
ostensible managers were in general of very suspicious characters, both as to morals and loyalty. The Union had actually set up a press of their own at Calbe, in the neighbourhood of Halberstadt. Every day there appeared stronger
proofs of a combination of the Journalists, Reviewers, and
even of the publishers and booksellers, to suppress the
writings which appeared in defense of the civil and ecclesiastical constitutions of the States of Germany. The extensive literary manufacture of Germany is carried on in such
a manner that it is impossible for any thing less than the
joint operation of the whole federated powers to prevent
this. The spirit of free thinking and innovating in religious
matters had been remarkable prevalent in the dominions
of the King of Prussia, having been much encouraged by
the indifference of the late King. One of the vilest things
published on this occasion was an abominable farce, called
the Religion Edict. This was traced to Bahrdt's Ruhe, and
the Doctor was arrested, and all his papers seized and
ransacked. The civil Magistrate was glad of an opportunity
of expiscating the German Union, which common fame
had also traced hither. The correspondence was accordingly
examined, and many discoveries were made, which there
was no occasion to communicate to the public, and the
prosecution of the business of the Union was by this means
stopped. But the persons in high office at Berlin agree in
saying that the Association of writers and other turbulent
persons in Germany has been but very faintly hit by this
blow, and is almost as active as ever.

The German Union appears a mean and precipitate Association. The Centre, the Archives, and the Secretary are
contemptible. All the Archives that were found were the

plans and lists of the members and a parcel of letters of correspondence. The correspondence and other business was managed by an old man in some very inferior office or judicatory, who lived at bed and board in Bahrdt's house for about six shillings a week, having a chest of papers and a writing desk in the corner of the common room of the house.

Bahrdt gives a long narration of his concern in the affair, but we can put little confidence in what he says; yet as we have no better authority, I shall give a very short abstract of it as follows.

He said, that he learned Cosmo-political Free Masonry in England, when he was there getting pupils for his academy—but neglected it on his return to Germany. Some time after his settlement he was roused by a visit from a stranger who passed for an Englishman; but whom he afterwards found to be a Dutch officer—(he gives a description which bears considerable resemblance to the Prince or General Salms who gave so much disturbance to the States-General) —He was still more excited by an anonymous letter giving him an account of a Society which was employed in the instruction of mankind, and a plan of their mode of operations, nearly the same with that of No. III.—He then set up a Lodge of Free Masonry on Cosmo-political principles, as a preparation for engaging in this great plan—he was stopped by the National Lodge, because he had no patent from it.—This obliged him to work in secret.—He met with a gentleman in a coffee-house, who entreated him to go on, and promised him great assistance—this he got from time to time, as he stood most in need of it, and he now found that he was working in concert with many powerful though unknown friends, each in his own circle. The plan of operation of the XXII was gradually unfolded to him, and he got solemn promises of being made acquainted with his colleagues—But he now found, that after he had so essentially served their noble cause, he was dropped by them in the hour of danger, and thus was made the sacrifice for the public good. The last packet which he received was a request from a *Friend to the Union* to print two performances sent him, with a promise of 100 dahlers for his trouble.—These were the abominable farce called the *Re-*

*ligion Edict,* and some Dissertations on that Royal Proclamation.

He then gives an account of his system of Free Masonry, not very different from Weishaupt's Masonic Christianity— and concludes with the following abstract of the advantages of the Union—Advancement of Science—A general interest and concern for Arts and Learning—Excitement of Talents —Check of Scribbling—Good Education—Liberty—Equality—Hospitality—Delivery of many from Misfortunes— Union of the Learned—and at last—perhaps—Amen.

What the meaning of this enigmatical conclusion is we can only guess—and our conjectures cannot be very favorable.

The narration, of which this is a very short index, is abundantly entertaining; but the opinion of the most intelligent is, that it is in a great measure fictitious, and that the contrivance of the Union is mostly his own. Although it could not be legally proved that he was the author of the farce, every person in court was convinced that he was, and indeed it is perfectly in Bahrdt's very singular manner. —This invalidates the whole of his story—and he afterwards acknowledges the farce (at least by implication) in several writings, and boasts of it.

For these reasons I have omitted the narration in detail. Some information, however, which I have received since, seems to confirm his account, while it diminishes its importance. I now find that the book called *Fuller Information* is the performance of a clergyman called *Schutz,* of the lowest class, and by no means of an eminent character— Another performance in the form of a dialogue between X, Y, and Z, giving nearly the same account, is by Pott, the dear friend of Bahrdt and of his Union, and author of the Commentary on the Edict. Schutz got his materials from one Roper, an expelled student of debauched morals, who subsisted by copying and vending filthy manuscripts. Bahrdt says, that he found him naked and starving, and, out of pity, took him into his house, and employed him as an amanuensis. Roper stole the papers at various times, taking them with him to Leipzig, whither he went on pretence of sickness. At last Schutz and he went to Berlin together, and gave the information on which Bahrdt was put in prison. In short they all appear to have been equally profligates and traitors to each other, and exhibit a dreadful, but I hope a useful picture of the influence of this Illumination which so wonderfully fascinates Germany.

This is all the direct information that I can pick up of the founder and the proceedings of the German Union. The project is coarse, and palpably mean, aiming at the dahlers of entry-money and of annual contribution, and at the publication and profitable sale of Dr. Bahrdt's books. This circumstance gives it strong features of its parentage. —Philo speaks of Bahrdt in his *Final Declaration* in terms of contempt and abhorrence. There is nothing ingenious, nothing new, nothing enticing, in the plans; and the immediate purpose of indulging the licentious taste of the public comes so frequently before the eye, that it bears all the marks of that grossness of mind, precipitancy, and impatient oversight that are to be found in all the voluminous writings of Dr. Bahrdt.—Many in Germany, however, ascribe the Union to Weishaupt, and say that it is the Illuminati working in another form. There is no denying that the principles, and even the manner of proceeding, are the same in every essential circumstance. Many paragraphs of the declarations circulated through Germany with the plans, are transcribed verbatim from Weishaupt's *Corrected System of Illuminatism.* Much of the work *On Instruction, and the Means for promoting it,* is very nearly a copy of the same work, blended with slovenly extracts from some of his own writings—There is the same series of delusions from the beginning, as in Illuminatism—Free Masonry and Christianity are compounded—first with marks of respect —then Christianity is twisted to a purpose foreign from it, but the same with that aimed at by Weishaupt—then it is thrown away altogether, and Natural Religion and Atheism substituted for it—For no person will have a moment's hesitation in saying, that this is the creed of the author of the books *On Instruction* and *On the Liberty of the Press.* Nor can he doubt that the political principles are equally anarchical with those of the Illuminati.—The endeavours also to get possession of public offices, of places of education—of the public mind, by the Reading Societies, and by

publications—are so many transcripts from the Illuminati.
—Add to this, that Dr. Bahrdt was an *Illuminatus*—and
wrote the *Better than Horus*, at the command of Weishaupt.
—Nay, it is well known that Weishaupt was twice or thrice
at Bahrdt's Ruhe during those transactions, and that he
zealously promoted the formation of Reading Societies in
several places.—But I am rather of the opinion that Weishaupt made those visits in order to keep Dr. Bahrdt within
some bounds of decency, and to hinder him from hurting
the cause by his precipitancy, when spurred on by the want
of money. Weishaupt could not work in such an unskilful
manner. But he would be very glad of such help as this
coarse tool could give him—and Bahrdt gave great help;
for, when he was imprisoned and his papers seized, his Archives, as he called them, shewed that there were many
Reading Societies which his project had drawn together.
The Prussian States had above thirty, and the number of
readers was astonishingly great—and it was found, that the
pernicious books had really found their way into every
hut. Bahrdt, by descending a story lower than Weishaupt,
has greatly increased the number of his pupils.

But, although I cannot consider the German Union as
a formal revival of the Order under another name, I
must hold those *United,* and the members of those Reading Societies, as *Illuminati* and *Minervals.* I must even consider
the Union as a part of Spartacus's work. The plans of Weishaupt were partly carried into effect in their different
branches—they were pointed out, and the way to carry
them on are distinctly described in the private correspondence of the Order—It required little genius to attempt them
in imitation. Bahrdt made the attempt, and in part succeeded. Weishaupt's hopes were well founded—The leaven
was not only distributed, but the management of the fermentation was now understood, and it went on apace.

It is to be remarked, that nothing was found among
Bahrdt's papers to support the story he writes in his diary
—no such correspondences—but enough for detecting
many of these societies. Many others however were found
unconnected with Bahrdt's Ruhe, not of better character,
either as to Morality or Loyalty, and some of them considerable and expensive; and many proofs were found of

a combination to force the public to a certain way of thinking, by the management of the Reviews and Journals. The extensive dealings of Nicholai of Berlin gave him great weight in the book-making trade, which in Germany surpasses all our conceptions. The catalogues of *new* writings in sheets, which are printed twice a-year for each of the fairs of Leipzig and Frankfort, would astonish a British reader by the number. The booksellers meet there, and in one glance see the whole republic of literature, and, like Roman senators, decide the sentiments of distant provinces. By thus seeing the whole together, their speculations are national, and they really have it in their power to give what turn they please to the literature and to the sentiments of Germany. Still however they must be induced by motives. The motive of a merchant is gain, and every object appears in his eye something by which money may be made. Therefore in a luxurious and voluptuous nation, licentious and free-thinking books will abound. The writers suggest, and the booksellers think how the thing will tickle. Yet it must not be inferred from the prevalence of such books, that such is the common sense of mankind, and that the writings are not the corrupters, but the corrupted, or that they are what they ought to be, because they please the public. We need only push the matter to an extremity, and its cause appears plain. Filthy prints will always create a greater crowd before the shop window than the finest performances of Woollet. Licentious books will be read with a fluttering eagerness, as long as they are not universally permitted; and pitiable will be the state of the nation when their number makes them familiar and no longer entertaining.

But although it must be confessed that great encouragement was given to the sceptical, infidel, and licentious writings in Germany, we see that it was still necessary to practice seduction. The *religionist* was made to expect some engaging exhibition of his faith. The *Citizen* must be told that his civil connections are respected, and will be improved; and *all* are told that good manners or virtue is to be supported. Man is supposed to be, in very essential circumstances, what he wishes to be, and feels he ought to be; and he is corrupted by means of falsehood and trick. The principles by which he is wheedled into wickedness in the first instance, are therefore such as are really addressed to the general sentiments of mankind: these therefore should be considered as more expressive of the public mind than those which he afterwards adopts, after this artificial education. Therefore Virtue, Patriotism, Loyalty, Veneration for true and undefiled Religion, are really acknowledged by those corrupters to be the *prevailing* sentiments; and they are good if this prevalence is to be the test of worth. The mind that is otherwise affected by them, and hypocritically uses them in order to get hold of the uninitiated, that he may in time be made to cherish the contrary sentiments, cannot be a good mind, notwithstanding any pretentions it may make to the love of mankind.

No man, not Weishaupt himself, has made stronger professions of benevolence, of regard for the happiness of mankind, and of every thing that is amiable, than Dr. Bahrdt. It may not be useless to enquire what effect such principles have had on his own mind, and those of his chief coadjutors. Deceit of every kind is dishonorable; and the deceit that is professedly employed in the proceedings of the Union is no exception. No pious fraud *whatever* must be used, and pure religion must be presented to the view without all disguise.

> "The more fair Virtue's seen, the more she charms.
> "Safe, plain, and easy, are her artless ways.
> "With face erect, her eyes look strait before;
> "For dauntless is her march, her step secure.
>
> "Not so pale Fraud—now here she turns, now there,
> "Still seeking darker shades, secure in none,
> "Looks often back, and wheeling round and round,
> "Sinks headlong in the danger she would shun."

The mean motive of the Protestant Sceptic is as inconsistent with our notions of honesty as with our notions of honor; and our suspicions are justly raised of the character of Dr. Bahrdt and his associates, even although we do not suppose that their aim is the total abolishing of religion. With propriety therefore may we make some enquiry about their lives and conduct. Fortunately this is easy in the present instance. A man that has turned every eye upon himself can hardly escape observation. But it is not so easy to get fair information. The peculiar situation of Dr. Bahrdt, and the cause between him and the public, are of all others the most productive of mistake, misrepresentation, obloquy, and injustice. But even here we are fortunate. Many remarkable parts of his life are established by the most respectable testimony, or by judicial evidences; and, to make all sure, he has written his own life. I shall insert nothing here that is not made out by the two last modes of proof, resting nothing on the first, however respectable the evidence may be. But I must observe, that his life was also written by his dear friend Pott, the partner of Walther the bookseller. The story of this publication is curious, and it is instructive.

Bahrdt was in prison, and in great poverty. He intended to write his own life, to be printed by Walther, under a fictitious name, and in this work he intended to indulge his spleen and his dislike of all those who had offended him, and in particular all priests, and rulers, and judges, who had given him so much trouble. He knew that the strange, and many of them scandalous anecdotes, with which he had so liberally interlarded many of his former publications, would set curiosity on tiptoe, and would procure a rapid sale as soon as the public should guess that it was his own performance, by the singular but significant name which the pretended author would assume. He had almost agreed with Walther for a thousand dahlers (about L. 200) when he was imprisoned for being the author of the farce so often named, and of the Commentary on the *Religion Edict,* written by Pott, and for the proceedings of the German Union. He was refused the use of pen and ink. He then applied to Pott, and found means to correspond with him, and to give him part of his life already written, and materials for the rest, consisting of stories, and anecdotes, and correspondence. Pott sent him several sheets, with which he was so pleased, that they concluded a bargain. Bahrdt says, that Pott was to have 400 copies, and that the rest was to go to the maintenance of Bahrdt and his family, consisting of his wife, daughter, a Christina and her children who lived with them, &c. Pott gives a different account, and the truth was different from both, but of little consequence to us. Bahrdt's papers had been seized, and searched for evidence of his transactions, but the strictest attention was paid to the precise points of the charge, and no paper was abstracted which did not relate to these.

All others were kept in a sealed room. Pott procured the removal of the seals, and got possession of them. Bahrdt says, that his wife and daughter came to him in prison, almost starving, and told him that now that the room was opened, Pott had made an offer to write for their support, if he had the use of these papers—that this was the conclusion of the bargain, and that Pott took away all the papers. N. B. Pott was the associate of Walther, who had great confidence in him (*Anecdotenbuch für meinen lieben Amtsbrüder, p.* 400.) and had conducted the business of Stark's book, as has been already mentioned. No man was better known to Bahrdt, for they had long acted together as chief hands in the Union. He would therefore write the life of its founder *con amore,* and it might be expected to be a rare and tickling performance. And indeed it was. The first part of it only was published at this time; and the narration reaches from the birth of the hero till his leaving Leipzig in 1768. The attention is kept fully awake, but the emotions which successfully occupy the mind of the reader, are nothing but strong degrees of aversion, disgust, and horror. The figure set up to view is a monster, clever indeed, and capable of great things; but lost to truth, to virtue, and even to the affectation of common decency—In short, a shameless profligate.—Poor Bahrdt was astonished —flared—but, having his wits about him, saw that this life would sell, and would also sell another.—Without loss of time, he said that he would hold Pott to his bargain— but he reckoned without his host. "No, no," said Pott, "You are not the man I took you for—your correspondence was put into my hands—I saw that you had deceived me, and it was my duty, as a man *who loves truth above all things,* to hinder you from deceiving the world. I have not written the book you desired me. I did not work for you, but for myself—therefore you get not a groschen." "Why, Sir," said Bahrdt "we both know that this wont do. You and I have already tried it. You received Stark's manuscript, to be printed by Walther—Walther and you sent it hither to Michaelis, that I might see it during the printing. I wrote an illustration and a key, which made the fellow very ridiculous, and they were printed together, with one title page. You know that we were cast in court. Walther was obliged to print the work as Stark first ordered, and we lost all our labour. So shall you now, for I will commence an action this instant, and let me see with what face you will defend your-self, within a few weeks of your last appearance in court." Pott said, "You may try this. My work is already sold, and dispersed over all Germany—and I have no objection to begin yours to-morrow—believe me, it will sell." Bahrdt pondered—and resolved to write one himself.

This is another specimen of the *Union*.

DR. CARL FRIEDERICH BAHRDT was born in 1741. His father was then a parish-minister, and afterwards Professor of Theology at Leipzig, where he died in 1775. The youth, when at College, enlisted in the Prussian service as a hussar, but was bought off by his father. He was M. A. in 1761. He became catechist in his father's church, was a popular preacher, and published sermons in 1765, and some con-troversial writings, which did him honor—But he then be-gan to indulge in conviviality, and in anonymous basquí-nades, uncommonly bitter and offensive. No person was safe—Professors—Magistrates—Clergymen—had his chief notice—also, students—and even comrades and friends. (Bahrdt says, that these things might cut to the quick, but they were all just.) Unluckily his temperament was what the atomical philosophers (who can explain every thing by æthers and vibrations) call sanguine. He *therefore* (his own word) was a passionate admirer of the ladies. Coming home from supper he frequently met a young Miss in the way to his lodgings, neatly dressed in a rose-coloured silk jacket and train, and a sable bonnet, costly, and like a lady. One evening (after some old Rhenish, as he says) he saw the lady home. Some time after, the mistress of the house, Madam Godschusky, came into his room, and said that the poor maiden was pregnant. He could not help that—but it was very unfortunate, and would ruin him if known.—He therefore gave the old lady a bond for 200 dahlers, to be paid by instalments of twenty-five.——"The girl was sensi-ble, and good, and as he had already paid for it, and her conversation was agreeable, he did not discontinue his acquaintance." A comrade one day told him, that one Bel, a magistrate, whom he had lampooned, knew the affair, and would bring it into court, unless he immediately retrieved the bond. This bond was the only evidence, but it was enough. Neither Bahrdt nor his friend could raise the

money. But they fell on another contrivance. They got
Madam Godschusky to meet them at another house, in
order to receive the money. Bahrdt was in a closet, and
his comrade wore a sword. The woman could not be prevailed on to produce the bond till Bahrdt should arrive, and
the money be put into her hands, with a present to herself.
The comrade tried to flutter her, and, drawing his sword,
shewed her how men fenced—made passes at the wall—
and then at her—but she was too firm—he then threw away
his sword, and began to try to force the paper from her.
She defended herself a good while, but at length he got the
paper out of her pocket, tore it in pieces, opened the closet-
door, and said, "There you b—there is the honorable fellow
whom you and your wh—have bullied—but it is with me
you have to do now, and you know that I can bring you to
the gallows." There was a great squabble to be sure, says
Bahrdt, but it ended, and I thought all was now over.—
But Mr. Bel had got word of it, and brought it into court
the very day that Bahrdt was to have made some very
reverend appearance at church. In short, after many attempts of his poor father to save him, he was obliged to
send in his gown and band, and to quit the place. It was
some comfort, however, that Madam Godschusky and the
young Miss did not fare much better. They were both imprisoned. Madam G. died some time after of some shocking
disease. The court-records give a very different account of
the whole, and particularly of the scuffle; but Bahrdt's story
is enough.

Bahrdt says, that his father was severe—but acknowledges that his own temperament was hasty (why does not
his father's temperament excuse something? *Vibratiunculæ*
will explain every thing or nothing.) *"Therefore* (again) I
sometimes forgot myself.—One day I laid a loaded pistol
on the table, and told him that he should meet with that if
he went on so. But I was only seventeen."

Dr. Bahrdt was, of course, obliged to leave the place.
His friends, and Semler in particular, an eminent theological writer, who had formed a very favorable opinion of his
uncommon talents, were assiduous in their endeavours to
get an establishment for him. But his high opinion of himself, his temper, impetuous, precipitant, and overbearing,

and a bitter satirical habit which he had freely indulged in his outset of life, made their endeavours very ineffectual.

At last he got a professorship at Erlangen, then at Erfurth, and in 1771, at Giessen. But in all these places, he was no sooner settled than he got into disputes with his colleagues and with the established church, being a strenuous partizan of the innovations which were attempted to be made in the doctrines of Christianity. In his anonymous publications, he did not trust to rational discussion alone, but had recourse to ridicule and personal anecdotes, and indulged in the most cutting sarcasms and gross scurrility.— Being fond of convivial company, his income was insufficient for the craving demand, and as soon as he found that anecdote and slander always procured readers, he never ceased writing. He had wonderful readiness and activity, and spared neither friends nor foes in his anonymous performances. But this could not last, and his avowed theological writings were such as could not be suffered in a Professor of Divinity. The very students at Giessen were shocked with some of his liberties. After much wrangling in the church-judicatories he was just going to be dismissed, when he got an invitation to Marschlins in Switzerland to superintend an academy. He went thither about the year 1776, and formed the seminary after the model of Basedow's Philanthropine, or academy, at Dessau, of which I have already given some account. It had acquired some celebrity, and the plan was peculiarly suited to Bahrdt's taste, because it left him at liberty to introduce any system of religious or irreligious opinions that he pleased. He resolved to avail himself of this liberty, and though a clergyman and Doctor of Theology, he would outstrip even Basedow, who had no ecclesiastical orders to restrain him. But he wanted the moderation, the prudence, and the principle of Basedow. He had, by this time, formed his opinion of mankind, by meditating on the feelings of his own mind. His theory of human nature was simple—"The leading propensities, says he, of the human mind are three—Instinctive liberty *(Freyheitstriebe)*—instinctive activity *(Triebe fur Thatigkeit)*—and instinctive love *(Liebes triebe.")* I do not wish to misunderstand him, but I can give no other translation.—"If a man is obstructed in the exercise of any of these propensities, he suffers an injury—The busi-

ness of a good education therefore is to teach us how they
are to be enjoyed in the highest degree."

We need not be surprised although the Doctor should
find it difficult to manage the Cyclopedia in his Philanthropine in such a manner as to give satisfaction to the neighbourhood, which was habituated to very different sentiments.—Accordingly he found his situation as uncomfort-
able as at Giessen. He says, in one of his latest performances, "that the Grisons were a strong instance of the immense importance of education. They knew nothing but
their handicrafts, and their minds were as coarse as their
persons." He quarrelled with them all, and was obliged
to abscond after lying some time in arrest.

He came to Durkheim or Turkheim, where his father
was or had been minister. His literary talents were well
known.—After some little time he got an association formed
for erecting and supporting a Philanthropine or house of
education. A large fund was collected, and he was enabled
to travel into Holland and England, to engage pupils, and
was furnished with proper recommendations.—On his return the plan was carried into execution. The castle or residence of Count Leining Hartzburgh at Heidesheim, having
gardens, park, and every handsome accommodation, had
been fitted up for it, and it was consecrated by a solemn
religious festival in 1778.

But his old misfortunes pursued him. He had indeed no
colleagues to quarrel with, but his avowed publications became every day more obnoxious—and when any of his
anonymous pieces had a great run, he could not stifle his
vanity and conceal the author's name.—Of these pieces,
some were even shocking to decency.—It was indifferent to
him whether it was friend or foe that he abused; and some
of them were so horribly injurious to the characters of the
most respectable men in the state, that he was continually
under the correction of the courts of justice. There was
hardly a man of letters that had ever been in his company
who did not suffer by it. For his constant practice was to
father every new step that he took towards Atheism on
some other person; and, whenever the reader sees, in the
beginning of a book, any person celebrated by the author

for sound sense, profound judgment, accurate reasoning, or praised for acts of friendship and kindness to himself, he may be assured that, before the close of the book, this man will convince Dr. Bahrdt in some private conversation, that some doctrine, cherished and venerated by all Christians, is a practice of knavish superstition. So lost was Dr. Bahrdt to all sense of shame. He said that he held his own opinions independent of all mankind, and was indifferent about their praise or their reproach.

Bahrdt's licentious, very licentious life, was the cause of most of these enormities. No income could suffice, and he wrote for bread. The abominable way in which the literary manufacture of Germany was conducted, made it impossible to hinder the rapid dispersion of his writings over all Germany; and the undelicate and coarse maw of the public was as ravenous as the sensuality of Dr. Bahrdt, who really battened in the Epicurean sty. The consequence of all this was that he was obliged to fly from Heidesheim, leaving his sureties in the *Philanthropine* to pay about 14,000 dahlers, besides debts without number to his friends. He was imprisoned at Dienheim, but was released I know not how, and settled at Halle. There he sunk to be a keeper of a tavern and billiard-table, and his house became the resort and the bane of the students in the University.—He was obliged therefore to leave the city. He had somehow got funds which enabled him to buy a little vineyard, prettily situated in the neighbourhood. This he fitted up with every accommodation that could invite the students, and called it *Bahrdt's Ruhe*. We have already seen the occupations of Dr. B. in this *Buen Retiro*—Can we call it *otium cum dignitate?* Alas no! He had not lived two years here, bustling and toiling for the German Union, sometimes without a bit of bread—when he was sent to prison at Halle, and then to Magdeburgh, where he was more than a year in jail. He was set at liberty, and returned to *Bahrdt's Ruhe,* not, alas, to live at ease, but to lie down on a sick bed, where, after more than a year's suffering encreasing pain, he died on the 23d of April 1793, the most wretched and loathsome victim of unbridled sensuality.

The account of his case is written by a friend, a Dr. Jung, who professes to defend his memory and his principles. The medical description melted my heart, and I am certain would make his bitterest enemy weep. Jung repeatedly says that the case was not venereal—calls it the vineyard disease—the quicksilver disease (he was dying of an unconquerable salivation) and yet, through the whole of his narration, relates symptoms and sufferings, which, as a medical man, he could not possibly mean to be taken in any other sense than as effects of pox. He meant to please the enemies of poor Bahrdt, knowing that such a man could have no friends, and being himself ignorant of what friendship or goodness is. The fate of this poor creature affected me more than any thing I have read of a great while. All his open enemies put together have not said so much ill of him as his trusted friend Pott, and another confident, whose name I cannot recollect, who published in his lifetime an anonymous book called *Bahrdt with the iron brow*—and this fellow Jung, under the absurd mask of friendship, exhibited the loathsome carcase for a florin, like a malefactor's at Surgeons Hall. Such were the fruits of the German Union, of that Illumination that was to refine the heart of man, and bring to maturity the seeds of native virtue, which are choaked in the hearts of other men by superstition and despotism. We see nothing but mutual treachery and base desertion.

I do not concern myself with the gradual perversion of Dr. Bahrdt's moral and religious opinions. But he affected to be the enlightener and reformer of mankind; and affirmed, that all the mischiefs in life originated from despotism supported by superstition. "In vain," says he, "do we complain of the inefficacy of religion. All positive religion is founded on injustice. No Prince has a right to prescribe or sanction any such system. Nor would he do it, were not the priests the firmest pillars of his tyranny, and superstition the strongest fetters for his subjects. He dares not show religion as she is, pure and undefiled—She would charm the eyes and the hearts of mankind, would immediately produce true morality, would open the eyes of freeborn man, would teach him what are his rights, and who are his oppressors, and Princes would vanish from the face of the earth."

Therefore, without troubling ourselves with the truth or falsehood of his religion of Nature, and assuming it as an indisputable point, that Dr. Bahrdt has seen it in this natural and so effective purity, it is surely a very pertinent question, "Whether has the sight produced on his mind an effect so far superior to the acknowledged faintness of the impression of Christianity on the bulk of mankind, that it will be prudent to adopt the plan of the German Union, and at once put an end to the divisions which so unfortunately alienate the minds of professing Christians from each other? The account here given of Dr. Bahrdt's life seems to decide the question.

But it will be said that I have only related so many instances of the quarrels of Priests and their slavish adherents with Dr. Bahrdt. Let us view him in his ordinary conduct, not as the Champion and Martyr of Illumination, but as an ordinary citizen, a husband, a father, a friend, a teacher of youth, a clergyman.

When Dr. Bahrdt was a parish-minister, and president of some inferior ecclesiastical district, he was empowered to take off the censures of the church from a young woman who had born a bastard child. By violence he again reduced her to the same condition, and escaped censure, by the poor girl's dying of a fever before her pregnancy was far advanced, or even legally documented. Also, on the night of the solemn farce of consecrating his Philanthropine, he debauched the maid-servant, who bore twins, and gave him up for the father. The thing, I presume, was not judiciously proved, otherwise he would have surely been disgraced; but it was afterwards made evident, by the letters which were found by Pott, when he undertook to write his life. A series of these letters had passed between him and one Graf a steward, who was employed by him to give the woman the small pittance by which she and the infants were maintained. Remonstrances were made when the money was not advanced; and there are particularly letters about the end of 1779, which show that Bahrdt had ceased giving any thing. On the     of February 1780, the infants (three years old) were taken away in the night, and were found exposed, the one at Ufstein, and the other at Worms, many miles distant from each other, and almost frozen to death. The first was found, by its moans, by a shoemaker in a field by the road-side, about six in the morning; the other was found by two girls between the hedges in a lane, set between two great stones, past all crying. The poor mother travelled up and down the country in quest of her infants, and hearing these accounts, found them both, and took one of them home; but not being able to maintain both, when Bahrdt's commissioner refused contributing any more, it remained with the good woman who had taken it in.

Bahrdt was married in 1772 while at Giessen; but after wasting the greatest part of his wife's little fortune left her by a former husband, he was provoked, by losing 1000 florins (about L. 110) in the hands of her brother, who would not pay it up. After this he used her very ill, and speaks very contemptuously of her in his own account of his life, calling her a dowdy, jealous, and every thing contemptible. In two infamous novels, he exhibits characters, in which she is represented in a most cruel manner; yet this woman (perhaps during the honey-moon) was enticed by him one day into the bath, in the pond of the garden of the Philanthropine at Heidesheim, and there, in the sight of all the pupils, did he (also undressed) toy with his naked wife in the water. When at Halle, he used the poor woman extremely ill, keeping a mistress in the house, and giving her the whole command of the family, while the wife and daughter were confined to a separate part of it. When in prison at Magdeburgh, the strumpet lived with him, and bore him two children. He brought them all to his house when he was set at liberty. Such barbarous usage made the poor woman at last leave him and live with her brother. The daughter died about a year before him, of an overdose of Laudanum given by her father, to procure sleep when ill of a fever. He ended his own wretched life in the same manner, unable, poor man, to bear his distress, without the smallest compunction or sorrow for his conduct: and the last thing he did was to send for a bookseller (Vipink of Halle, who had published some of his vile pieces) and recommend his strumpet and her children to his protection, without one thought of his injured wife.

I shall end my account of this profligate monster with a specimen of his way of using his friends.

"Of all the acquisitions which I made in England, Mr. ————— (the name appears at full length) was the most important. This person was accomplished in the highest degree. With sound judgment, great genius, and correct taste, he was perfectly a man of the world. He was my friend, and the only person who warmly interested himself for my institution. To his warm and repeated recommendations I owe all the pupils I got in England, and many most respectable connections; for he was universally esteemed as a man of learning and of the most unblemished worth. He was my friend, my conductor, and I may say my preserver; for when I had not bread for two days, he took me to his house, and supplied all my wants. This gentleman was a clergyman, and had a small but genteel and selected congregation, a flock which required strong food. My friend preached to them pure natural religion, and was beloved by them. His sermons were excellent, and delivered with native energy and grace, because they came from the heart. I had once the honor of preaching for him. But what a difference—I found myself afraid—I feared to speak too boldly, because I did not know where I was, and thought myself speaking to my crouching countrymen. But the liberty of England opens every heart, and makes it accessible to morality. I can give a very remarkable instance.

"The women of the town in London do not, to be sure, meet with my unqualified approbation in all respects. But it is impossible not to be struck with the propriety and decency of their manners, so unlike the clownish impudence of our German wh ————. I could not distinguish them from modest women, otherwise than by their greater attention and eagerness to shew me civility. My friend used to laugh at my mistakes, and I could not believe him when he told me that the lady who had kindly shewed the way to me, a foreigner, was a votary of Venus. He maintained that English liberty naturally produced morality and kindness. I still doubted, and he said that he would convince me by my own experience. These girls are to be seen in crouds every evening in every quarter of the town. Although some of them may not have even a shift, they come out in the evening dressed like princesses, in hired clothes, which are entrusted to them without any fear of their making off with them. Their fine shape, their beautiful skin, and dark brown hair, their swelling bosom so prettily set off by their black silk dress, and above all, the gentle sweetness of their manners, makes an impression in the highest degree favorable to them. They civilly offer their arm, and say, "My dear, will you give me a glass of wine." If you give them no encouragement, they pass on, and give no farther trouble. I went with my friend to Covent Garden, and after admiring the innumerable beauties we saw in the piazzas, we gave our arm to three very agreeable girls, and immediately turned in to a temple of the Cytherean Goddess, which is to be found at every second door of the city, and were shown into a parlour elegantly carpeted and furnished, and lighted with wax, with every other accommodation at hand. My friend called for a pint of wine, and this was all the expence, for which we received so much civility. The conversation and other behaviour of the ladies was agreeable in the highest degree, and *not a word* passed that would have distinguished them from nuns, or that was not in the highest degree mannerly and elegant. We parted in the street—and such is the liberty of England, that my friend ran not the smallest risk of suffering either in his honor or usefulness.—Such is the effect of freedom."

We may be sure, the poor man was astonished when he saw his name before the public as one of the enlighteners of Christian Europe. He is really a man of worth, and of the most irreproachable character, and knew that whatever might be the protection of British liberty, such conduct would ruin him with his own hearers, and in the minds of all his respectable countrymen. He therefore sent a vindication of his character from his slanderous abuse to the publishers of the principal newspapers and literary journals in Germany. The vindication is complete, and B. is convicted of having related what he *could not possibly have seen*. It is worthy of remark, that the vindication did not appear in the *Berlin Monatschrift,* nor in any of the Journals which make favorable mention of the performances of the Enlighteners.

"Think not, indignant reader," says Arbuthnot, "that this man's life is useless to mortals." It shows in a strong light the falsity of all his declamations in favor of his so much praised natural religion and universal kindness and humanity. No man of the party writes with more persuasive energy, and, though his petulance and precipitant self-conceit lead him frequently astray, no man has occasionally put all the arguments of these philosophers in a clearer light; yet we see that all is false and hollow. He is a vile hypocrite, and the real aim of all his writings is to make money, by fostering the sensual propensities of human nature, although he sees and feels that the completion of the plan of the German Union would be an event more destructive and lamentable than any that can be pointed out in the annals of superstition. I will not say that all partisans of Illumination are hogs of the sty of Epicurus like this wretch. But the reader must acknowledge that, in the institution of Weishaupt, there is the same train of sensual indulgence laid along the whole, and that purity of heart and life is no part of the morality that is held forth as the perfection of human nature. The final abolition of Christianity is undoubtedly one of its objects—whether as an end of their efforts, or as a mean for the attainment of some end still more important. Purity of heart is perhaps the most distinctive feature of Christian morality. Of this Dr. Bahrdt seems to have had no conception; and his institution, as well as his writings, show him to have been a very coarse sensualist. But his taste, though coarse, accorded with what Weishaupt considered as a ruling propensity, by which he had the best chance of securing the fidelity of his subjects.—Craving desires, beyond the bounds of our means, were the natural consequences of indulgence—and since the purity of Christian morality stood in his way, his first care was to clear the road by rooting it out altogether—What can follow but general dissoluteness of manners?

Nothing can more distinctly prove the crooked politics of the Reformers than this. It may be considered as the mainspring of their whole machine. Their pupils were to be led by means of their meaner desires, and the aim of their conductors was not to inform them, but merely to lead them; not to reform, but to rule the world.—They would reign, though in hell, rather than serve in heaven.—Dr. Bahrdt was a true Apostle of Illuminatism; and though his torch was made of the grossest materials, and "served only to discover sights of woe," the horrid glare darted

into every corner, rousing hundreds of filthy vermin, and
directing their flight to the rotten carrion where they could
best deposit their poison and their eggs; in the breasts, to
wit, of the sensual and profligate, there to fester and burst
forth in a new and filthy progeny: and it is astonishing what
numbers were thus roused into action. The scheme of Reading Societies had taken prodigiously, and became a very
profitable part of the literary trade of Germany. The booksellers and writers soon perceived its importance, and acted
in concert.

I might fill a volume with extracts from the criticisms
which were published on the *Religion Edict* so often mentioned already. The Leipzig catalogue for one year contained 173. Although it concerned the Prussian States alone,
these appeared in every corner of Germany; nay, also in
Holland, in Flanders, in Hungary, in Switzerland, in Courland, and in Livonia. This shows it to have been the operation of an Associated Band, as was intimated to the King
with so much petulance by Mirabeau. There was (past all
doubt) such a combination among the innumerable scribblers who supplied the fairs of Leipzig and Frankfort.
Mirabeau calls it a *Conjuration des Philosophes,* an expression very clear to himself, for the miriads of garreteers
who have long fed the craving mouth of Paris ("always
thirsting after some new thing") called themselves philosophers, and, like the gangs of St. Gile's, conversed with each
other in a cant of their own, full of *moral,* of *energie,* of
*bienveillance,* &c. &c. &c. unintelligible or misunderstood
by other men, and used for the purpose of deceit. While
Mirabeau lived too, they formed a *Conjuration.* The 14th
of July 1790 the most solemn invocation of the Divine
presence ever made on the face of this earth, put an end
to the propriety of this appellation; for it became necessary
(in the progress of political Illumination) to declare that
oaths were nonsense, because the invoked was a creature of
the imagination, and the grand federation, like Weishaupt
and Bahrdt's Masonic Christianity, is declared, to those
initiated into the higher mysteries, to be a lie. But if we
have no longer a *Conjuration des Philosophes,* we have a
gang of scribblers that has got possession of the public mind
by their management of the literary journals of Germany,
and have made licentious sentiments in politics, in morals,

and in religion, as familiar as were formerly the articles of ordinary news. All the sceptical writings of England put together will not make half the number that have appeared in Protestant Germany during the last twelve or fifteen years. And, in the Criticisms on the Edict, it is hard to say whether infidelity or disloyalty fills the most pages.

To such a degree had the Illuminati carried this favorite and important point that they obtained the direction even of those whose office it was to prevent it. There is at Vienna, as at Berlin, an office for examining and licensing writings before they can have their course in the market. This office publishes annually an index of forbidden books. In this index are included the account of the last *Operations of Spartacus and Philo in the Order of Illuminati,* and a dissertation on *The Final Overthrow of Free Masonry,* a most excellent performance, showing the gradual corruption and final perversion of that society to a seminary of sedition. Also the Vienna *Magazine of Literature and Arts,* which contains many accounts of the interferences of the Illuminati in the disturbances of Europe. The Censor who occasioned this prohibition was an *Illuminatus,* named *Retzer.* He makes a most pitiful and Jesuitical defence, showing himself completely versant in all the chicane of the *Illuminati,* and devoted to their Infidel principles. (See *Rel. Begebenh.* 1795. p. 493.)

There are two performances which give us much information respecting the state of moral and political opinions in Germany about this time. One of them is called, *Proofs of a hidden Combination to destroy the Freedom of Thought and Writing in Germany.* These proofs are general, taken from many concurring circumstances in the condition of German literature. They are convincing to a thinking mind, but are too abstracted to be very impressive on ordinary readers. The other is the *Appeal to my Country* (which I mentioned in the former part of this work.) This is much more striking, and, in each branch of literature, gives a progressive account of the changes of sentiment, all supported by the evidence of the books themselves. The author puts it past contradiction, that in every species of literary composition into which it was possible, without palpable absurdity, to introduce licentious or seditious principles, it was done. Many romances, novels, journies through Germany and other countries,* are written on purpose to attach praise or reproach to certain sentiments, characters, and pieces of conduct. The Prince, the nobleman, is made despotic, oppressive, unfeeling, or ridiculous—the poor, and the men of talents, are unfortunate and neglected —and here and there a fictitious Graf or Baron is made a divinity, by philanthropy expressed in romantic charity and kindness, or ostentatious indifference for the little honors which are so precious in the eyes of a German.—In short, the system of Weishaupt and Knigge is carried into vigorous effect over all. In both these performances, and indeed in a vast number of other pieces, I see that the influence of Nicholai is much commented on, and considered as having had the chief hand in all those innovations.

Thus I think it clearly appears, that the suppression of the Illuminati in Bavaria and of the Union of Brandenburgh, were insufficient for removing the evils which they had introduced. The Elector of Bavaria was obliged to issue another proclamation in November 1790, warning his subjects of their repeated machinations, and particularly enjoining the Magistrates to observe carefully the assemblies in the Reading Societies, which were multiplying in his States. A similar proclamation was made and repeated by the Regency of Hanover, and it was on this occasion that Mauvillon impudently avowed the most anarchical opinions. —But Weishaupt and his agents were still busy and successful. The habit of plotting had formed itself into a regular system. Societies now acted every where in secret, in correspondence with similar societies in distant places. And thus a mode of co-operation was furnished to the discontented, the restless, and the unprincipled in all places, without even the trouble of formal initiations, and without any external appearances by which the existence and occupations of the members could be distinguished. The Hydra's teeth were already sown, and each grew up, independent of the rest, and soon sent out its own offsets.—In all places where such secret practices were going on, there did not

*A plan adopted within these few years in our own country, which, if prosecuted with the same industry with which it has been begun, will soon render our circulating Libraries so many Nurseries of Sedition and Impiety. (See Travels Into Germany by Este.)

fail to appear some individuals of more than common zeal and activity, who took the lead, each in his own circle. This gives a consistency and unity to the operations of the rest, and they, encouraged by this co-operation, could now attempt things which they would not have otherwise ventured on. It is not till this state of things obtains, that this influence becomes sensible to the public. Philo, in his public declaration, unwarily lets this appear. Speaking of the numerous little societies in which their principles were cultivated, he says, "we thus begin to be formidable." It may now alarm—but it is now too late. The same germ is now sprouting in another place.

I must not forget to take notice that about this time (1787 or 1788) there appeared an invitation from a Baron or Prince S——, Governor of the Dutch fortress H——, before the troubles in Holland to form a society *for the Protection of Princes.*—The plan is expressed in very enigmatical terms, but such as plainly show it to be merely an odd title, to catch the public eye; for the Association is of the same seditious kind with all those already spoken of, viz. professing to enlighten the minds of men, and making them imagine that all their hardships proceed from superstition, which subjects them to useless and crafty priests; and from their own indolence and want of patriotism, which make them submit to the mal-administration of ministers. The Sovereign is supposed to be innocent, but to be a cypher, and every magistrate, who is not chosen by the people actually under him, is held to be a despot, and is to be bound hand and foot.—Many circumstances concur to prove that the projector of this insidious plan is the Prince Salms, who so assiduously fomented all the disturbances in the Dutch and Austrian Netherlands. He had, before this time, taken into his service Zwack, the Cato of the Illuminati. The project had gone some length when it was discovered and suppressed by the States.

Zimmerman, who had been president of the Illuminati in Manheim, was also a most active person in propagating their doctrines in other countries. He was employed as a missionary, and erected some Lodges even in Rome—also at Neufchatel—and in Hungary. He was frequently seen in the latter place by a gentleman of my acquaintance, and preached up all the ostensible doctrines of Illuminatism in the most public manner, and made many proselytes. But when it was discovered that their real and fundamental doctrines were different from those which he professed in order to draw in proselytes, Zimmerman left the country in haste.—Some time after this he was arrested in Prussia for seditious harangues—but he escaped, and has not been heard of since.—When he was in Hungary he boasted of having erected above an hundred Lodges in different parts of Europe, some of which were in England.

That the Illuminati and other hidden Cosmo-political societies had some influence in bringing about the French Revolution, or at least in accelerating it, can hardly be doubted.—In reading the secret correspondence, I was always surprised at not finding any reports from France, and something like a hesitation about establishing a mission there; nor am I yet able thoroughly to account for it. But there is abundant evidence that they interfered, both in preparing for it in the same manner as in Germany, and in accelerating its progress. Some letters in the Brunswick Journal from one *Campe, w*ho was an inspector of the seminaries of education, a man of talents, and an *Illuminatus,* put it beyond doubt. He was residing in Paris during its first movements, and gives a minute account of them, lamenting their excesses, on account of their imprudence, and the risk of shocking the nation, and thus destroying the project, but justifying the motives, on the true principles of Cosmo-politism. The Vienna Zeitschrift, and the Magazine of Literature and Fine Arts for 1790, and other pamphlets of that date, say the same thing in a clearer manner. I shall lay together some passages from such as I have met with, which I think will shew beyond all possibility of doubt, that the Illuminati took an active part in the whole transaction, and may be said to have been its chief contrivers. I shall premise a few observations, which will give a clearer view of the matter.

# CHAP. IV.

## The French Revolution.

DURING these dissensions and discontents, and this general fermentation of the public mind in Germany, political occurrences in France gave exercise and full scope for the operation of that spirit of revolt which had long growled in secret in the different corners of that great empire. The Cosmo-political and sceptical opinions and sentiments so much cultivated in all the Lodges of the *Philalethes* had by this time been openly professed by many of the sages of France, and artfully interwoven with their statistical œconomics. The many contests between the King and the Parliament of Paris about the registration of his edicts, had given occasion to much discussion, and had made the public familiarly acquainted with topics altogether unsuitable to the absolute monarchy of France.

This acquaintance with the natural expectations of the subject, and the expediency of a candid attention on the part of Government to these expectations, and a view of Legislation and Government founded on a very liberal interpretation of all these things, was prodigiously promoted by the rash interference of France in the dispute between Great Britain and her colonies. In this attempt to ruin Britain, even the court of France was obliged to preach the doctrines of Liberty, and to take its chance that Frenchmen would consent to be the only slaves. But their officers and soldiers who returned from America, imported the American principles, and in every company found hearers who listened with delight and regret to their fascinating tale of American independence. During the war, the Minister, who had too confidently pledged himself for the destruction of Britain, was obliged to allow the Parisians to amuse themselves with theatrical entertainments, where English law was represented as oppression, and every fretful ex-

travagance of the Americans was applauded as a noble
struggle for native freedom.——All wished for a taste of that
liberty and equality which they were allowed to applaud
on the stage; but as soon as they came from the theatre
into the street, they found themselves under all their former restraints. The sweet charm had found its way into
their hearts, and all the luxuries of France became as dull
as common life does to a fond girl when she lays down
her novel.

In this irritable state of mind a spark was sufficient for
kindling a flame. To import this dangerous delicacy of
American growth, France had expended many millions,
and was drowned in debts. The mad prodigality of the
Royal Family and the Court had drained the treasury, and
forestalled every livre of the revenue. The edicts for new
taxes and forced loans were most unwelcome and oppressive.

The *Avocats au parlement* had nothing to do with state-
affairs, being very little more than barristers in the highest
court of justice; and the highest claim of the Presidents
of this court was to be a sort of humble counsellors to the
King in common matters. It was a very strange inconsistency in that ingenious nation to permit such people to touch
on those state-subjects; for, in fact, the King of France was
an absolute Monarch, and the subjects were slaves. This is
the result of all their painful research, notwithstanding that
glimmerings of natural justice and of freedom are to be
met with in their records. There could not be found in their
history so much as a tolerable account of the manner of
calling the nation together, to learn from the people how
their chains would best please their fancy. But all this was
against nature, and it was necessary that it should come
to an end, the first time that the Monarch confessed that
he could not do every thing unless they put the tools into
his hands. As things were approaching gradually but rapidly
to this condition, the impertinent interference (for so a
Frenchman, subject of the Grand Monarch, *must* think it)
of the advocates of the Parliament of Paris was popular in
the highest degree; and it must be confessed, that in general
it was patriotic, however inconsistent with the constitution.

They felt themselves pleading the cause of humanity and natural justice. This would embolden honest and worthy men to speak truth, however unwelcome to the court. In general, it must also be granted that they spoke with caution and with respect to the sovereign powers: and they had frequently the pleasure of being the means of mitigating the burdens of the people. The Parliament of Paris, by this conduct, came to be looked up to as a sort of mediator between the King and his subjects; and as the avocats saw this, they naturally rose in their own estimation far above the rank in which the constitution of their government had placed them. For it must always be kept in mind, that the robe was never considered as the dress of a Nobleman, although the cassock was. An advocate was merely not a roturier; and though we can hardly conceive a profession more truly honorable than the dispensing of distributive justice, nor any skill more congenial to a rational mind than that of the practical morality which we, in theory, consider as the light by which they are always conducted; and although even the artificial constitution of France had long been obliged to bow to the dictates of nature and humanity, and to confer nobility, and even title, on such of the professors of the municipal law as had, by their skill and their honorable character, risen to the first offices of their profession, yet the Noblesse de la Robe never could incorporate with the Noblesse du Sang, nor even with the Noblesse de l'Epée. The descendants of a Marquis de la Robe never could rise to certain dignities in the church and at court. The avocats de parlement felt this, and smarted under the exclusion from court-honors; and though they eagerly courted such nobility as they could attain, they seldom omitted any opportunity that occurred during their junior practice of exposing the arrogance of the Noblesse, and the dominion of the court. This increased their popularity, and in the present situation of things, being certain of support, they went beyond their former cautious bounds, and introduced in their pleadings, and particularly in their joint remonstrances against the registration of edicts, all the wire-drawn morality, and cosmo-political jurisprudence, which they had so often rehearsed in the Lodges, and which had of late been openly preached by the economists and philosophers.

A signal was given to the nation for engaging "en masse" in political discussion. The *Notables* were called upon to come and advise the King; and the points were laid before them, in which his Majesty (infallible till now) acknowledged his ignorance or his doubts. But who were the Notables? Were they more knowing than the King, or less in need of instruction? The nation thought otherwise; nay, the court thought otherwise; for, in some of the royal proclamations on this occasion, men of letters were invited to assist with their counsels, and to give what information their reading and experience should suggest as to the best method of convoking the States General, and of conducting their deliberations. When a Minister thus solicits advice from all the world how to govern, he most assuredly declares his own incapacity, and tells the people that now they must govern themselves. This however was done, and the Minister, Neckar, the Philosopher and Philanthropist of Geneva, set the example, by sending in *his* opinion, to be laid on the council-table with the rest. On this signal, counsel poured in from every garret, and the press groaned with advice in every shape. Ponderous volumes were written for the Bishop or the Duke; a handsome 8vo for the *Notable* Officer of eighteen; pamphlets and single sheets for the loungers in the *Palais Royal*. The fermentation was astonishing, but it was no more than should have been expected from the most cultivated, the most ingenious, and the least bashful nation on earth. All wrote, and all read. Not contented with bringing forth all the fruits which the Illumination of these bright days of reason had raised in such abundance in the conservatories of the *Philalethes,* and which had been gathered from the writings of Voltaire, Diderot, Rousseau, Raynal, &c. the patriotic counsellors of the Notables had ransacked all the writings of former ages. They discovered THAT FRANCE HAD ALWAYS BEEN FREE! One would have thought that they had travelled with Sir John Mandeville in that country where even the speeches of former times had been frozen, and were now thawing apace under the beams of the sun of Reason. For many of these essays were as incongruous and mal-à-propos as the broken sentences recorded by Mr. Addison in the Spectator. A gentleman who was in Paris at this time, a person of great judgment, and well informed in every thing respecting the constitution and present condition of his country, assured me that this invitation, followed by the memorial of Mr. Neckar, operated like an electrical shock. In the course of four or five days, the appearance of Paris was completely changed. Every where one saw crowds staring at papers pasted on the walls—breaking into little parties—walking up and down the streets in eager conversation—adjourning to coffee-houses—and the conversation in all companies turned to politics alone; and in all these conversations, a new vocabulary, where every second word was Morality, Philanthropy, Toleration, Freedom, and Equalisation of property. Even at this eary period persons were listened to without censure, or even surprise, who said that it was nonsense to think of reforming their government, and that it must be completely changed. In short, in the course of a month, a spirit of licentiousness and a rage for innovation had completely pervaded the minds of the Parisians. The most conspicuous proof of this was the unexpected fate of the Parliament. It met earlier than usual, and to give greater eclat to its patriotic efforts, and completely to secure the gratitude of the people, it issued an arret on the present state of the nation, containing a number of resolutions on the different leading points of national liberty. A few months ago these would have been joyfully received as the Magna Charta of Freedom, and really contained all that a wise people should desire; but because the Parliament had some time before given it as their opinion as the constitutional counsel of the Crown, that the States should be convoked on the principles of their last meeting in 1614, which preserved the distinctions of rank, all their past services were forgotten—all their hard struggle with the former administration, and their unconquerable courage and perseverance, which ended only with their downfall, all were forgotten; and those distinguished members whose zeal and sufferings ranked them with the most renowned heroes and martyrs of patriotism, were now regarded as the contemptible tools of Aristocracy. The Parliament now set, in a fiery troubled sky—to rise no more.

Of all the barristers in the Parliament of Paris, the most conspicuous for the display of the enchanting doctrines of Liberty and Equality was Mr. Duval, son of an Avocat in the same court, and ennobled about this time under the name of Despresmenil. He was member of a Lodge of the *Amis*

*Reunis* at Paris, called the *Contract Social,* and of the Lodge of *Chevaliers Bienfaisants* at Lyons. His reputation as a barrister had been prodigiously encreased about this time by his management of a cause, where the descendant of the unfortunate General Lally, after having obtained the restoration of the family honors, was striving to get back some of the estates. Mr. Lally Tollendahl had even trained himself to the profession, and pleaded his own cause with astonishing abilities. But Despresmenil had near connections with the family which was in possession of the estates, and opposed him with equal powers, and more address. He was on the side which was most agreeable to his favorite topics of declamation, and his pleadings attracted much notice both in Paris and in some of the provincial Parliaments. I mention these things with some interest, because this was the beginning of that marked rivalship between Lally Tollendahl and Despresmenil, which made such a figure in the journals of the National Assembly. It ended fatally for both. Lally Tollendahl was obliged to quit the Assembly, when he saw it determined on the destruction of the monarchy and of all civil order, and at last to emigrate from his country with the loss of all his property, and to subsist on the kindness of England. Despresmenil attained his meredian of popularity by his discovery of the secret plan of the Court to establish the *Cour pleniere,* and ever after this took the lead in all the strong measures of the Parliament of Paris, which was now overstepping all bounds of moderation or propriety, in hopes of preserving its influence after it had rendered itself impotent by an unguarded stroke. Despresmenil was the first martyr of that Liberty and Equality which it was now boldly preaching, having voluntarily surrendered himself a prisoner to the officer sent to demand him from the Parliament. He was also a martyr to any thing that remained of the very shadow of liberty after the Revolution, being guillotined by Robespierre.

I have already mentioned the intrigues of Count Mirabeau at the Court of Berlin, and his seditious preface and notes on the anonymous letters on the Rights of the Prussian States. He also, while at Berlin, published an *Essai sur la Secte des Illuminés,* one of the strangest and most impudent performances that ever appeared. He there describes a sect existing in Germany, called the *Illuminated*, and says, that they are the most absurd and gross fanatics imaginable, waging war with every appearance of Reason, and maintaining the most ridiculous superstitions. He gives some account of these, and of their rituals, ceremonies, &c. as if he had seen them all. His sect is a confused mixture of Christian superstitions, Rosycrucian nonsense, and every thing that can raise contempt and hatred. But no such Society ever existed, and Mirabeau confided in his own powers of deception, in order to screen from observation those who were known to be Illuminati, and to hinder the rulers from attending to their real machinations, by means of this Ignis fatuus of his own brain. He knew perfectly that the Illuminati were of a stamp diametrically opposite; for he was illuminated by Mauvillon long before.—He gained his point in some measure, for Nicholai and others of the junto immediately adopted the whim, and called them *Obscuranten,* and joined with Mirabeau in placing on the list of *Obscuranten* several persons whom they wished to make ridiculous.

Mirabeau was not more discontented with the Court of Berlin for the small regard it had testified for his eminent talents, than he was with his own Court, or rather with the minister Calonne, who had sent him thither. Calonne had been greatly dissatisfied with his conduct at Berlin, where his self-conceit, and his private projects, had made him act in a way almost contrary to the purposes of his mission. Mirabeau was therefore in a rage at the minister, and published a pamphlet, in which his celebrated memorial on the state of the nation, and the means of relieving it, was treated with the utmost severity of reproach; and in this contest his mind was wrought up to that violent pitch of opposition which he ever after maintained. To be noticed, and to lead, were his sole objects—and he found that taking the side of the discontented was the best field for his eloquence and restless ambition.—Yet there was no man that was more devoted to the principles of a court than Count Mirabeau, provided he had a share in the administration; and he would have obtained it, if any thing moderate would have satisfied him—but he thought nothing worthy of him but a place of active trust, and a high department. For such offices all knew him to be totally unfit. He wanted knowledge of great things, and was learned only in the bustling detail of intrigue, and at any time would sacrifice every thing to have an opportunity of exercising his brilliant eloquence, and indulging his passion for satire and reproach.—The greatest obstacle to his advancement was the abject worthlessness of his character. What we usually call profligacy, viz. debauchery, gaming, impiety, and every kind of sensuality were not enough—he was destitute of decency in his vices—tricks which would disgrace a thief-catcher, were never boggled at in order to supply his expences—For instance—His father and mother had a process of separation—Mirabeau had just been liberated from prison for a gross misdemeanour, and was in want of money—He went to his father, sided with him in invectives against his mother, and, for 100 guineas, wrote his father's memorial for the court.—He then went to his mother, and by a similar conduct got the same sum from her—and both memorials were presented. Drinking was the only vice in which he did not indulge—his exhausted constitution did not permit it. His brother the Viscount, on the contrary, was apt to exceed in jollity. One day the Count said to him, "How can you, Brother, so expose yourself?" "What! says the Viscount, how insatiable you are—Nature has given you every vice, and having left me only this one, you grudge it me." When the elections were making for the States-General, he offered himself a candidate in his own order at Aix—But he was so abhorred by the Noblesse, that they not only rejected him, but even drove him from their meetings. This affront settled his measures, and he determined on their ruin. He went to the Commons, disclaimed his being a gentleman, set up a little shop in the market-place of Aix, and sold trifles—and now, fully resolved what line he should pursue, he courted the Commons, by joining in all their excesses against the Noblesse, and was at last returned a member of the Assembly.

From this account of Mirabeau we can easily foretell the use he would make of the Illumination which he had received in Germany. Its grand truths and just morality seem to have had the same effects on his mind as on that of Weishaupt or Bahrdt.

In the year 1786, Mirabeau, in conjunction with the

Duke de Lauzun and the Abbé Perigord, afterwards Bishop of Autun (the man so puffed in the National Assemblies as the brightest pattern of humanity) reformed a Lodge of Philalethes in Paris, which met in the Jacobin College or Convent. It was one of the *Amis Reunis,* which had now rid itself of all the insignificant mysticism of the sect. This was now become troublesome, and took up the time which would be much better employed by the *Chevaliers du Soleil,* and other still more refined champions of reason and universal citizenship. Mirabeau had imparted to it some of that Illumination which had beamed upon him when he was in Berlin. In 1788 he and the Abbé were Wardens of the Lodge. They found that they had not acquired all the dexterity of management that he understood was practised by his Brethren in Germany, for keeping up their connection, and conducting their correspondence. A letter was therefore sent from this Lodge, signed by these two gentlemen, to the Brethren in Germany, requesting their assistance and instruction. In the course of this year, and during the sitting of the Nobles, A DEPUTATON WAS SENT from the German Illuminati to catch this glorious opportunity of carrying their plan into full execution with the greatest eclat.

Nothing can more convincingly demonstrate the early intentions of a party, and this a great party, in France to overturn the constitution completely, and plant a democracy or oligarchy on its ruins. The Illuminati had no other object. They accounted all Princes usurpers and tyrants, and all privileged orders as their abettors. They intended to establish a government of Morality, as they called it *(Sittenregiment)* where talents and character (to be estimated by their own scale, and by themselves) should alone lead to preferment. They meant to abolish the laws which protected property accumulated by long continued and successful industry, and to prevent for the future any such accumulation. They intended to establish universal Liberty and Equality, the imprescriptible Rights of Man (at least they pretended all this to those who were neither Magi nor Regentes.) And, as necessary preparations for all this, they intended to root out all religion and ordinary morality, and even to break the bonds of domestic life, by destroying the veneration for marriage-vows, and by taking the education of children out of the hands of the parents. *This was all that the Illuminati could teach,* and THIS WAS PRECISELY WHAT FRANCE HAS DONE.

I cannot proceed in the narration without defiling the page with the detested name of *Orleans,* stained with every thing that can degrade or disgrace human nature. He only wanted Illumination, to shew him in a system all the opinions, dispositions, and principles which filled his own wicked heart. This contemptible being was illuminated by Mirabeau, and has shown himself the most zealous disciple of the Order. In his oath of allegiance he declares, "That the interests and the object of the Order shall be rated by him above all other relations, and that he will serve it with his honor, his fortune, and his blood."—He has kept his word, and has sacrificed them all—And he has been treated in the true spirit of the Order—used as a mere tool, cheated and ruined.—For I must now add, that the French borrowed from the Illuminati a maxim, unheard of in any other association of banditti, viz. that of cheating each other. As the managers had the sole possession of the higher mysteries, and led the rest by principles which they held to be false, and which they employed only for the purpose of securing the co-operation of the inferior Brethren, so Mirabeau, Sieyes, Pethion, and others, led the Duke of Orleans at first by his wicked ambition, and the expectation of obtaining that crown which they intended to break in pieces, that they might get the use of his immense fortune, and of his influence on the thousands of his depending sycophants, who ate his bread and pandered to his gross appetites. Although we very soon find him acting as an *Illuminatus,* we cannot suppose him so lost to common sense as to contribute his fortune, and risk his life, merely in order that the one should be afterwards taken from him by law, and the other put on a level with that of his groom or his pimp. He surely hoped to obtain the crown of his indolent relation. And indeed Mirabeau said to Bergasse, that "when the project was mentioned to the Duke of Orleans, he received it with all possible favor," *(avec toute la grace imaginable.)* During the contests between the Court and the Parliament of Paris, he courted popularity with an indecency and folly that nothing can explain but a mad and fiery ambition which blinded his eyes to all consequences. This is put out of doubt by his behaviour at Versailles on the dreadful 5th and 6th of October 1789. The depositions at the Chatelet prove in the most incontestable manner, that during the horrors of these two days he was repeatedly seen, and that whenever he was recognised by the croud, he was huzzaed with *Vive Orleans, Vive notre Roi Orleans*, &c.—He then withdrew, and was seen in other places. While all about the unfortunate Royal Family were in the utmost concern for their fate, he was in gay humour, chatting on indifferent subjects. His last appearance in the evening of the 5th was, about nine o'clock, conversing in a corner with men disguised in mean dress, and some in women's clothes; among whom were Mirabeau, Barnave, Duport, and other deputies of the Republican party—and these men were seen immediately after, concealed among the lines of the *Regiment de Flandre*, the corruption of which they had that day completed. He was seen again next morning conversing with the same persons in women's dress. And when the insulted Sovereign was dragged in triumph to Paris, Orleans was again seen, skulking in a balcony behind his children, to view the procession of devils and furies; anxiously hoping all the while that some disturbance would arise in which the King might perish.—I should have added that he was seen in the morning at the top of the stairs, pointing the way with his hand to the mob, where they should go, while he went by another road to the King. In short, he went about trembling like a coward, waiting for the explosion which might render it safe for him to shew himself. Mirabeau said to him, "The fellow carries a loaded pistol in his bosom, but will never dare to pull the trigger." He was saved, notwithstanding his own folly, by being joined in the accusation with Mirabeau, who could not rescue himself without striving also for Orleans, whom he despised, while he made use of his fortune.—In short, Orleans was but half illuminated at this time, and hoped to be King or Regent.

Yet he was deeply versed in the preparatory lessons of Illuminatism, and well convinced of its fundamental truths. He was well assured of the great influence of the women in society, and he employed this influence like a true disciple of Weishaupt. Above three hundred nymphs from the Purlieus of the Palais Royal were provided with ecus and Louis d'ors, by his grand procureur the Abbés Sieyes, and were sent to meet and to illuminate the two battalions of the

*Regiment de Flandre*, who were coming to Versailles for the protection of the Royal Family. The privates of one of these regiments came and informed their officers of this attempt made on their loyalty.—45,000 livres were given them at St. Deny's, to make them disband themselves—and the poor lads were at first dazzled by the name of a sum that was not familiar to them—but when some thinking head among them told them that it only amounted to two Louis d'ors a-piece, they disclosed the bribery. They were then offered 90,000, but never saw it. (Depositions at the Chatelet, No. 317.) Mademoiselle Therouane, the *favorita* of the day at the Palais Royal, was the most active person of the armed mob from Paris, dressed *en Amazonne,* with all the elegance of the opera, and turned many young heads that day which were afterwards taken off by the guillotine. The Duke of Orleans acknowledged, before his death, that he had expended above L. 50,000 Sterling in corrupting the *Gardes Françoises*. The armed mob which came from Paris to Versailles on the 5th of October, importuning the King for bread, had their pockets filled with crown-pieces; and Orleans was seen on that day by two gentlemen, with a bag of money so heavy that it was fastened to his clothes with a strap, to hinder it from being oppressive, and to keep it in such a position that it should be accessible in an instant. (See the Depositions at the Chatelet, No. 177.)

But such was the contempt into which his gross profligacy, his cowardice, and his niggardly disposition, had brought him with all parties, that, if he had not been quite blinded by his wicked ambition, and by his implacable resentment of some bitter taunts he had gotten from the King and Queen, he must have seen very early that he was to be sacrificed as soon as he had served the purpoies of the faction. At present, his assistance was of the utmost consequence. His immense fortune, much above three millions Sterling, was almost exhausted during the three first years of the Revolution. But (what was of more consequence) he had almost unbounded authority among the Free Masons.

In this country we have no conception of the authority of a National Grand Master. When Prince Ferdinand of Brunswick, by great exertions among the jarring sects in

Germany, had got himself elected Grand Master of the *Strict Observanz*, it gave serious alarm to the Emperor, and to all the Princes of Germany, and contributed greatly to their connivance at the attempts of the *Illuminati* to discredit that party. In the great cities of Germany, the inhabitants paid more respect to the Grand Master of the Masons than to their respective Princes. The authority of the D. of Orleans in France was still greater, in consequence of his employing his fortune to support it. About eight years before the Revolution he had (not without much intrigue and many bribes and promises) been elected Grand Master of France, having under his directions all the *Improved* Lodges. The whole Association was called the *Grand Orient de la France*, and in 1785 contained 266 of these Lodges (see *Freymaurerische Zeitung, Neuwied,* 1787.) Thus he had the management of all those Secret Societies; and the licentious and irreligious sentiments which were currently preached there, were sure of his hearty concurrence. The same intrigue which procured him the supreme chair, must have filled the Lodges with his dependents and emissaries, and these men could not better earn their pay, than by doing their utmost to propagate infidelity, immorality, and impurity of manners.

But something more was wanted: Disrespect for the higher Orders of the State, and disloyalty to the Sovereign. —It is not so easy to conceive how these sentiments, and particularly the latter, could meet with toleration, and even encouragement, in a nation noted for its professions of veneration for its Monarch, and for the pride of its Noblesse. Yet I am certain, that such doctrines were habitually preached in the Lodges of *Philalethes*, and *Amis Reunis de la Verité*. That they should be very current in Lodges of lowborn Literati, and other Brethren in inferior stations, is natural, and I have already said enough on this head. But the French Lodges contained many gentlemen in easy, in affluent circumstances. I do not expect such confidence in my assertions, that even in these the same opinions were very prevalent. I was therefore much pleased with a piece of information which I got while these sheets were printing off, which corroborates my assertions.

This is a performance called *La voile retirée, ou le Se-*

*cret de la Revolution expliqué par la Franc Maçonnerie.*
It was written by a Mr. Lefranc, President of the Seminary
of the *Eudists* at Caen in Normandy, and a second edition
was published at Paris in 1792. The author was butchered
in the massacre of September. He says, that on the death
of a friend, who had been a very zealous Mason, and many
years Master of a respectable Lodge, he found among his
papers a collection of Masonic writings, containing the
rituals, catechisms, and symbols of every kind, belonging
to a long train of degrees of Free Masonry, together with
many discourses delivered in different Lodges, and minutes
of their proceedings. The perusal filled him with astonish-
ment and anxiety. For he found that doctrines were taught,
and maxims of conduct were inculcated, which were subversive of religion and of all good order in the state; and
which not only countenanced disloyalty and sedition, but
even invited to it. He thought them so dangerous to the
state, that he sent an account of them to the Archbishop of
Paris long before the Revolution, and always hoped that
that Reverend Prelate would represent the matter to his
Majesty's Ministers, and that they would put an end to the
meetings of this dangerous Society, or would at least restrain them from such excesses. But he was disappointed,
and therefore thought it his duty to lay them before the
public.*

Mr. Lefranc says expressly, that this shocking perversion
of Free Masonry to seditious purposes was, in a great
measure, but a late thing, and was chiefly brought about
by the agents of the Grand Master, the Duke of Orleans.
He was, however, of opinion that the whole Masonic Fraternity was hostile to Christianity and to good morals, and
that it was the contrivance of the great schismatic Faustus

---

*Had the good man been spared but a few months, his surprise at
this neglect would have ceased. For, on the 19th of November 1793,
the Archbishop of Paris came to the Bar of the Assembly, accompanied by his Vicar and eleven other Clergymen, who there renounced
their Christianity and their clerical vows; acknowledging that they
had played the villain for many years against their consciences, teaching what they knew to be a lie, and were now resolved to be honest
men. The Vicar indeed had behaved like a true *Illuminatus* some
time before, by running off with another man's wife and his strong
box.—None of them, however, seem to have attained the higher mysteries, for they were all guillotined not long after.

Socinus, who being terrified by the fate of Servetus, at Geneva, fell on this method of promulgating his doctrines among the great in secret. This opinion is but ill supported, and is incompatible with many circumstances in Free Masonry—But it is out of our way at present. Mr. Lefranc then takes particular notice of the many degrees of Chivalry cultivated in the Lodges, and shows how, by artful changes in the successive explanations of the same symbols, the doctrines of Christianity, and of all revealed religion, are completely exploded, and the *Philosophe Inconnu* becomes at last a professed Atheist.—He then takes notice of the political doctrines which are in like manner gradually unfolded, by which "patriotism and loyalty to the Prince are declared to be narrow principles, inconsistent with universal benevolence, and with the native and imprescriptible rights of man; civil subordination is actual oppression, and Princes are *ex officio* usurpers and tyrants." These principles he fairly deduces from the Catechisms of the *Chevalier du Soleil,* and of the *Philosophe Inconnu.* He then proceeds to notice more particularly the intrigues of the Duke of Orleans. From these it appears evident that his ambitious views and hopes had been of long standing, and that it was entirely by his support and encouragement that seditious doctrines were permitted in the Lodges. Many noblemen and gentlemen were disgusted and left these Lodges, and advantage was taken of their absence to *improve* the Lodges still more, that is, to make them still more anarchical and seditious. Numbers of paltry scribblers who haunted the Palais Royal, were admitted into the Lodges, and there vented their poisonous doctrines. The Duke turned his chief attention to the French guards, introducing many of the privates and inferior officers into the obscure and even the more respectable Lodges, so that the officers were frequently disgusted in the Lodges by the insolent behaviour of their own soldiers, under the mask of Masonic Brotherhood and Equality—and this behaviour became not unfrequent even out of doors. He asserts with great confidence that the troops were much corrupted by these intrigues—and that when they sometimes declared, on service, that they would not fire *on their Brethren*, the phrase had a particular reference to their Masonic Fraternity, because they recognized many of their Brother Masons in every crowd.—

And the corruption was by no means confined to Paris and its neighbourhood, but extended to every place in the kingdom where there was a Municipality and a Mason Lodge.

Mr. Lefranc then turns our attention to many peculiarities in the Revolution, which have a resemblance to the practices in Free Masonry. Not only was the arch rebel the Duke of Orleans the Grand Master, but the chief actors in the Revolution, Mirabeau, Condorcet, Rochefoucault, and others, were distinguished office-bearers in the great Lodges. He says that the distribution of France into departments, districts, circles, cantons, &c. is perfectly similar, with the same denominations, to a distribution which he had remarked in the correspondence of the Grand Orient.*—The President's hat in the National Assembly is copied from that of a *Tres Venerable Grand Maitre.*—The scarf of a Municipal Officer is the same with that of a Brother Apprentice.—When the Assembly celebrated the Revolution in the Cathedral, they accepted of the highest honors of Masonry by passing under the *Arch of Steel,* formed by the drawn swords of two ranks of Brethren.—Also it is worthy of remark, that the National Assembly protected the meetings of Free Masons, while it peremptorily prohibited every other private meeting. The obligation of laying aside all stars, ribbands, crosses, and other honorable distinctions under the pretext of Fraternal Equality, was not merely a prelude, but was intended as a preparation for the destruction of all civil distinctions, which took place almost at the beginning of the Revolution—*and the first proposal of a surrender,* says Mr. Lefranc, *was made by a zealous Mason.* —He farther observes, that the horrible and sanguinary oaths, the daggers, death-heads, cross-bones, the imaginary combats with the murderers of Hiram, and many other gloomy ceremonies, have a natural tendency to harden the heart, to remove its natural disgust at deeds of horror, and have paved the way for those shocking barbarities which have made the name of Frenchman abhorred over all Europe. These deeds were indeed perpetrated by a mob of fanatics; but the principles were promulgated and fostered by persons who style themselves philosophers.

*I cannot help observing, that it is perfectly similar to the arrangement and denominations which appear in the secret correspondence of the Bavarian Illuminati.

I see more evidence of these important facts in another book just published by an emigrant gentleman (Mr. Latocnaye.) He confirms my repeated assertions, that all the irreligious and seditious doctrines were the subjects of perpetual harangues in the Mason Lodges, and that all the principles of the Revolution, by which the public mind was as it were set on fire, were nothing but enthusiastic amplifications of the common-place cant of Free Masonry, and arose naturally out of it. He even thinks "that this *must of necessity* be the case in every country where the minds of the lower classes of the State are in any way considerably fretted or irritated; it is almost impossible to avoid being drawn into this vortex, whenever a discontented mind enters into a Mason Lodge. The stale story of brotherly love, which at another time would only lull the hearer asleep, now makes him prick up his ears, and listen with avidity to the silly tale, and he cannot hinder fretting thoughts from continually rankling in his mind."

Mr. Latocnaye says expressly, "That notwithstanding the general contempt of the public for the Duke of Orleans, his authority as Grand Master of the Masons gave him the greatest opportunity that a seditious mind could desire for helping forward the Revolution. He had ready to his hand a connected system of hidden Societies, protected by the State, habituated to secrecy and artifice, and already tinged with the very enthusiasm he wished to inspire. In these he formed political committees, into which only his agents were admitted. He filled the Lodges with the French guards, whom he corrupted with money and hopes of preferment: and by means of the Abbé Sieyes, and other emissaries, they were harangued with all the sophistical declamation, or cant of Masonry."

Mr. Latocnaye says, that all this was peculiar to the Lodges of the Grand Orient; but that there were many (not very many, if we judge by the Neuwied almanac, which reckons only 289 in all France in 1784, of which 266 were of the Grand Orient) Lodges who continued on the old plan of amusing themselves with a little solemn trifling. He coincides with Mr. Lefranc in the opinion that the awful and gloomy rituals of Masonry, and particularly the severe trials of confidence and submission, must have a great tendency to harden the heart, and fit a man for atrocious actions. No one can doubt of this who reads the following instance:

"A candidate for reception into one of the highest Orders, after having heard many threatenings denounced against all who should betray the Secrets of the Order, was conducted to a place where he saw the dead bodies of several who were said to have suffered for their treachery. He then saw his own brother tied hand and foot, begging his mercy and intercession. He was informed that this person was about to suffer the punishment due to this offence, and that it was reserved for him (the candidate) to be the instrument of this just vengeance, and that this gave him an opportunity of manifesting that he was completely devoted to the Order. It being observed that his countenance gave signs of inward horror (the person in bonds imploring his mercy all the while) he was told, that in order to spare his feelings, a bandage should be put over his eyes. A dagger was then put into his right hand, and being hood-winked, his left hand was laid on the palpitating heart of the criminal, and he was then ordered to strike. He instantly obeyed; and when the bandage was taken from his eyes, he saw that it was a lamb that he had stabbed. Surely such trials and such wanton cruelty are only fit for training conspirators."

Mr. Latocnaye adds, that "when he had been initiated, an old gentleman asked him what he thought of the whole?" He answered, "A great deal of noise, and much nonsense." "Nonsense, said the other, don't judge so rashly, young man; I have worked these twenty-five years, and the farther I advanced, it interested me the more; but I stopped short, and nothing shall prevail on me to advance a step farther." In another conversation the gentleman said, "I imagine that my stoppage was owing to my refusal about nine years ago, to listen to some persons who made to me, out of the Lodge, proposals which were seditious and horrible; for ever since that time I have remarked, that my higher Brethren treat me with a much greater reserve than they had done before; and that, under the pretext of further instruction, they have laboured to confute the notions which I had already acquired, by giving some of the most delicate subjects a different turn. I saw that they wanted to remove some suspicions which I was beginning to form concerning the ultimate scope of the whole."

I imagine that these observations will leave no doubt in the mind of the reader with respect to the influence of the secret Fraternity of Free Masonry in the French Revolution, and that he will allow it to be highly probable that the infamous Duke of Orleans had, from the beginning, entertained hopes of mounting the throne of France. It is not my province to prove or disprove this point, only I think it no less evident, from many circumstances in the transactions of those tumultuous days, that the active leaders had quite different views, and were impelled by fanatical notions of democratic felicity, or more probably, by their own ambition to be the movers of this vast machine, to overturn the ancient government, and erect a republic, of which they hoped to be the managers.* Mirabeau had learned when in Germany, that the principles of anarchy had been well digested into a system, and therefore wished for some instructions as to the subordinate detail of the business, and for this purpose requested a deputation from the *Illuminati*.

In such a cause as this, we may be certain that no ordinary person would be sent. One of the deputies was Amelius, the next person in the order to Spartacus and Philo. His worldly name was Johann. J. C. Bode, at Weimar, privy-counsellor to the Prince of Hesse-Darmstadt (See *Fragmente der Biographie des verstorbenes-Freyherr Bode in Weimar, mit zuverlassigen Urkunden, 8vo. Riom.* 1795. See also *Endliche Shickfall der Freymaurerey,* 1794; also

---

*The depositions at the Chatelet, which I have already quoted, give repeated and unequivocal proofs, that he, with a considerable number of the deputies of the National Assembly, had formed this plot before the 5th of October 1789. That trial was conducted in a strange manner, partly out of respect for the Royal Family, which still had some hearts affectionately attached to it, and to the monarchy, and partly by reason of the fears of the members of this court. There was now no safety for any person who differed from the opinion of the frantic populace of Paris. The chief points of accusation were written in a schedule which is not published, and the witnesses were ordered to depose on these in one general Yes or or No; so that it is only the least important part of the evidence that has been printed. I am well informed that the whole of it is carefully preserved, and will one day appear.

*Wiener Zeitschrift fur* 1793.)—This person has played a principal part in the whole scheme of Illumination. He was a person of considerable and showy talents as a writer. He had great talents for conversation, and had kept good company. With respect to his mystical character, his experience was great. He was one of the Templar Masons, and among them was *Eques à Liliis Convallium*. He had speculated much about the origin and history of Masonry, and when at the Willemsbad convention, was converted to Illuminatism. He was the great instigator of Nicholai, Gedicke, and Biester, to the hunt after Jesuits, which so much occupied them, and suggested to Nicholai his journey through Germany. Leuchtsenring, whom I mentioned before, was only the letter-carrier between Bode and these three authors. He was just such a man as Weishaupt wished for; his head filled with Masonic fanaticism, attaching infinite importance to the frivolities of Masonry, and engaged in an enthusiastic and fruitless research after its origin and history. He had collected, however, such a number of archives (as they were called) of Free Masonry, that he sold his manuscript to the Duke of Saxe Gotha (into whose service Weishaupt engaged himself when he was driven from Bavaria) for 1500 dahlers. This little anecdote shows the high importance attributed to these matters by persons of whom we should expect better things. Bode was also a most determined and violent materialist. Besides all these qualities, so acceptable to the Illuminati, he was a discontented Templar Mason, having been repeatedly disappointed of the preferment which he thought himself entitled to. When he learned that the first operations of the Illuminati were to be the obtaining the sole direction of the Mason Lodges, and of the whole Fraternity, his hopes revived of rising to some of the Commanderies, which his enthusiasm, or rather fanaticism, had made him hope to see one day regained by the Order—but when he found that the next and favorite object was to root out the *Strict Observanz* altogether, he started back. But Philo saw that the understanding (shall we call it) that can be dazzled with one whim, may be dazzled with another, and he now attached him to Illuminatism, by a magnificent display of a world ruled by the Order, and conducted to happiness by means of Liberty and Equality. This did the business, as we see by the private correspondence, where Philo informs Spartacus of his first difficulties with Amelius. Amelius was gained over in August 1782, and we see by the same correspondence, that the greatest affairs were soon entrusted to him—he was generally employed to deal with the great. When a Graf or a Baron was to be wheedled into the Order, Amelius was the agent.—He was also the chief operator in all their contests with the Jesuits and the Rosycrucians. It was also Bode that procured the important accession of Nicholai to the Order. This he brought about through Leuchtsenring; and lastly, his numerous connections among the Free Masons, together with Knigge's influence among them, enabled the Illuminati to worm themselves into every Lodge, and at last gave them almost the entire command of the Fraternity.

Such was the first of the deputies to France. The other was a Mr. Bussche, called in the Order Bayard; therefore probably a man of respectable character; for most of Spartacus's names were significant, like his own. He was a military man, Lieutenant-Colonel in the service of Hesse-Darmstadt. This man also was a discontented Templar Mason, and his name in that Fraternity had been *Eques a Fontibus Eremi*. He was Illuminated by Knigge. He had also been unsuccessful both at court and in the field, in both of which situations he had been attempting to make a distinguished figure. He, as well as Bode, were immersed in debts. They were therefore just in the proper temper for Cosmo-political enterprise.

They went to Paris in the end of 1788, while the Notables were sitting, and all Paris was giving advice. The alarm that was raised about Animal Magnetism, which was indeed making much noise at that time, and particularly in Paris, was assigned by them as the great motive of the journey. Bode also said that he was anxious to learn what were the corrections made on the system of the *Chevaliers Bienfaisants*. They had taken that name at first, to screen themselves from the charges against them under the name of Templars. They had corrected something in their system when they took the name *Philalethes*. And now when the schisms of the *Philalethes* were healed, and the Brethren again united under the name of *Amis Reunis*, he suspected that Jesuits had interfered; and because he had heard that the principles of the *Amis Reunis* were very noble, he wished to be more certain that they were purged of every thing Jesuitical.

The deputies accordingly arrived at Paris, and immediately obtained admission into these two Fraternities.* They found both of them in the ripest state for Illumination, having shaken off all the cabalistical, chemical, and mystical whims that had formerly disturbed them, and would now take up too much of their time. They were now cultivating with great zeal the philosophico-political doctrines of universal citizenship. Their leaders, to the number of twenty, are mentioned by name in the Berlin Monatschrift for 1785, and among them are several of the first actors in the French Revolution. But this is nothing distinctive, because persons of all opinions were Masons.

The *Amis Reunis* were little behind the Illuminati in every thing that was irreligious and anarchical, and had no inclination for any of the formalities of ritual, &c. They were already fit for the higher mysteries, and only wanted to learn the methods of business which had succeeded so well in spreading their doctrines and maxims over Germany. Besides, their doctrines had not been digested into a system, nor had the artful methods of leading on the pupils from bad to worse been practised. For hitherto, each individual had vented in the Lodges his own opinions, to unburden his own mind, and the Brethren listened for instruction and mutual encouragement. Therefore, when Spartacus's plan was communicated to them, they saw at

*To prevent interruptions, I may just mention here the authorities for this journey and co-operation of the two deputies.

1. *Ein wichtiger Ausschluss über ein noch wenig bekannte Veranlassung der Französchen Revolution*, in the Vienna Zeitschrift for 1793, p. 145.

2. *Endliche Shickfall des Freymaurer-Ordens,* 1794, p. 19.

3. *Neueste Arbeitung des Spartacus und Philo*, Munich, 1793, p. 151—154.

4. *Historische Nachrichten über die Franc Revolution 1792, von Girkinner, var. loc.*

5. *Revolutions Almanach für 1792—4. Gottingen, var. loc.*

6. *Beytrage zur Biographie des verstorbenes Frey-Herr v. Bode,* 1794.

7. *Magazin des Literatur et Kunst,* for 1792, 3, 4, &c &c.

once its importance, in all its branches, such as the use of the Mason Lodges, to fish for Minervals—the rituals and ranks to entice the young, and to lead them by degrees to opinions and measures, which, at first sight, would have shocked them. The firm hold which is gotten of the pupils, and indeed of all the inferior classes, by their reports in the course of their pretended training in the knowledge of themselves and of other men—and, above all, the provincial arrangement of the Order, and the clever subordination and entire dependence on a select band or Pandæmonium at Paris, which should inspire and direct the whole.—I think (although I have not express assertions of the fact) from the subsequent conduct of the French revolters, that even at this early period, there were many in those societies who were ready to go every length proposed to them by the Illuminati, such as the abolition of royalty and of all privileged orders, as tyrants by nature, the annihilation and robbery of the priesthood, the rooting out of Christianity, and the introduction of Atheism, or a philosophical chimera which they were to call Religion. Mirabeau had often spoken of the last branch of the Illuminated principles, and the conversations held at Versailles during the awful pauses of the 5th of October (which are to be seen in the evidence before the Chatelet in the Orleans process) can hardly be supposed to be the fancies of an accidental mob.

Mirabeau was, as I have said, at the head of this democratic party, and had repeatedly said, that the only use of a King was to serve as a pageant, in order to give weight to public measures in the opinion of the populace.—And Mr. Latocnaye says, that this party was very numerous, and that immediately after the imprudent or madlike invitation of every scribbler in a garret to give his advice, the party did not scruple to speak their sentiments in public, and that they were encouraged in their encomiums on the advantages of a virtuous republican government by Mr. Necker, who had a most extravagant and childish predilection for the constitution of Geneva, the place of his nativity, and was also much tinged with the Cosmo-political philosophy of the times. The King's brothers, and the Princes of the blood, presented a memorial to his Majesty, which concluded by saying, that "the effervescence of the public opinions had come to such a height that the most dangerous principles, imported from foreign parts, were avowed in print with perfect impunity—that his Majesty had unwarily encouraged every fanatic to dictate to him, and to spread his poisonous sentiments, in which the rights of the throne were not only disrespected, but were even disputed—that the rights of the higher classes in the state ran a great risk of being speedily suppressed, and that nothing would hinder the sacred right of property from being ere long invaded, and the unequal distribution of wealth from being thought a proper subject of reform."

When such was the state of things in Paris, it is plain that the business of the German deputies would be easily transacted. They were received with open arms by the *Philalethes,* the *Amis de la Verité,* the *Social Contract,* &c. and in the course of a very few weeks in the end of 1788, and the beginning of 1789 (that is, before the end of March) the whole of the Grand Orient, including the *Philalethes, Amis Reunis, Martinistes,* &c. had the secrets of Illumination communicated to them. The operation naturally began with the Great National Lodge of Paris, and those in immediate dependence on it. It would also seem, from many circumstances that occurred to my observation, that the Lodges in Alsace and Lorraine were illuminated at this time, and not long before, as I had imagined. Strasburg I know had been illuminated long ago, while Philo was in the Order. A circumstance strikes me here as of some moment. The sects of *Philalethes* and *Amis Reunis* were refinements engrafted on the system of the *Chevaliers Bienfaisants* at Lyons. Such refinements never fail to be considered as a sort of heresy, and the professors will be beheld with a jealous and unfriendly eye by some, who will pride themselves on adhering to the old faith. And the greater the success of the heresy, the greater will be the animosity between the parties.—May not this help to explain the mutual hatred of the Parisians and the Lyonnois, which produced the most dreadful atrocities ever perpetrated on the face of the earth, and made a shambles and a desert of the finest city of France?

The first proceeding by the advice of the deputies was the formation of a Political Committee in every Lodge.

This committee corresponded with the distant Lodges, and in it were discussed and settled all the political principles which were to be inculcated on the members. The author of the *Neueste Arbutung* says expressly, that "he was thoroughly instructed in this, that it was given in charge to these committees to frame general rules, and to carry through the great plan *(grand œuvre)* of a general overturning of religion and government." The principal leaders of the subsequent Revolution were members of these committees. Here were the plans laid, and they were transmitted through the kingdom by the Corresponding Committees.

Thus were the stupid Bavarians (as the French were once pleased to call them) their instructors in the art of overturning the world. The French were indeed the first who put it in practice. These committees arose from the Illuminati in Bavaria, who had by no means given over working; and these committees produced the Jacobin Club. It is not a frivolous remark, that the Masonic phrase of the persons who wish to address the Brethren, *"S. je demande la parole,* which the F. S. reports to the V. G. M. and which he announces to the Brethren thus, *"Mes freres, frere tel demande la parole, la parole lui est accordée,"*) is exactly copied by the Jacobin Club. There is surely no natural connection between Free Masonry and Jacobinism—but we see the link—Illuminatism.—

The office-bearers of one of the Lodges of Philalethes in Paris were *Martin, Willermooz* (who had been deputy from the *Chevaliers Bienfaisants* to the Willemsbad Convention) *Chappe, Minet, de la Henriere,* and *Savatier de l'Ange.\** In another (the *Contract Social*) the political committee consisted of *La Fayette, Condorcet, Pethion, d'Orleans, Abbé Bertholis, d'Aiguillon, Bailly, Marq. de la*

---

\*Minet was (I think) at this time a player. He was son of a surgeon at Nantes—robbed his father and fled—enlisted in Holland—deserted and became smuggler—was taken and burnt in the hand—became player, and married an actress—then became priest—and was made Bishop of Nantes by Coustard in discharge of a debt of L. 500. Mr. Latocnaye often saw Coustard kneel to him for benediction. It cannot be supposed that he was much venerated in his pontificals in his native city.—It seems Minet, Minet, is the call of the children to a kitten—This was prohibited at Nantes, and many persons whipped for the freedom used with his name.

*Salle, Despresmenil.* This particular Lodge had been founded and conducted by one *De Leutre,* an adventurer and cheat of the first magnitude, who sometimes made a figure, and at other times was without a shilling. At this very time he was a spy attached to the office of the police of Paris.* The *Duke of Orleans* was Warden of the Lodge. The *Abbé Sieyes* was a Brother Orator, but not of this Lodge, nor (I think) of the former. It was probably of the one conducted by Mirabeau and the Abbé Perigord. But it appears from the piece from which I am at present borrowing, that Sieyes was present in the meetings of both Lodges, probably as visiting Brother, employed in bringing them to common measures. I must observe, that the subsequent conduct of some of these men does not just accord with my conjecture, that the principles of the Illuminati were adopted in their full extent. But we know that all the Bavarian Brethren were not equally illuminated, and it would be only copying their teachers if the cleverest of these their scholars should hold a *sanctum sanctorum* among themselves, without inviting all to the conference. Observe too that the chief lesson which they were now taking from the Germans was *the method of doing business,* of managing their correspondence, and of procuring and training pupils. A Frenchman does not think that he needs instruction in any thing like principle or science. He is ready on all occasions to be the instructor.

Thus were the Lodges of France converted in a very short time into a set of secret affiliated societies, corresponding with the mother Lodges of Paris, receiving from thence their principles and instructions, and ready to rise up at once when called upon, to carry on the great work of overturning the state.

*He now (or very lately) keeps the best company, and lives in elegence and affluence in London.

> *Augur, schœnobates medicus, magus, omnia novit*
> *Graculus esuriens; in cœlum jusseris, ibit.†*
> *Ingenium velox audacia perdita, sermo*
> *Promptus.———*

Juvenal.

†All sciences a hungry Frenchman knows.
  And bid him go to hell—to hell he goes.

*Johnson's Translation.*

Hence it has arisen that the French aimed, in the very beginning, at overturning the whole world. In all the revolutions of other countries, the schemes and plots have extended no farther than the nation where they took their rise. But here we have seen that they take in the whole world. They have repeatedly declared this in their manifestos, and they have declared it by their conduct. This is the very aim of the Illuminati.—Hence too may be explained how the revolution took place almost in a moment in every part of France. The revolutionary societies were early formed, and were working in secret before the opening of the National Assembly, and the whole nation changed, and changed again, and again, as if by beat of drum. Those duly initiated in this mystery of iniquity were ready every where at a call. And we see Weishaupt's wish accomplished in an unexpected degree, and the debates in a club giving laws to solemn assemblies of the nation, and all France bending the neck to the city of Paris. The members of the club are Illuminati, and so are a great part of their correspondents.—Each operates in the state as a Minerval would do in the Order, and the whole goes on with systematic regularity. The famous Jacobin Club was just one of these Lodges, as has been already observed; and as, among individuals, one commonly takes the lead, and contrives for the rest, so it has happened on the present occasion, that this Lodge, supported by Orleans and Mirabeau, was the one that stepped forth and shewed itself to the world, and thus became the oracle of the party; and all the rest only echoed its discourses, and at last allowed it to give law to the whole, and even to rule the kingdom. It is to be remarked too that the founders of the club at Mentz were Illuminati (*Relig. Begebenh.* 1793. p. 448.) before the Revolution, and corresponded with another Lodge at Strasburg; and these two produced mighty effects during the year 1790. In a performance called *Memoires Posthumes de Custine* it is said that when that General was bending his course to Holland, the Illuminati at Strasburg, Worms, and Spire immediately formed clubs, and invited him into that quarter, and, by going to Mentz and encouraging their Brethren in that city, they raised a party against the garrison, and actually delivered up the place to the French army.

A little book, just now printed with the title *Paragraphen,* says, that Zimmerman, of whom I have spoken more than once, went to France to preach liberty. He was employed as a missionary of Revolution in Alsace, where he had formerly been a most successful missionary of Illuminatism. Of his former proceedings the following is a curious anecdote. He connected himself with a highly accomplished and beautiful woman, whose conversation had such charms, that he says she gained him near a hundred converts in Spire alone. Some persons of high rank, and great exterior dignity of character, had felt more tender impressions— and when the lady informed them of certain consequences to their reputation, they were glad to compound matters with her friend Mr. Zimmerman, who either passed for her husband, or took the scandal on himself. He made above 1500 Louis d'ors in this way. When he returned, as a preacher of Revolution, he used to mount the pulpit with a sabre in his hand, and bawl out, "Behold, Frenchmen, this is your God. This alone can save you." The author adds, that when Custine broke into Germany, Zimmerman got admission to him, and engaged to deliver Manheim into his hands. To gain this purpose, he offered to set some corners of the city on fire, and assured him of support. Custine declined the offer.—Zimmerman appeared against him before the Revolutionary Tribunal, and accused him of treachery to his cause.—Custine's answer is remarkable. "Hardly," said he, "had I set my foot in Germany, when this man, and all the fools of his country, besieged me, and would have delivered up to me their towns and villages— What occasion had I to do any thing to Manheim, when the Prince was neutral?" Zimmerman found his full account in Robespierre's bloody sway—but the spurt of his atrocities was also the whole of Zimmerman's career. He was arrested, but again liberated, and soon after again imprisoned, after which I can learn no more of him. The same thing is positively asserted in another performance, called *Cri de la Raison,* and in a third, called *Les Masques arrachées.* Observe too, that it is not the clubs merely that are accused of this treachery, but the Illuminati. *De la Metherie* also, in his preface to the *Journal de Physique* for 1790, says expressly that "the cause and arms of France were powerfully supported in Germany by a sect of philosophers called the Illuminated." In the preface to the *Journal* for 1792, he says, that "Letters and deputations were received by the Assembly from several Corresponding Societies in England, felicitating them on the triumph of Reason and Humanity, and promising them their cordial assistance." He read some of these manifests, and says, that "one of them recommended strongly the political education of the children, who should be taken from the parents, and trained up for the state." Another lamented the baleful influence of property, saying that "the efforts of the Assembly would be fruitless, till the fence was removed with which the laws so anxiously secured inordinate wealth. They should rather be directed to the support of talents and virtue; because property would always support itself by the too great influence which it had in every corrupted state. The laws should prevent the too great accumulation of it in particular families."—In short, the counsel was almost verbatim what the Abbé Cossandey declared to have been the doctrine preached in the meetings of the Illuminati, which terrified him and his colleagues, and made them quit the Association. Anarcharsis Cloots, born in Prussian Westphalia, a keen Illuminatus, came to Paris for the express purpose of forwarding the *great work,* and by intriguing in the style of the Order, he got himself made one of the Representatives of the Nation. He seems to have been one of the completest fanatics in Cosmo-politism, and just such a tool as Weishaupt would choose to employ for a coarse and arduous job. He broke out at once into all the silly extravagance of the unthinking herd, and his whole language is just the jargon of Illumination. Citizen of the World—Liberty and Equality, the imprescriptible Rights of Man—Morality, dear Morality—Kings and Priests are useless things—they are Despots and Corrupters, &c.—He declared himself an atheist, and zealously laboured to have atheism established by law. He conducted that farcical procession in the true style of the most childish ritual of Philo, where counterfeited deputies from all quarters of the world, in the dresses of their countries, came to congratulate the nation for its victory over Kings and Priests. It is also worthy of remark, that by this time Leuchtsenring, whom we have seen so zealous an *Illuminatus,* after having been as zealous a Protestant, tutor of Princes, Hofrath and Hofmeister, was now a secretary or clerk in one of the Bureaus of the National Assembly of France.

I may add as a finishing touch, that the National Assembly of France was the only body of men that I have ever heard of who openly and systematically proposed to employ assassination, and to institute a band of patriots, who should exercise this profession either by sword, pistol, or poison;—and though the proposal was not completed, it might be considered as the sentiments of the meeting; for it was only delayed till it should be considered how far it might not be imprudent, because they might expect reprisals. The Abbé Dubois engaged to poison the Comte d'Artois; but was himself robbed and poisoned by his accomplices.—There were strong reasons for thinking that the Emperor of Germany was poisoned—and that Mirabeau was thus tricked by his pupil Orleans, also Madame de Favras and her son.—This was copying the Illuminati very carefully.

After all these particulars, can any person have a doubt that the Order of Illuminati formally interfered in the French Revolution, and contributed greatly to its progress? There is no denying the insolence and oppression of the Crown and the Nobles, nor the misery and slavery of the people, nor that there were sufficient provocation and cause for a total change of measures and of principles. But the rapidity with which one opinion was declared in every corner, and that opinion as quickly changed, and the change announced every where, and the perfect conformity of the principles, and sameness of the language, even in arbitrary trifles, can hardly be explained in any other way. It may indeed be said, *"que les beaux genies se rencontrent*—that wits jump. The principles are the same, and the conduct of the French has been such as the Illuminati would have exhibited; but this is all—the Illuminati no longer existed." Enough has been said on this last point already.—The facts are as have been narrated. The Illuminati continued *as an Order,* and even held assemblies, though not so frequently nor so formally as before, and though their *Areopagus* was no longer at Munich. But let us hear what the French themselves thought of the matter.

In 1789, or the beginning of 1790, *a manifest was sent from the* GRAND NATIONAL LODGE *of Free Masons* (so it is entitled) *at Paris, signed by the Duke of Orleans as*

*Grand Master, addressed and sent to the Lodges in all the respectable cities of Europe, exhorting them to unite for the support of the French Revolution, to gain it friends, defenders, and dependents; and according to their opportunities, and the practicability of the thing, to kindle and propagate the spirit of revolution through all lands.* This is a most important article, and deserves a very serious attention. I got it first of all in a work called, *Hochste wichtige Erinnerungen zur rechten Zeit uber einige der allerernsthaftesten Angelegenheiten dieses Zeitalters, von L. A. Hoffmann,* Vienna, 1795.

The author of this work says, "That every thing he advances in these memorandums is consistent with his own personal knowledge, and that he is ready to give convincing proofs of them to any respectable person who will apply to him personally. He has already given such convincing documents to the Emperor, and to several Princes, that many of the machinations occasioned by this manifesto have been detected and stopped; and he would have no scruple at laying the whole before the public, did it not unavoidably involve several worthy persons who had suffered themselves to be misled, and heartily repented of their errors." He is naturally (being a Catholic) very severe on the Protestants (and indeed he has much reason) and by this has drawn on himself many bitter retorts. He has however defended himself against all that are of any consequence to his good name and veracity, in a manner that fully convinces any impartial reader, and turns to the confusion of the slanderers.

Hoffmann says, that "he saw some of those manifests; that they were not all of one tenor, some being addressed to friends, of whose support they were already assured." One very important article of their contents is *Earnest exhortations to establish in every quarter secret schools of political education, and schools for the public education of the children of the people, under the direction of well-principled masters; and offers of pecuniary assistance for this purpose, and for the encouragement of writers in favor of the Revolution, and for indemnifying the patriotic booksellers who suffer by their endeavours to suppress publications which have an opposite tendency.* We know very well that the immense revenue of the Duke of Orleans was scattered among all the rabble of the *Palais Royal*. Can we doubt of its being employed in this manner? Our doubts must vanish, when we see that not long after this it was publicly said in the National Assembly "that this method was the most effectual for accomplishing their purpose of setting Europe in a flame." "But much expence," says the speaker, "will attend it, and much has already been employed, which cannot be named, because it is given in secret." The Assembly had given the Illumination war-hoop—*"Peace with cottages, but war with palaces."*—A *pouvoir revolutionnaire* is mentioned, which supersedes all narrow thoughts, all ties of morality. Lequinio publishes the most detestable book that ever issued from a printing press, *Les Prejugés vaincus,* containing all the principles, and expressed in the very words of Illuminatism.

Hoffmann says, that the French *Propaganda* had many emissaries in Vienna, and many Friends whom he could point out. Mirabeau in particular had many connections in Vienna, and to the certain knowledge of Hoffmann, carried on a great correspondence in cyphers. The progress of Illumination had been very great in the Austrian States, and a statesman gave him accounts of their proceedings *(qui font redresser les cheveux)* which make one's hair stand on end. "I no longer wonder," says he, "that the *Neueste Arbutung des Spartacus und Philo* was forbidden. O ye almighty *Illuminati,* what can you not accomplish by your serpent-like insinuation and cunning!" Your leaders say, "This book is dangerous, because it will teach wicked men the most refined methods of rebellion, and it must never get into the hands of the common people. They have said so with the most impudent face to some Princes, who did not perceive the deeper-laid reason for suppressing the book. The leaders of the *Illuminati* are, not without reason, in anxiety, lest the inferior classes of their own Society should make just reprisals for having been so basely tricked, by keeping them back, and in profound ignorance of their real designs; and for working on them, by the very goodness of their hearts, to their final ruin; and lest the Free Masons, whom they have also abused, should think of revenging themselves, when the matchless villany of their deceivers has been so clearly exposed. It is in vain for them to talk of the danger of instructing the people in the methods of fomenting rebellion by this book. The aims are too apparent, and even in the neighbourhood of Regensburg, where the strength of the *Illuminati* lay, every person said aloud, that the Illuminatism discovered by this book was High Treason, and the most unheard-of attempt to annihilate every religion and every civil government." He goes on: "In 1790 I was as well acquainted with the spirit of the Illumination-system as at present, but only not so documented by their constitutional acts, as it is now by the *Neuste Arbeitung des Spartacus und Philo.* My masonic connections were formerly extensive, and my publication entitled *Eighteen Paragraphs concerning Free Masonry,* procured me more acquaintance with Free Masons of the greatest worth, and of *Illuminati* equally upright, persons of respectability and knowledge, who had discovered and repented the trick and inveigling conduct of the Order. All of us jointly swore opposition to the *Illuminati,* and my friends considered me as a proper instrument for this purpose. To whet my zeal, they put papers into my hands which made me shudder, and raised my dislike to the highest pitch. I received from them lists of the members, and among them saw names which I lamented exceedingly. Thus stood matters in 1790, when the French Revolution began to take a serious turn. The intelligent saw in the open system of the Jacobins the complete hidden system of the Illuminati. We knew that this system included the whole world in its aims, and France was only the place of its first explosion. The Propaganda works in every corner to this hour, and its emissaries run about in all the four quarters of the world, and are to be found in numbers in every city that is a seat of government."

"He farther relates how they in Vienna wanted to enlist him, and, as this failed, how they have abused him even in the foreign newspapers.

"I have personal knowledge (continues he) that in Germany a second Mirabeau, Mauvillon, had proposed in detail a plan of revolution, entirely and precisely suited to the present state of Germany. This he circulated among several Free Mason Lodges, among all the Illuminated Lodges which still remained in Germany, and through the hands of all the emissaries of the Propaganda, who had been already dispatched to the frontiers (*vorposten*) of every district of the empire, with means for stirring up the people." (N. B. in 1792 Mauvillon, finding abundant support and encouragement in the appearance of things round him, when the French arms had penetrated every where, and their invitations to revolt had met with so hearty a reception from the discontented in every state, came boldly forward, and, in the Brunswick Journal for March 1792, declared that "he heartily rejoiced in the French Revolution, wished it all success, and thought himself liable to no reproach when he declared his hopes that a similar revolution would speedily take place in Germany.")

In the Hamburgh Political Journal, August, September, and October 1790, there are many proofs of the machinations of emissaries from the *Mason Lodges* of Paris among the German Free Masons—See pages 836, 963, 1087, &c. It appears that a club has taken the name of *Propaganda,* and meets once a-week at least, in the form of a Mason Lodge. It consists of persons of all nations, and is under the direction of the Grand Master, the Duke of Orleans. De Leutre is one of the Wardens. They have divided Europe into colonies, to which they give revolutionary names, such as the *Cap,* the *Pike,* the *Lantern,* &c. They have ministers in these colonies. (One is pointed out in Saxony, by marks which I presume are well understood.) A secret press was found in Saxe Gotha, furnished with German types, which printed a seditious work called the *Journal of Humanity.* This journal was found in the mornings lying in the streets and highways. The house belonged to an *Illuminatus* of the name of Duport, a poor schoolmaster—he was associated with another in Strasburg, who was also an *Illuminatus.*— His name was Meyer, the writer of the Strasburg Newspaper. He had been some time a teacher in Salzmann's academy, who we see was also an *Illuminatus,* but displeased with their proceedings almost at the first. (Private Correspondence.)

"I have personal knowledge (continues Professor Hoffmann) that in 1791, during the temporary dearth at Vienna, several of these emissaries were busy in corrupting the minds of the poor, by telling them that in like manner the court had produced a famine in Paris in 1789. I detected some of them, and exposed them in my *Patriotic Remarks on the present Dearth,* and had the satisfaction of seeing my endeavours of considerable effect."

Surely these facts show that the Anarchists of France knew of the German Illuminati, and confided in their support. They also knew to what particular Lodges they could address themselves with safety and confidence.—But what need is there of more argument, when we know the zeal of the Illuminati, and the unhoped for opportunity that the Revolution had given them of acting with immediate effect in carrying on their great and darling work? Can we doubt that they would eagerly put their hand to the plough? And, to complete the proof, do we not know from the lists found in the secret correspondence of the Order, that they already had Lodges in France, and that in 1790 and 1791, many Illuminated Lodges in Germany, viz. at Mentz, Worms, Spire, Frankfort, actually interfered, and produced great effects. In Switzerland too they were no less active. They had Lodges at Geneva and at Bern. At Bern two Jacobins were sentenced to several years imprisonment, and among their papers were found their patents of Illumination. I also see the fate of Geneva ascribed to the operations of Illuminati residing there by several writers—particularly by Girtanner, and by the Gottingen editor of the Revolution Almanac.

I conclude this article with an extract or two from the proceedings of the National Assembly and Convention, which make it evident that their principles and their practice are precisely those of the Illuminati, on a great scale.

When the assumption of the Duchy of Savoy as an 84th Department was debated, Danton said to the Convention,

"In the moment that we send freedom to a nation on our frontier, we must say to them, You must have no more Kings—for if we are surrounded by tyrants, their coalition puts our own freedom in danger.—When the French nation sent us hither, it created a great committee for the general insurrection of the people."

On the 19th of November 1792, it was decreed, "That the Convention, in the name of the French nation, tenders help and fraternity to all people who would recover their liberty."

On the 21st of November, the President of the Convention said to the pretended deputies of the Duchy of Savoy, "Representatives of an independent people, important to mankind was the day when the National Convention of France pronounced its sentence, *Royal dignity is abolished.* —From that day many nations will in future reckon the era of their political existence.—From the beginning of civil establishments Kings have been in opposition to their nations—but now they rise up to annihilate Kings.—Reason, when she darts her rays into every corner, lays open eternal truths—She alone enables us to pass sentence on despots, hitherto the scare-crow of other nations."

But the most distinct exhibition of principle is to be seen in a report from the diplomatic committee, who were commissioned to deliberate on the conduct which France was to hold with other nations. On this report was founded the decree of the 15th of December 1793. The Reporter addresses the Convention as follows.

"The Committees of Finance and War ask in the beginning, What is the object of the war which we have taken in hand? Without all doubt the object is THE ANNIHILATION OF ALL PRIVILEGES, WAR WITH THE PALACES, PEACE WITH THE COTTAGES. These are the principles on which *your declaration of war* is founded. All tyranny, all privilege must be treated as an enemy in the countries where we set our foot. This is the genuine result of our principles.— But it is not with Kings alone that we are to wage war— were these our sole enemies, we should only have to bring down ten or twelve heads. We have to fight with all their accomplices, with the privileged orders, who devour and have oppressed the people during many centuries.

We must therefore declare ourselves for a revolutionary power in all the countries into which we enter (loud applauses from the Assembly)—Nor need we put on the cloak of humanity—we disdain such little arts.—We must clothe ourselves with all the brilliancy of reason, and all the force of the nation. We need not mask our principles—the despots know them already. The first thing we must do is to ring the alarum bell, for insurrection and uproar.—We must, in a solemn manner, let the people see the banishment of their tyrants and privileged casts—otherwise, the people, accustomed to their fetters, will not be able to break their bonds.—It will effect nothing, merely to excite a rising of the people—this would only be giving them words instead of standing by them.

"And since, in this manner, we ourselves are the Revolutionary Administration, all that is against the rights of the people must be overthrown, at our entry—We must display our principles by actually destroying all tyranny; and our generals, after having chased away the tyrants and their satellites, must proclaim to the people that they have brought them happiness; and then, on the spot, they must suppress tithes, feudal rights, and every species of servitude."

"But we shall have done nothing if we stop here. Aristocracy still domineers—we must therefore suppress all authorities existing in the hands of the upper classes.—When the Revolutionary Authority appears, there must nothing of the old establishment remain.—A popular system must be introduced—every office must be occupied by new functionaries—and the Sansculottes must every where have a share in the Administration.

"Still nothing is done, till we declare aloud the *precision* of our principles to such as want only a half freedom.—We must say to them—if you think of compromising with the privileged casts, we cannot suffer such dealing with tyrants—They are our enemies, and we must treat them as enemies, because they are neither for Liberty nor Equality.—Show yourselves disposed to receive a free constitution—and the Convention will not only stand by you, but will give you permanent support; we will defend you against the vengeance of your tyrants, against their attacks, and against their return.—Therefore abolish from among you the Nobles—and every ecclesiastical and military incorporation. They are incompatible with Equality.—Henceforward you are citizens, all equal in rights—equally called upon to rule, to defend, and to serve your country.—The agents of the French Republic will instruct and assist you in forming a free constitution, and assure you of happiness and fraternity."

This Report was loudly applauded, and a decree formed in precise conformity to its principles.—Both were ordered to be translated into all languages, and copies to be furnished to their generals, with orders to have them carefully dispersed in the countries which they invaded.

And, in completion of these decrees, their armies found it easy to collect as many discontented or worthless persons in any country as sufficed for setting up a tree of liberty. This they held as a sufficient call for their interference.— Sometimes they performed this ceremony themselves—a representation was easily made up in the same way—and then, under the name of a free constitution, the nation was forced to acquiesce in a form dictated at the point of the bayonet, in which they had not the smallest liberty to choose—and they were plundered of all they had, by way of compensating to France for the trouble she had taken.— And this they call Liberty.—It needs no comment.—

Thus I have attempted to prove that the present awful situation of Europe, and the general fermentation of the public mind in all nations, have not been altogether the natural operations of discontent, oppression, and moral corruption, although these have been great, and have operated with fatal energy; but that this political fever has been carefully and systematically heightened by bodies of men, who professed to be the physicians of the State, and, while their open practice employed cooling medicines, and a treatment which all approved, administered in secret the most inflammatory poisons, which they made up so as to flatter the diseased fancy of the patient. Although this was not a plan begun, carried on, and completed by the same persons, it was undoubtedly an uniform and consistent scheme, proceeding on the same unvaried principle, and France undoubtedly now smarts under all the woes of German Illumination.

I beg leave to suggest a few thoughts, which may enable us to draw some advantage from this shocking mass of information.

---

### General Reflections.

**I.** I may observe, in the *first* place, and I beg it may be particularly attended to, that in all those villainous machinations against the peace of the world, the attack has been first made on the principles of Morality and Religion. The conspirators saw that till these are extirpated, they have no chance of success; and their manner of proceeding shews that they consider Religion and Morality as inseparably connected together. We learn much from this—*Fas est et ab hoste doceri.*—They endeavour to destroy our religious sentiments, by first corrupting our morals. They try to inflame our passions, that when the demands from this quarter become urgent, the restraints of Religion may immediately come in sight, and stand in the way. They are careful, on this occasion, to give such a view of those restraints, that the real origin of them does not appear.— We are made to believe that they have been altogether the contrivance of Priests and despots, in order to get the command of us. They take care to support these assertions by facts, which, to our great shame, and greater misfortune, are but too numerous.—Having now the passions on their side, they find no difficulty in persuading the voluptuary, or the discontented, that tyranny actually exerted, or resolved on in future, is the sole origin of religious restraint. He seeks no further argument, and gives himself no trouble to find any. Had he examined the matter with any care, he would find himself just brought back to those very feelings of moral excellence and moral depravity that he wishes to get rid of altogether; and these would tell him that pure Religion does not lay a single restraint on us that a noble nature would not have laid on itself—nor enjoins a single duty which an ingenuous and warm heart would not be ashamed to find itself deficient in. He would then see that all the sanctions of Religion are fitted to his high rank in the scale of existence. And the more he contemplates his future prospects, the more they brighten upon his view, the more attainable they appear, and the more he is able to know what they may probably be. Having attained this happy state of mind (an attainment in the power of any kind heart that is in earnest in the enquiry) he will think that no punishment is too great for the unthankful and groveling soul which can forego such hopes, and reject these noble proffers, for the comparatively frivolous and transitory gratifications of life. He is not frightened into worthy and virtuous conduct by fears of such merited punishment; but, if not enticed into it by his high expectations, he is, at least, retained in the paths of virtue by a kind of manly shame.

But all this is overlooked, or is kept out of sight, in the instructions of Illuminatism. In these the eye must be kept always directed to the Despot. This is the bugbear, and every thing is made to connect with present or future tyranny and oppression—Therefore Religion is held out as a combination of terrors—the invention of the state-tools, the priests. But it is not easy to stifle the suggestions of Nature—therefore no pains are spared to keep them down, by encreasing the uncertainty and doubts which arise in the course of all speculations on such subjects. Such difficulties occur in all scientific discussions.—Here they must be numerous and embarrassing—for in this enquiry we come near the first principles of things, and the first principles of human knowledge. The geometer does not wonder at mistakes even in *his* science, the most simple of all others. Nor does the mechanic or the chemist reject all his science, because he cannot attain clear conceptions of some of the natural relations which operate in the phenomena under his consideration. Nor do any of these students of nature brand with the name of fool, or knave, or bigot, another person who has drawn a different conclusion from the phenomenon.——In one point they all agree—they find themselves possessed of faculties which enable them to speculate, and to discover; and they find, that the operation of those faculties is quite unlike the things which they contemplate by their means—*and they feel a satisfaction in the possession of them,* and in this distinction.——But this seems a misfortune to our Illuminators. I have long been struck with this. If by deep meditation I have solved a problem which has baffled the endeavours of others, I should hardly thank the person who convinced me that my success was entirely owing to the particular state of my health, by which my brain was kept free from many irritations to which other persons are exposed. Yet this is the conduct of the Illuminated—They are abundantly self-conceited; and yet they continually endeavour to destroy all grounds of self-estimation.—They rejoice in every discovery that is reported to them of some resemblance, unnoticed before, between mankind and the inferior creation, and would be happy to find that the resemblance is complete. It is very true, Mr. Pope's "Poor Indian, with untutor'd mind," had no objection to his dog's going to heaven with him;

> "And thinks, admitted to that equal sky,
> "His faithful dog shall bear his company."

This is not an abject, but it is a modest sentiment. But our high-minded philosophers, who, with Beatrice in the play, "cannot brook obedience to a wayward piece of marl," if it be in the shape of a Prince, have far other notions of the matter. Indeed they are not yet agreed about it. Mr. de la Metherie hopes, that before the enlightened Republic of France has got into its teens, he shall be able to tell his fellow-citizens, in his *Journal de Physique,* that particular form of crystallization which men have been accustomed to call God.—Dr. Priestly again deduces all intelligence from elastic undulations, and will probably think, that his own great discoveries have been the quiverings of some fiery marsh *miasma.* While Pope's poor Indian hopes to take his dog to heaven with him, these Illuminators hope to die like dogs, and that both soul and body shall be as if they never had been.

Is not this a melancholy result of all our Illumination? It is of a piece with the termination of the ideal Philosophy, viz. professed and total ignorance. Should not this make us start back and hesitate, before we pout like wayward children at the rubs of civil subordination, and before we make a sacrifice to our ill humour of all that we value ourselves for? Does it not carry ridicule and absurdity in its forehead?—Such assertion of personal worth and dignity (always excepting Princes and priests) and such abject acknowledgements of worthlessness.—Does not this, of itself, show that there is some radical fault in the whole? It has all arisen from what they have called *Illumination,* and this turns out to be worse than darkness—But we also know that it has all arisen from self-conceited discontent, and that it has been brought to its present state by the rage of speculation. We may venture to put the question to any man's conscience—whether discontent did not precede his doubts about his own nature, and whether he has not *encouraged* the train of argument that tended to degrade him. "Thy wish was father, Harry, to that thought."— Should not this make us distrust, at least, the operations of this faculty of our mind, and try to moderate and check this darling propensity? It seems a misfortune of the age —for we see that it is a natural source of disturbance and revolution. But here it will be immediately said, "What, must we give over thinking—be no longer rational creatures, and believe every lie that is told us?" By no means. Let us be *really* rational creatures—and, taught by experience, let us, in all our speculations on subjects which engage the passions, guard ourselves with the most anxious care against the risk of having our judgments warped by our desires. There is no propensity of our nature of which the proper and modest indulgence is not beneficial to man, and which is not hurtful, when this indulgence is carried too far. And if we candidly peruse the page of history, we shall be convinced that the abuse is great in proportion as the subject is important. What has been so ruinously perverted as the religious principle? What horrid superstition has it not produced? The Reader will not, I hope, take it amiss that I presume to direct his attention to some maxims which ought to conduct a prudent man in his indulgence of a speculative disposition, and apply them to the case in hand.

Whoever will for a while cast off his attention from the common affairs of life, the *Curæ hominum, et rerum pondus inane,* and will but reflect a little on that wonderful principle within him, which carries him over the whole universe, and shows him its various relations—Whoever also remarks what a *less than nothing* he is, when compared with this unmeasurable scene—Whoever does this, cannot but feel an inexpressible pleasure in the contemplation.— He must rise in his own estimation, and be disposed to cherish with fondness this principle which so eminently raises him above all around him. Of all the sources of human vanity this is surely the most manly, the most excusable, and the most likely to be extravagantly indulged.—We may be certain that it will be so indulged, and that men will frequently speculate for the sake of speculation alone, and that they will have too much confidence in the results of this favorite occupation.—As there have been ages of indolent and abject credulity and superstition, it is next to certain that there are also times of wild and extravagant speculation—and when we see it becoming a sort of general passion, we may be certain that this is a case in point.

This can hardly be denied to be the character of the present day. It is not denied. On the contrary it is gloried in, as the prerogative of the 18th century. All the speculations of antiquity are considered as glimmerings (with the exceptions of a few brighter flashes) when compared with our present meridian splendor. We should therefore listen with caution to the inferences from this boasted Illumination. Also, when we reflect on what passes in our own minds, and on what we observe in the world, of the mighty influence of our desires and passions on our judgments, we should carefully notice whether any such warping of the belief is probable in the present case. That it is so is almost certain—for the general and immediate effect of this Illumination is to lessen or remove many restraints which the sanctions of religion lay on the indulgence of very strong passions, and to diminish our regard for a certain purity or correctness of manners, which religion recommends, as the only conduct suited to our noble natures, and as absolutely necessary for attaining that perfection and happiness of which we are capable.—For surely if we take away religion, it will be wisdom "to eat and to drink, since tomorrow we die." If moreover, we see this Illumination extolled above all science, as friendly to virtue as improving the heart, and as producing a just morality, which will lead to happiness, both for ourselves and others, but perceive at the same time that these assertions are made at the expence of principles, which our natural feelings force us to venerate as supreme and paramount to all others, we may then be certain that our informer is trying to mislead and deceive us.—For all virtue and goodness, both of heart and conduct, is in perfect harmony, and there is no jarring or inconsistency. But we must pass this sentence on the doctrines of this Illumination. For it is a melancholy truth that they have been preached and recommended, for the most part, by clergymen, parish-ministers, who, in the presence of invoked Deity, and in the face of the world, have set their solemn seal to a system of doctrines directly opposite to those recommended in their writings; which doctrines they solemnly profess to believe, and solemnly swear to inculcate.—Surely the informations and instructions of such men should be rejected.—Where shall we find their real opinions? In their solemn oaths?—or in these infidel dissertations?—In either case, they are deceivers, whether mislead by vanity, or by the mean desire of church-emoluments; or they are prostitutes, courting the society of the wealthy and sensual. Honesty, like justice, admits of no degrees. A man is honest, or he is a knave—and who would trust a knave? But such men are unsuitable instructors for another reason—they are unwise; for, whatever they may think, they are not respected as men of worth, but are inwardly despised as parasites, by the rich, who admit them into their company, and treat them with civility, for their own reasons. We take instructions not merely from the knowing—the learned—but from the wise—not therefore from men who give such evidences of weakness.

Such would be the conduct of a prudent man, who listens to the instructions of another with the serious intention of profiting by them. In the present case, he sees plain proofs of degraded self estimation, of dishonesty, and of mean motives. But the prudent man will go further—he will remark that dissolute manners, and actions which are inevitably subversive of the peace and order, nay, of the very existence of society, are the natural and necessary consequences of irreligion. Should any doubt of this remain in his mind; should he sometimes think of an Epectetus, or one or two individuals of antiquity, who were eminently virtuous, without the influence of religious sanctions, he should recollect, that the Stoics were animated by the thought, that while the wise man was playing the game of life, the gods were looking on, and pleased with his skill. Let him read the beautiful account given by Dr. Smith, of the rise of the Stoic philosophy, and he will see that it was an artificial, but noble attempt of a few exalted minds, enthusiasts in virtue, aiming to steel their souls against the dreadful but unavoidable misfortunes to which they were continually exposed by the daily recurring revolutions in the turbulent democracies of ancient Greece. There a Philosopher was this day a Magistrate, and the next day a captive and a slave. He would see, that this fair picture of mental happiness and independence was fitted for the contemplation of only a few choice spirits, but had no influence on the bulk of mankind. He must admire the noble characters who were animated by this manly enthusiasm, and who have really exhibited some wonderful pictures of virtuous heroism; but he will regret, that the influence of these manly, these natural principles, was not more extensive. He will say to himself, "How will a whole nation act, when religious sanctions are removed, and men are actuated by reason alone?"—He is not without instruction on this important subject. France has given an awful lesson to surrounding nations, by shewing them what is the natural effect of shaking off the religious principle, and the veneration for that pure morality which characterises Christianity. By a decree of the Convention (June 6, 1794) it is declared, that there is nothing criminal in the promiscuous commerce of the sexes, and therefore nothing that derogates from the female character, when woman forgets that she is the depositary of all domestic satisfaction—that her honor is the sacred bond of social life—that on her modesty and delicacy depend all the respect and confidence that will make a man attach himself to her society, free her from labour, share with her the fruits of all his own exertions, and work with willingness and delight, that she may appear on all occasions his equal, and the ornament of all his acquisitions. In the very argument which this selected body of senators has given for the propriety of this decree, it has degraded woman below all estimation. "It is to prevent her from murdering the fruit of unlawful love, by removing her shame, and by relieving her from the fear of want." The senators say, "the Republic wants citizens, and therefore must not only remove this temptation of shame, but must take care of the mother while she nurses the child. It is the property of the nation, and must not be lost." The woman all the while is considered only as the she animal, the breeder of Sansculottes. This is the *just* morality of

Illumination. It is really amusing (for things revolting to nature now amuse) to observe with what fidelity the principles of the *Illuminati* have expressed the sentiments which take possession of a people who have shaken off the sanctions of religion and morality. The following is part of the address to *Psycharion* and the company mentioned in page 148: "Once more, Psycharion, I indulge you with a look behind you to the flowry days of childhood. Now look forward, *young woman!* the holy circle of the marriageable *(mannbaren)* welcome you.———Young men, honor the young woman, the future breeder *(gebaererin)!"* Then, to all.—"Rejoice in the dawn of Illumination and Freedom. Nature at last enjoys her sacred never-fading rights. Long was her voice kept down by civil subordination; but the days of your majority now draw nigh, and you will no longer, under the authority of guardians, account it a reproach to consider with enlightened eyes the secret workshops of Nature, and to enjoy your work and duty." Minos thought this very fine, but it raised a terrible disturbance, and broke up the assembly. Such are the effects of this boasted enlightening of the human mind with respect to religion and morality. Let us next consider what is the result of the mighty information which we have got in respect of our social or political connections.

II. We have learned the sum-total of this political Illumination, and see that, if true, it is melancholy, destructive of our present comforts, numerous as they are, and affords no prospect of redress from which we can profit, but, on the contrary, plunges mankind into contest, mutual injury, and universal misery, and all this for the *chance* only of prevailing in the contest, and giving our posterity a *chance* of going on in peace, if no change shall be produced, as in former times, by the efforts of ambitious men. But the Illumination appears to be partial, nay false. What is it? It holds out to the Prince nothing but the resignation of all his possessions, rights, and claims, sanctioned by the quiet possession of ages, and by all the feelings of the human heart which give any notion of right to his lowest subject. All these possessions and claims are discovered to have arisen from usurpations, *and are therefore tyranny*. It has been discovered, that all subordinate subjections were enforced, *therefore their continuance is slavery*. But both of these historical assertions are in a great degree false, and the inferences from them are unreasonable. The world has gone on as we see it go on at present. Most principalities or sovereignties have arisen as we see personal authorities and influence arise every day among ourselves. Business for the whole must be done. Most men are sufficiently occupied by their private affairs, and they are indolent even in these—they are contented when another does the thing for them. There is not a little village, nor a society of men, where this is not seen every day. Some men have an enjoyment in this kind of vicarious employment. All men like influence and power, and thus are compensated for their trouble. Thus many petty managers of public affairs arise in every country. The mutual animosities of individuals, and still more, the animosities of tribes, clans, and different associations, give rise to another kind of superiors—to leaders, who direct the struggles of the rest, whether for offence or defence. The descendants of Israel said, "they wanted a man to go out before the people, like other nations." As the small business of a few individuals requires a manager or a leader, so do some more general affairs of these petty superiors, and many of these also are indolent enough to wish this trouble taken off their hands; and thus another rank of superiors arises, and a third, and so on, till a great State may be formed; and in this gradation each class is a competent judge of the conduct of that class only which is immediately above it. All this may arise, and has often arisen, from voluntary concession alone. This concession may proceed from various causes—from confidence in superior talents—from confidence in great worth—most generally from the respect or deference which all men feel for great possessions. This is frequently founded in self-interest and expectations of advantage; but it is natural to man, and perhaps springs from our instinctive sympathy with the satisfactions of others—we are unwilling to disturb them, and even wish to promote them.

But this subordination may arise, and has often arisen, from other causes—from the love of power and influence, which makes some men *eager* to lead others, or even to manage their concerns. We see this every day, and it may be perfectly innocent. It often arises from the desire of gain of one kind or another. Even this may frequently be indulged with perfect innocence, and even with general advantage. Frequently, however, this subordination is produced by the love of power or of gain pushed to an immoderate degree of ambition, and rendered unjust. Now there arise oppression, tyranny, sufferings, and slavery. Now appears an opposition between the rights or claims of the ruler and of the people. Now the rulers come to consider themselves as a different class, and their transactions are now only with each other.—Prince becomes the rival or the enemy of Prince; and in their contests one prevails, and the dominion is enlarged. This rivalship may have begun in any rank of superiors, even between the first managers of the affairs of the smallest communities; and it must be remarked that they only are the immediate gainers or losers in the contest, while those below them live at ease, enjoying many advantages of the delegation of their own concerns.

No human society has ever proceeded purely in either of these two ways, but there has always been a mixture of both.—But this process is indispensably necessary for the formation of a great nation and for all the consequences that result only from such a coalition.—Therefore it is necessary for giving rise to all those comforts, and luxuries, and elegances, which are to be found only in great and cultivated states. It is necessary for producing such enjoyments as we see around us in Europe, which we prize so highly, and for which we are making all this stir and disturbance. I believe that no man who expects to be believed will flatly say that human nature and human enjoyments are not meliorated by this cultivation.—It seems to be the intention of nature, and, notwithstanding the follies and vices of many, we can have little hesitation in saying that there are in the most cultivated nations of Europe, and even in the highest ranks of these nations, men of great virtue and worth and of high accomplishment—Nor can we deny that such men are the finest specimens of human nature. Rousseau wrote a whimsical pamphlet in which he had the vanity to think that he had proved that all these fruits of cultivation were losses to humanity and to virtue—Yet Rousseau could not be contented with the society of the rude and unpolished, although he pretended that he was almost the sole worshipper of pure virtue.—He supported himself, not by assisting the simple peasant, but by writing music for the pampered rich.

This is the circumstance entirely overlooked, or artfully kept out of sight, in the boasted Illumination of these days. No attention is paid to the important changes which have happened in national greatness, in national connection, in national improvement—yet we never think of parting with any of the advantages, real or imaginary, which these changes have produced—nor do we reflect in order to keep a great nation together—to make it act with equality, or with preponderancy, among other nations, the individual exertions must be concentrated, must be directed—and that this requires a ruler vested with supreme power, and *interested by some great and endearing motive,* such as hereditary possession of this power and influence, to maintain and defend this coalition of men.—All this is overlooked, and we attend only to the subordination which is indispensably necessary. Its grievances are immediately felt, and they are heightened ten fold by a delicacy or sensibility which springs from the great improvements in the accommodations and enjoyments of life, which the gradual usurpation and subsequent subordination have produced and continue to support. But we are determined to have the elegance and grandeur of a palace without the prince.—We will not give up any of our luxuries and refinements, yet will not support those high ranks and those nice minds which produced them, and which must continue to keep them from degenerating into barbarous simplicity and coarse sensuality. —We would keep the philosophers, the poets, the artists, but not the Mœcenases.—It is very true that in such a state there would be no *Conjuration des Philosophes;* for in such a state this vermin of *philosophes* and scribblers would not have existed.—In short, we would have what is impossible.

I have no hesitation in saying, that the British Constitution is the form of government *for a great and refined nation,* in which the ruling sentiments and propensities of human nature seem most happily blended and balanced. There is no occasion to vaunt it as the ancient rights of Britons, the wisdom of ages, &c. It has attained its present pitch of perfection by degrees, and this not by the efforts of wisdom, but by the struggles of vice and folly, working on a rich fund of good nature, and of manly spirit, that are conspicuous in the British character. I do not hesitate to say that this is the *only* form of government which will admit and give full exercise to all the respectable propensities of our nature, with the least chance of disturbance, and the greatest probability of man's arriving at the highest pitch of improvement in every thing that raises him above the beasts of the field. Yet there is no part of it that may not, that is not, abused, by pushing it to an improper length, and the same watchful care is necessary for preserving our inestimable blessings that was employed in acquiring them. —This is to be done, not flying at once to an abstract theory of the rights of man.—There is an evident folly in this procedure. What is this theory? It is the best general sketch that we can draw of social life, deduced from our knowledge of human nature.—And what is this knowledge? It is a well digested abstract, or rather a declaration *of what we have observed* of human actions. What is the use therefore of this intermediate picture, this theory of the rights of man?—It has a chance of being unlike the original—it must certainly have imperfections.—Therefore it can be of no use to us.—We should go at once to the original—we should consider how men *have acted*—what *have* been their mutual expectations—their fond propensities—what of these are inconsistent with each other—what are the degrees of indulgence which *have been* admitted in them all without disturbance. I will venture to say that whoever does this, will find himself imperceptibly set down in the British parliament of King, Lords, and Commons, all looking at each other with somewhat of a cautious or jealous eye, while the rest of the nation are sitting, "each under his own vine, and under his own fig-tree, and there is none to make him afraid."

A most valuable result of such contemplation will be a thorough conviction that the grievance which is most clamorously insisted on is the inevitable consequence of the liberty and security which we enjoy. I mean ministerial corruption, with all the dismal tale of placemen, and pensioners, and rotten boroughs, &c. &c. These are never seen in a despotic government—there they are not wanted— nor can they be very apparent in an uncultivated and poor state—but in a luxurious nation, where pleasures abound, where the returns of industry are secure; here an individual looks on every thing as his own acquisition—he does not *feel* his relation to the state—has no patriotism—thinks that he would be much happier if the state would let him alone.—He is fretted by the restraints which the public weal lays on him—therefore government and governors appear as checks and hindrances to his exertions—hence a general inclination to resist administration.—Yet public business must be done, that we may lie down and rise again in safety and peace.—Administration must be supported—there are always persons who wish to possess the power that is exercised by the present ministers, and would turn them out. —How is all this to be remedied?—I see no way but by applying to the selfish views of individuals—by rewarding the friends of administration—this may be done with perfect virtue—and from this the selfish will conceive hopes, and will support a virtuous ministry—but they are as ready to help a wicked one.—This becomes the greatest misfortune of a free nation.—Ministers are tempted to bribe— and, if a systematic opposition be considered as a necessary part of a practical constitution, it is almost indispensable —and it is no where so prevalent as in a pure democracy.— Laws may be contrived to make it very troublesome—but can never extirpate it, nor greatly diminish it—this can be done only by despotism, or by national virtue.—It is a shameful complaint—we should not reprobate a few ministers, but the thousands who take the bribes.—Nothing tends so much to diminish it in a corrupted nation as great limitations to the eligibility of representatives—and this is the beauty of our constitution.

*We have not discovered,* therefore, by this boasted Illumination, that Princes and superiors are useless, and must vanish from the earth; nor that the people have now attained full age, and are fit to govern themselves. We want only to revel for a little on the last fruits of national cultivation, which we would quickly consume, and never allow to be raised again.—No matter how this progress began, whether from concession or usurpation—We possess it, and if wise, we will preserve it, by preserving its indispensable supports. They have indeed been frequently employed very improperly, but their most pernicious abuse has been this breed of scribbling vermin, which have made the body-politic smart in every limb.

Hear what opinion was entertained of the sages of France by their Prince, the Father of Louis XVI. the unfortunate martyr of Monarchy. "By the principles of our new Philosophers, the Throne no longer wears the splendour of divinity. They maintain that it arose from violence, and that by the same justice that force erected it, force may again shake it, and overturn it. The people can never give up their power. They only let it out for their own advantage, and always retain the right to rescind the contract, and resume it whenever their personal advantage, their only rule of conduct, requires it. Our philosophers teach in public what our passions suggest only in secret. They say to the Prince that all is permitted only when all is in his power, and that his duty is fulfilled when he has pleased his fancy. Then, surely, if the laws of self-interest, that is, the self-will of human passions, shall be so generally admitted, that we thereupon forget the eternal laws of God and of Nature, all conceptions of right and wrong, of virtue and vice, of good and evil, must be extirpated from the human heart. The throne must totter, the subjects must become unmanageable and mutinous, and their ruler hard-hearted and inhuman. The people will be incessantly either oppressed, or in an uproar."—"What service will it be if I order such a book to be burnt—the author can write another by to-morrow." This opinion of a Prince is unpolished indeed, and homely, but it is just.

Weishaupt grants that "there will be a terrible convulsion, and a storm—but this will be succeeded by a calm—the unequal will now be equal—and when the cause of dissension is thus removed, the world will be in peace." True, when the causes of dissension are removed. Thus, the destruction of our crop by vermin is at an end when a flood has swept every thing away—but as new plants will spring up in the waste, and, if not instantly devoured, will again cover the ground with verdure, so the industry of man, and his desire of comfort and consideration, will again accumulate in the hands of the diligent a greater proportion of the good things of life. In this infant state of the emerging remains of former cultivation, comforts, which the present inhabitants of Europe would look on with contempt, will be great, improper, and hazardous acquisitions. The principles which authorise the proposed dreadful equalisation will as justly entitle the idle or unsuccessful of future days to strip the possessor of his advantages, and things must ever remain on their savage level.

III. I think that the impression which the insincerity of conduct of those instructors will leave on the mind, must be highly useful. They are evidently teaching what they do not believe themselves—and here I do not confine my remark to their preparatory doctrines, which they afterwards explode. I make it chiefly with respect to their grand ostensible principle, which pervades the whole, a principle which they are obliged to adopt against their will. They know that the principles of virtue are rooted in the heart and that they can only be smothered—but did they pretend to eradicate them and proclaim *hominem homini lupum,* all would spurn at their instruction. We are wheedled, by tickling our fancy with the notion that sacred virtue is not only secure, but that it is only in such hearts that it exerts its native energy. Sensible that the levelling maxims now spoken of, are revolting to the mind, the Illuminators are under the necessity of keeping us from looking at the shocking picture, by displaying a beautiful scene of Utopian happiness—and they rock us asleep by the eternal lullaby of morality and universal philanthropy. Therefore the foregoing narration of the personal conduct of these instructors and reformers of the world, is highly useful. All this is to be brought about by the native loveliness of pure virtue, purged of the corruptions which superstitious fears have introduced, and also purged of the selfish thoughts which are avowed by the advocates of what their opponents call true religion. This is said to hold forth eternal rewards to the good, and to threaten the wicked with dreadful punishment. Experience has shown how inefficient such motives are. Can they be otherwise, say our Illuminators? Are they not addressed to a principle that is ungenerous and selfish? But our doctrines, say they, touch the hearts of the worthy. Virtue is beloved for her own sake, and all will yield to her gentle sway. But look, Reader, look at Spartacus the murderer—at Cato the keeper of poisons and the thief—Look at Tiberius, at Alcibiades, and the rest of the Bavarian Pandemonium.—Look at Poor Bahrdt.—Go to France—

look at Lequinio—at Condorcet.*—Look at the Monster Orleans.—All were liars. Their divinity had no influence on their profligate minds. They only wanted to wheedle you, by touching the strings of humanity and goodness which are yet braced up in your heart, and which will still yield sweet harmony if you will accompany their notes with those of religion, and neither clog them with the groveling pleasures of sense, nor damp the whole with the thought of eternal silence.

A most worthy and accomplished gentleman, who took refuge in this country, leaving behind him his property, and friends to whom he was most tenderly attached, often said to me that nothing so much affected him as the revolution in the hearts of men.—Characters which were unspotted, hearts thoroughly known to himself, having been tried by many things which search the inmost folds of selfishness or malevolence—in short, persons whose judgments were excellent, and on whose worth he could have rested his honor and his life, so fascinated by the contagion, that they came at last to behold, and even to commit the most atrocious crimes with delight.—He used sometimes to utter a sigh which pierced my heart, and would say, that it was caused by some of those things that had come across his thoughts. He breathed his last among us, declaring that it was impossible to recover peace of mind, without a total oblivion of the wickedness and miseries he had beheld.— What a valuable advice, "Let him that thinketh he standeth, take heed lest he fall."—When the prophet told Hazael that he would betray his Prince, he exclaimed, "Is thy servant a dog, that he should do such a thing?" Yet next day he murdered him.

Never, since the beginning of the world, has true religion received so complete an acknowledgment of her excellence, as has been extorted from the fanatics who have attempted to destroy her. Religion stood in their way, and the wretch

---

*De la Metherie says (*Journ. de Phys. Nov.* 1792) that Condorcet was brought up in the house of the old Duke of Rochefoucault, who treated him as his son—got Turgot to create a lucrative office for him, and raised him to all his eminence—yet he pursued him with malicious reports—and actually employed ruffians to assassinate him. Yet is Condorcet's writing a model of humanity and tenderness.

Marat, as well as the steady villain Weishaupt, saw that they could not proceed till they had eradicated all sentiments of the moral government of the universe. Human nature, improved as it has been by Religion, shrunk from the tasks that were imposed, and it must therefore be brutalized—The grand confederation was solemnly sworn to by millions in every corner of France—but, as Mirabeau said of the declaration of the Rights of Man, it must be made only the "Almanac of the bygone year"—Therefore Lequinio must write a book, declaring oaths to be nonsense, unworthy of sansculottes, and all religion to be a farce.— Not long after, they found that they had some use for a God—but he was gone—and they could not find another. —Their constitution was gone—and they have not yet found another.—What is now left them on which they can depend for awing a man into a respect for truth in his judicial declarations?—what but the honor of a Citizen of France, who laughs at all engagements, which he has broken again and again.—Religion has taken off with her every sense of human duty.—What can we expect but villany from an Archbishop of Paris and his chapter, who made a public profession that they had been playing the villains for many years, teaching what they thought to be a bundle of lies? What but the very thing which they have done, cutting each others throats. Have not the enlightened citizens of France applauded the execution of their fathers? Have not the furies of Paris denounced their own children?— But turn your eyes from the horrifying spectacle, and think on your own noble descent and alliance. You are not the accidental productions of a fatal chaos, but the work of a Great Artist, creatures that are cared for, born to noble prospects, and conducted to them by the plainest and most simple precepts, "to do justly, to love mercy, and to walk humbly before God," not bewildered by the false and fluttering glare of French Philosophy, but conducted by this clear, single light, perceivable by all, "Do to others what you should reasonably expect them to do to you."

> Think not the Muse whose sober voice you hear,
>     Contracts with bigot frown her sullen brow.
> Casts round Religion's orb the mists of Fear,
>     Or shades with horror what with smiles should glow.

No—she would warm you with seraphic fire,
    Heirs as ye are of Heaven's eternal day,
Would bid you boldly to that Heaven aspire,
    Not sink and slumber in your cells of clay.

Is this the bigot's rant? Away ye vain,
    Your doubts, your fears, in gloomy dulness sleep;
Go—soothe your souls in sickness, death, or pain,
    With the sad solace of eternal sleep.

Yet know, vain sceptics, know, th' Almighty Mind,
    Who breath'd on man a portion of his fire.
Bade his free soul, by earth nor time confin'd,
    To Heaven, to immortality aspire.

Nor shall this pile of hope his bounty rear'd,
    By vain philosophy be e'er destroy'd;
Eternity, by all or hop'd or fear'd,
    Shall be by all or suffer'd or enjoy'd.

                                        MASON.

The unfortunate Prince who has taken refuge in this kingdom, and whose situation among us is an illustrious mark of the generosity of the nation, and of the sovereignty of its laws, said to one of the Gentlemen about him, that "if this country was to escape the general wreck of nations, it would owe its preservation to Religion."—When this was doubted, and it was observed, that there had not been wanting many Religionists in France: "True," said the Prince, "but they were not in earnest.—I see here a serious interest in the thing. The people know what they are doing when they go to church—they understand something of it, and take an interest in it." May his observation be just, and his expectations be fulfilled!

IV. I would again call upon my countrywomen with the most earnest concern, and beseech them to consider this subject as of more particular importance to themselves than even to the men.—While woman is considered as a respectable moral agent, training along with ourselves for endless improvement; then, and only then, will she be considered by lordly man as his equal;—then, and only then, will she be allowed to have any rights, and those rights be respected. Strip women of this prerogative, and they become the drudges of man's indolence, or the pampered playthings of his idle hours, subject to his caprices, and slaves to his mean passions. Soon will their present empire of gallantry

be over. It is a refinement of manners which sprang from
Christianity; and when Christianity is forgotten, this artificial diadem will be taken from their heads, and, unless
they adopt the ferocious sentiments of their Gallic neighbours, and join in the general uproar, they will sink into the
insignificance of the women in the turbulent republics of
Greece, where they are never seen in the busy haunts of
men, if we except four or five, who, during the course of
as many centuries, emerged from the general obscurity, and
appear in the historic page, by their uncommon talents,
and by the sacrifice of what my fair countrywomen still
hold to be the ornament of their sex. I would remind them
that they have it in their power to retain their present
honorable station in society. They are our early instructors,
and while mothers in the respectable stations of life continued to inculcate on the tender minds of their sons a
veneration for the precepts of Religion, their plient children, receiving their instructions along with the affectionate
caresses of their mothers, got impressions which long retained their force, and which protected them from the
impulses of youthful passions, till ripening years fitted
their minds for listening to serious instruction from their
public teachers. Sobriety and decency of manners were
then no slur on the character of a youth, and he was thought
capable of struggling for independence, or pre-eminence, fit
either for supporting or defending the state, although he
was neither a toper nor a rake. I believe that no man who
has seen thirty or forty years of life will deny that the manners of youth are sadly changed in this respect. And, without presuming to say that this has proceeded from the
neglect, and almost total cessation of the moral education
of the nursery, I think myself well warranted, from my
own observation, to say that this education and the sober
manners of young men have quitted us together.

Some will call this prudery, and croaking. But I am
almost transcribing from Cicero, and from Quintilian.—
Cornelia, Aurelia, Attia, and other ladies of the first rank,
are praised by Cicero only for their *eminence* in this respect; but not because they were *singular*. Quintilian says
that in the time immediately prior to his own, it had been
the general practice of the ladies of rank to superintend
the moral education both of sons and daughters. But of

late, says he, they are so engaged in continual and corrupting amusements, such as the shows of gladiators, horse-racing, and deep play, that they have no time, and have yielded their places to Greek governesses and tutors, outcasts of a nation more subdued by their own vices than by the Roman arms. I dare say this was laughed at, as croaking about the corruption of the age. But what was the consequence of all this?—The Romans became the most abandoned voluptuaries, and, to preserve their mean pleasures, they crouched as willing slaves to a succession of the vilest tyrants that ever disgraced humanity.

What a noble fund of self-estimation would our fair partners acquire to themselves, if, by reforming the manners of the young generation, they should be the means of restoring peace to the world! *They have it in their power,* by the renewal of the good old custom of early instruction, and perhaps still more, by impressing on the minds of their daughters the same sentiments, and obliging them to respect sobriety and decency in the youth, and pointedly to withhold their smiles and civilities from all who transgress these in the smallest degree. This is a method of proceeding that *will most certainly be victorious.* Then indeed will the women be the saviours of their country. While therefore the German fair have been repeatedly branded with having welcomed the French invaders,* let our Ladies stand up for the honor of free-born Britons, by turning against the pretended enlighteners of the world, the arms which nature has put into their hands, and which those profligates have presumptuously expected to employ in extending their influence over mankind. The empire of beauty is but short, but the empire of virtue is durable; nor is there an instance to be met with of its decline. If it be yet possible to reform the world, it is possible for the fair. By the constitution of human nature, they must always appear as the ornament of human life, and be the objects of fondness and affection; so that if any thing can make head against

*I have met with this charge in many places; and one book in particular, written by a Prussian General Officer, who was in the country over-run by the French troops, gives a detail of the conduct of the women that is very remarkable. He also says, that infidelity has become very prevalent among the ladies in the higher circles. Indeed this melancholy account is to be found in many passages of the private correspondence of the Illuminati.

the selfish and overbearing dispositions of man, it is his respectful regard for the sex. But mere fondness has but little of the rational creature in it, and we see it harbour every day in the breast that is filled with the meanest and most turbulent passions. No where is it so strong as in the harems of the east; and as long as the women ask nothing of the men but fondness and admiration, they will get nothing else—they will never be respected. But let them rouse themselves, assert their dignity, by shewing their own elevated sentiments of human nature, and by acting up to this claim, and they may then command the world.

V. Another good consequence that should result from the account that has been given of the proceedings of this conspiracy is, that since the fascinating picture of human life, by which men have been wheedled into immediate anarchy and rebellion, is insincere, and a mere artificial creature of the imagination, it can have no steadiness, but must be changed by every freak of fancy, or by every ingenious sophist, who can give an equal plausibility to whatever suits his present views. It is as much an airy phantom as any other whim of Free Masonry, and has no prototype, no original pattern in human nature, to which recourse may always be had, to correct mistakes, and keep things in a constant tenor. Has not France given the most unequivocal proofs of this? Was not the declaration of the Rights of Man, the production of their most brilliant Illuminators, a picture *in abstracto*, where man was placed at a distance from the eye, that no false light of local situation might pervert the judgment or engage the passions? Was it not declared to be the masterpiece of human wisdom? Did not the nation consider it at leisure? and having it continually before their eyes, did they not, step by step, give their assent to the different articles of their Constitution, derived from it, and fabricated by their most choice Illuminators? And did not this Constitution draw the applauses of the bright geniuses of other nations, who by this time were busy in persuading, each his countrymen, that they were ignoramuses in statistics, and patient slaves of oppression or of ancient prejudices? Did not panegyrics on it issue from every garret in London? Where is it now? where is its successor? Has any one plan of government subsisted, except while it was supported by the incontroulable and inexorable power of the guillotine? Is not the present administration of France as much as ever the object of discontent and of terror, and its coercions as like as ever to the summary justice of the Parisian mob? Is there any probability of its permanency in a state of peace, when the fears of a foreign enemy no longer give a consolidation to their measures, and oblige them either to agree among themselves, or immediately to perish?

VI. The above accounts evince in the most uncontrovertible manner the dangerous tendency of all mystical societies, and of all associations who hold secret meetings. We see that their uniform progress has been from frivolity and nonsense to wickedness and sedition. Weishaupt has been at great pains to show the good effects of secrecy in the Association, and the arguments are valid for his purpose.—But all his arguments are so many dissuasive advices to every thinking and sober mind. The man who really wishes to discover an abstruse truth will place himself, if possible, in a *calm* situation, and will by no means expose himself to the impatient hankering for secrets and wonders—and he will always fear that a thing which resolutely conceals itself cannot bear the light. All who have seriously employed themselves in the discovery of truth have found the great advantages of open communication of sentiment. And it is against common sense to imagine that there is any thing of vast importance to mankind which is yet a secret, and which must be kept a secret in order to be useful. This is against the whole experience of mankind—And surely to hug in one's breast a secret of such mighty importance, is to give the lie to all our professions of brotherly love. What a solecism! a secret to enlighten and reform the whole world.—We render all our endeavours impotent when we grasp at a thing beyond our power. Let an association be formed with a serious plan for reforming its own members, and let them extend their numbers in proportion as they succeed—this might do some good.—But must the way of doing this be a secret?—It may be to many—who will not look for it where it is to be found—It is this,

"Do good—seek peace—and pursue it."

But it is almost affronting the reader to suppose arguments necessary on this point. If there be a necessity for secrecy, the purpose of the Association is either frivolous, or it is selfish.

Now, in either case, the danger of such secret assemblies is manifest.—Mere frivolity can never seriously occupy men come to age. And accordingly we see that in every quarter of Europe where Free Masonry has been established, the Lodges have become seedbeds of public mischief. I believe that no ordinary Brother will say, that the occupations in the Lodges are any thing better than frivolous, very frivolous indeed. The distribution of charity needs be no secret, and it is but a very small part of the employment of the meeting.—This being the case, it is in human nature that the greater we suppose the frivolity of such an association to be, the greater is the chance of its ceasing to give sufficient occupation to the mind, and the greater is the risk that the meetings may be employed to other purposes which require concealment. When this happens, self-interest alone must prompt and rule, and now there is no length that some men will not go, when they think themselves in no danger of detection and punishment. The whole proceedings of the secret societies of Free Masons on the Continent (and I am authorised to say, of some Lodges in Britain) have taken one turn, and this turn is perfectly natural. In all countries there are men of licentious morals. Such men wish to have a safe opportunity of indulging their wits in satire and sarcasm; and they are pleased with the support of others.—The desire of making proselytes is in every breast—and it is whetted by the restraints of society.—And all countries have discontented men, whose grumblings will raise discontent in others, who might not have attended to some of the trifling hardships and injuries they met with, had they not been reminded of them. To be discontented, and not to think of schemes of redress, is what we cannot think natural or manly;—and where can such sentiments and schemes find such safe utterance and such probable support as in a secret society? Free Masonry is innocent of all these things; but Free Masonry has been abused, and at last totally perverted—and so will and must any such secret association, as long as men are licentious in their opinions or wicked in their dispositions.

It were devoutly to be wished therefore that the whole

Fraternity would imitate the truly benevolent conduct of those German Lodges who have formally broken up, and made a patriotic sacrifice of their amusement to the safety of the state. I cannot think the sacrifice great or costly. It can be no difficult matter to find as pleasant a way of passing a vacant hour—and the charitable deeds of the members need not diminish in the smallest degree. Every person's little circle of acquaintance will give him opportunities of gratifying his kind dispositions, without the chance of being mistaken in the worth of the person on whom he bestows his favors. There is no occasion to go to St. Petersburg for a poor Brother, nor to India for a convert to Christianity, as long as we see so many sufferers and infidels among ourselves.

But not only are secret societies dangerous, but all societies whose object is mysterious. The whole history of man is a proof of this position. In no age or country has there ever appeared a mysterious association which did not in time become a public nuisance. Ingenious or designing men of letters have attempted to show that some of the ancient mysteries were useful to mankind, containing rational doctrines of natural religion. This was the strong hold of Weishaupt, and he quotes the Eleusinian, the Pythagorean, and other mysteries. But surely their external signs and tokens were every thing that is shocking to decency and civil order. It is uncommon presumption for the learned of the 18th century to pretend to know more about them than their contemporaries, the philosophers, the law-givers of antiquity. These give no such account of them. I would desire any person who admires the ingenious dissertations of Dr. Warburton to read a dull German book, called *Caracteristik der Mysterien der Altern*, published at Frankfort in 1787. The author contents himself with a patient collection of every scrap of every ancient author who has said any thing about them. If the reader can see any thing in them but the most absurd and immoral polytheism and fable, he must take words in a sense that is useless in reading any other piece of ancient composition. I have a notion that the Dionysiacs of Ionia had some scientific secrets, viz. all the knowledge of practical mechanics which was employed by their architects and engineers, and that they were really a Masonic Fraternity. But, like the *Illuminati*, they tagged to the secrets of Masonry the secret of drunkenness and debauchery; they had their Sister Lodges, and at last became rebels, subverters of the States where they were protected, till aiming at the dominion of all Ionia, they were attacked by the neighbouring States and dispersed. They were Illuminators too, and wanted to introduce the worship of Bacchus over the whole country, as appears in the account of them given by *Strabo*.—Perhaps the Pythagoreans had also some scientific secrets! but they too were Illuminators, and thought it their duty to overset the State, and were themselves overset.

Nothing is so dangerous as a mystic Association. The object remaining a secret in the hands of the managers, the rest simply put a ring in their own noses, by which they may be led about at pleasure; and still panting after the secret, they are the better pleased the less they see of their way. A mystical object enables the leader to shift his ground as he pleases, and to accommodate himself to every current fashion or prejudice. This again gives him almost unlimited power; for he can make use of these prejudices to lead men by troops. He finds them already associated by their prejudices, and waiting for a leader to concentrate their strength and set them in motion. And when once great bodies of men are set in motion, with a creature of their fancy for a guide, even the engineer himself cannot say, "Thus far shalt thou go, and no farther."

VII. We may also gather from what we have seen, that all declamations on universal philanthropy are dangerous. Their natural and immediate effect on the mind is to increase the discontents of the unfortunate, and of those in the laborious ranks of life. No one, even of the Illuminators, will deny that these ranks must be filled, if society exists in any degree of cultivation whatever, and that there will always be a greater number of men who have no farther prospect. Surely it is unkind to put such men continually in mind of a state in which they might be at their ease; and it is unkindness unmixed, because all the change that they will produce will be, that James will serve John, who formerly was the servant of James. Such declamations naturally tend to cause men to make light of the obligations and duties of common patriotism, because these are represented as subordinate and inferior to the greater and more noble affection of universal benevolence. I do not pretend to say that patriotism is founded in a rationally-perceived pre-eminence or excellence of the society with which we are connected. But if it be a fact that society will not advance unless its members take an interest in it, and that human nature improves only in society, surely this interest should be cherished in every breast. Perhaps national union arises from national animosity;—but they are plainly distinguishable, and union is not necessarily productive of injustice. The same arguments that have any force against patriotism are equally good against the preference which natural instinct gives parents for their children; and surely no one can doubt of the propriety of maintaining this in its full force, subject however to the precise laws of justice.

But I am in the wrong to adduce paternal or filial affection in defence of patriotism and loyalty, since even those natural instincts are reprobated by the *Illuminati,* as hostile to the all-comprehending philanthropy. Mr. de la Metherie says, that among the memorials sent from the clubs in England to the National Assembly, he read two (printed) in which the Assembly was requested to establish a community of wives, and to take children from their parents, and educate them for the nation. In full compliance with this dictate of universal philanthropy, Weishaupt would have murdered his own child and his concubine—and Orleans voted the death of his near relation.

Indeed, of all the consequences of Illumination, the most melancholy is this revolution which it seems to operate in the heart of man—this forcible sacrifice of every affection of the heart to an ideal divinity, a mere creature of the imagination.—It seems a prodigy, yet it is a matter of experience, that the farther we advance, or vainly suppose that we do advance, in the knowledge of our mental powers, the more are our moral feelings flattened and done away. I remember reading, long ago, a dissertation on the nursing of infants by a French academician, Le Cointre of Versailles. He indelicately supports his theories by the case of his own son, a weak puny infant, whom his mother was obliged to keep continually applied to her bosom, so that she rarely could get two hours of sleep during the time of suckling him. Mr. Le Cointre says, that she contracted for this infant *"une partialité tout-à-fait deraisonable."*—Plato, or Socrates, or Cicero, would probably have explained this by the habitual exercise of pity, a very endearing emotion.—But our Academician, better illuminated, solves it by stimuli on the *papillæ*, and on the nerves of the skin, and by the meeting of the humifying *aura*, &c. and does not seem to think that young Le Cointre was much indebted to his mother. It would amuse me to learn that this was the wretch Le Cointre, Major of the National Guards of Versailles, who countenanced and encouraged the shocking treason and barbarity of those ruffians on the 5th and 6th of October 1789. Complete freezing of the heart would (I think) be the consequence of a theory which could perfectly explain the affections by vibrations or crystallizations.—Nay, any very perfect theory of moral sentiments must have something of this tendency.—Perhaps the ancient systems of moral philosophy, which were chiefly searches after the *fummum bonum,* and systems of moral duties, tended more to form and strengthen the heart, and produce a worthy man, than the most perfect theory of modern times, which explains every phenomenon by means of a nice anatomy of our affections.

So far therefore as we are really more illuminated, it may chance to give us an easier victory over the natur or instinctive attachments of mankind, and make the sacrifice to universal philanthropy less costly to the heart. I do not however pretend to say that this is really the case: but I think myself fully warranted to say, that increase of virtuous affections in general has not been the fruit of modern Illumination. I will not again sicken the reader, by calling his attention to Weishaupt and his associates or successors. But let us candidly contemplate the world around us, and particularly the perpetual advocates of universal philanthropy. What have been the general effects of their continual declamations? Surely very melancholy; nor can it easily be otherwise.— An ideal standard is continually referred to. This is made gigantic, by being always seen indistinctly, as thro' a mist, or rather a fluttering air. In comparison with this, every feeling that we have been accustomed to respect vanishes as insignificant; and, adopting the Jesuitical maxim, that "the great end sanctifies every

mean," this sum of Cosmo-political good is made to eclipse
or cover all the present evils which must be endured for it.
The fact now is, that we are become so familiarised with
enormities, such as brutality to the weaker sex, cruelty to
old age, wanton refinement on barbarity, that we now hear
unmoved accounts of scenes, from which, a few years ago,
we would have shrunk back with horror. With cold hearts,
and a metaphysical scale, we measure the present miseries
of our fellow-creatures, and compare them with the accumulated miseries of former times, occasioned through a
course of ages, and ascribed to the ambition of Princes.
In this artificial manner are the atrocities of France ex-
tenuated; and we struggle, and partly succeed, in reasoning
ourselves out of all the feelings which link men together in
society.—The ties of father, husband, brother, friend—all
are abandoned for an emotion which we must even strive
to excite—universal philanthropy. But this is sad perversion
of nature. "He that loveth not his brother whom he hath
seen, how can he love God whom he hath not seen?"—
Still less can he love this ideal being, of which he labours
to conjure up some indistinct and fleeting notion. It is also
highly absurd; for, in trying to collect the circumstances
which constitute the enjoyments of this Citizen of the
World, we find ourselves just brought back to the very
moral feelings which we are wantonly throwing away. Weishaupt allures us by the happiness of the patriarchal life as
the *summum bonum* of man. But if it is any thing more
than eating and sleeping, and bullying with the neighbouring patriarchs, it must consist in the domestic and neighbourly affections, and every other agreeable moral feeling,
all which are to be had in our present state in greater
abundance.

But this is all a pretence;—the wicked corrupters of mankind have no such views of human felicity, nor would they
be contented with it;—they want to intrigue and to lead;—
and their patriarchal life answers the same purpose of
tickling the fancy as the Arcadia of the poets. Horace shows
the frivolity of these declamations, without formally
enouncing the moral, in his pretty Ode,

*Beutus ille qui procul negotiis.*

The usurer, after expatiating on this Arcadian felicity,

hurries away to change, and puts his whole cash again out to usury.

Equally ineffective are the declamations of Cosmo-politism on a mind filled with selfish passions;—they just serve it for a subterfuge.—The ties of ordinary life are broken in the first place, and the Citizen of the World is a wolf of the desert.

The unhappy consequence is, that the natural progress of liberty is retarded. Had this *ignis fatuus* not appeared and misled us, the improvements which true Illumination has really produced, the increase in sciences and arts, and the improvement in our estimate of life and happiness, would have continued to work silently and gradually in all nations; and those which are less fortunate in point of government would also have improved, bit by bit, without losing any sensible portion of their present enjoyments in the possession of riches, or honors, or power. Those pretensions would gradually have come to balance each other, and true liberty, such as Britons enjoy, might have taken place over all.

Instead of this, the inhabitants of every State are put into a situation where every individual is alarmed and injured by the success of another, because all pre-eminence is criminal. Therefore there must be perpetual jealousy and struggle. Princes are now alarmed, since they see the aim of the lower classes, and they repent of their former liberal concessions. All parties maintain a sullen distance and reserve;—the people become unruly, and the Sovereign hard-hearted; so that liberty, such as *can* be enjoyed in peace, is banished from the country.

VIII. When we see how eagerly the Illuminati endeavoured to insinuate their Brethren into all offices which gave them influence on the public mind, and particularly into seminaries of education, we should be particularly careful to prevent them, and ought to examine with anxious attention the manner of thinking of all who offer themselves for teachers of youth. There is no part of the secret correspondence of Spartacus and his Associates, in which we see more varied and artful methods for securing pupils, than in his own conduct respecting the students in the University, and the injunctions he gives to others. There are two men, Socher and Drexl, who had the general inspection of the schools in the Electorate. They are treated by Spartacus as persons of the greatest consequence, and the instructions given them stick at no kind of corruption. Weishaupt is at pains, by circuitous and mean arts, to induce young gentlemen to come under his care, and, to one whom he describes in another letter as a little master who must have much indulgence, he causes it to be intimated, that in the quarters where he is to be lodged, he will get the key of the street-door, so that he can admit whom he will. In all this canvassing he never quits the great object, the forming the mind of the young man according to the principles of universal Liberty and Equality, and to gain this point, scruples not to flatter, and even to excite his dangerous passions. We may be certain, that the zeal of Cosmo-politism will operate in the same way in other men, and we ought therefore to be solicitous to have all that are the instructors of youth, persons of the most decent manners. No question but sobriety and hypocrisy may inhabit the same breast. But its immediate effect on the pupil is at least safe, and it is always easy for a sensible parent to represent the restrictions laid on the pupil by such a man as the effects of uncommon anxiety for his safety. Whereas there is no cure for the lax principles that may steal upon the tender mind that is not early put on its guard. Weishaupt undoubtedly thought that the principles of civil anarchy would be easiest inculcated on minds that had already shaken off the restraints of Religion, and entered into habits of sensual indulgence. We shall be safe if we trust his judgment in this matter.—We should be particularly observant of the character and principles of *Men of Talents,* who offer themselves for these offices, because *their* influence must be very great. Indeed this anxiety should extend to all offices which in any way give the holders any remarkable influence on the minds of considerable numbers. Such should always be filled by men of immaculate characters and approved principles; and, in times like the present, where the most essential questions are the subjects of frequent discussion, we should always consider with some distrust the men who are very cautious in declaring their opinions on these questions.

It is a great misfortune undoubtedly to feel ourselves in a situation which makes us damp the enjoyments of life with so much suspicion. But the history of mankind shows us that many great revolutions have been produced by remote and apparently frivolous causes. When things come to a height it is frequently impossible to find a cure—at any rate *medicina sero paratur*, and it is much better to prevent the disease—*principiis obsta*—*venienti occurrite marbo*.

IX. Nor can it be said that these are vain fears. We know that the enemy is working among us, and that there are many appearances in these kingdoms which strongly resemble the contrivance of this dangerous Association. We know that before the Order of Illuminati was broken up by the Elector of Bavaria, there were several Lodges in Britain, and we may be certain that they are not all broken up. I know that they are not, and that within these two years some Lodges were ignorant, or affected to be so, of the corrupted principles and dangerous designs of the Illuminati. The constitution of the Order shows that this may be, for the Lodges themselves were illuminated by degrees. But I must remark that we can hardly suppose a Lodge to be established in any place, unless there be some very zealous Brother at hand to instruct and direct it. And I think that a person can hardly be advanced as far as the rank of Scotch Knight of the Order, and be a safe man either for our church or state. I am very well informed that there are several thousands of subscribing Brethren in London alone, and we can hardly doubt but that many of that number are well advanced. The vocabulary also of the Illuminati is current in certain societies among us. These societies have taken the very name and constitution of the French and German societies. Corresponding—Affiliated—Provincial—Rescript—Convention—Reading Societies—Citizen of the World—Liberty and Equality, the Imprescriptible Rights of Man, &c. &c. And must it not be acknowledged that our public arbiters of literary merit have greatly changed their manner of treatment of theological and political writings of late years? Till Paine's Age of Reason appeared, the most sceptical writings of England kept within the bounds of decency and of argument, and we have not, in the course of two centuries, one piece that should be compared with many of the blackguard productions of the German presses.

Yet even those performances generally met with sharp reproof as well as judicious refutation. This is a tribute of commendation to which my country is most justly entitled. In a former part of my life I was pretty conversant in writings of this kind, and have seen almost every English performance of note. I cannot express the surprise and disgust which I felt at the number and the gross indecency of the German dissertations which have come in my way since I began this little history—and many of the titles which I observe in the Leipzig catalogues are such as I think no British writer would make use of. I am told that the licentiousness of the press has been equally remarkable in France, even before the Revolution.—May this sense of propriety and decency long continue to protect us, and support the national character for real good breeding, as our attainments in manly science have hitherto gained us the respect of the surrounding nations.

I cannot help thinking that British sentiment, or British delicacy, is changed; for Paine's book is treated by most of our Reviewers with an affected liberality and candour; and is laid before the public as quite new matter, and a fair field for discussion—and it strikes me as if our critics were more careful to let no fault of his opponents pass unnoticed than to expose the futility and rudeness of this indelicate writer. In the reviews of political writings we see few of those kind endeavours, which real love for our constitutional government would induce a writer to employ in order to lessen the fretful discontents of the people; and there is frequently betrayed a satisfaction at finding administration in straits, either through misconduct or misfortune. Real love for our country and its government would (I think) induce a person to mix with his criticisms some sentiments of sympathy with the embarassment of a minister loaded with the business of a great nation, in a situation never before experienced by any minister. The critic would recollect that the minister was a man, subject to error, but not necessarily nor altogether base. But it seems to be an assumed principle with some of our political writers and reviewers that government must always be in fault, and that every thing needs a reform. Such were the beginnings on the continent, and we cannot doubt but that attempts are made to influence the public mind in this

country, in the very way that has been practised abroad.—
Nay,

X. The detestable doctrines of Illuminatism have been
openly preached among us. Has not Dr. Priestly said (I
think in one of his letters on the Birmingham riots) "That
if the condition of other nations be as much improved
as that of France will be by the change in her system of
government, the great crisis, dreadful as it may appear, will
be a consummation devoutly to be wished for;—and though
calamitous to many, perhaps to many innocent persons,
will be eventually glorious and happy."—Is not this equivalent to Spartacus saying, "True—there will be a storm, a
convulsion—but all will be calm again?"—Does Dr. Priestly
think that the British will part more easily than their neighbours in France with their property and honors, secured
by ages of peaceable possession, protected by law, and
acquiesced in by all who wish and hope that their own
descendants may reap the fruits of their honest industry?
—Will they make a less manly struggle?—Are they less
numerous?—Must his friends, his patrons, whom he has
thanked, and praised, and flattered, yield up all peaceably,
or fall in the general struggle? This writer has already given
the most promising specimens of his own docility in the
principles of Illuminatism, and has already passed through
several degrees of initiation. He has refined and refined on
Christianity, and boasts, like another Spartacus, that he has,
at last, hit on the true secret.—Has he not been preparing
the minds of his readers for Atheism by his theory of mind,
and by his commentary on the unmeaning jargon of Dr.
Hartley? I call it unmeaning jargon, that I may avoid giving it a more apposite and disgraceful name. For, if intelligence and design be nothing but a certain modification
of the *vibratiunculæ* or undulations of any kind, what is
supreme intelligence, but a more extensive, and (perhaps
they will call it) refined undulation, pervading or mixing
with all others? Indeed it is in this very manner that the
universal operation of intelligence is pretended to be explained. As any new or partial undulation may be super-
induced on any other already existing, and this without the
least disturbance or confusion, so may the inferior intel-
ligences in the universe be only superinductions on the
operations of this supreme intelligence which pervades them

all.—And thus an undulation (of what? surely of something prior to and independent of this modification) is the cause of all the beings in the universe, and of all the harmony and beauty that we observe.—And this undulation is the object of love, and gratitude, and confidence (that is, of other kinds of undulations.) Fortunately all this has no meaning.—But surely, if anything can tend to diminish the force of our religious sentiments, and make all Dr. Priestly's discoveries in Christianity insignificant, this will do it.

Were it possible for the departed soul of Newton to feel pain, he would surely recollect with regret that unhappy hour, when, provoked by Dr. Hooke's charge of plagiarism, he first threw out his whim of a vibrating æther, to show what might be made of an hypothesis.—For Sir Isaac Newton must be allowed to have paved the way for much of the atomical philosophy of the moderns. Newton's æther is assumed as a *fac totum* by every precipitate sciolist, who in despite of logic, and in contradiction to all the principles of mechanics, gives us theories of muscular motion, of animal sensation, and even of intelligence and volition, by the undulations of ætherial fluids. Not one of a hundred of these theorists can go through the fundamental theorem of all this doctrine, the 47th prop. of the 2d book of the Principia, and not one in a thousand know that Newton's investigation is inconclusive.—Yet they talk of the effects and modifications of those undulations as familiarly and confidently as if they could demonstrate the propositions in Euclid's Elements.

Yet such is the reasoning that satisfies Dr. Priestly. But I do not suppose that he has yet attained his acmé of Illumination. His genius has been cramped by British prejudices.—These need not sway his mind any longer. He is now in that *"rará temporis (et loci) felicitate, ubi sentire quæ velis, et quæ sentias dicere licet,"*—in the country which was honored by giving the world the first avowed edition of the *Age of Reason,* with the name of the shop and publisher. I make no doubt but that his mind will now take a higher flight—and we may expect to see him fire "that train by which he boasted that he would blow up the religious establishment of his stupid and enslaved native country.—Peace be with him.—But I grieve that he has left any of his friends and abettors among us.—A very eminent one said in a company a few days ago, that "he would willingly wade to the knees in blood to overturn the establishment of the Kirk of Scotland." I understand that he proposes to go to India, and there to preach Christianity to the natives. Let me beseech him to recollect that among us Christianity is still considered as the gospel of peace, and that it strongly dissuades us from bathing our feet in blood.

I understand that more apostles of this mission are avowed enemies of all religious establishments, and indeed of all establishments of any kind. But, as I do not see a greater chance of one pastor or one patriarch being in the right, either as to religious or political matters, than a number of pastors or patriarchs, who have consulted together, and compared and accommodated their opinions; and as I can find nothing but quarrels and ill-will among independents, I should be sorry to have any of our establishments destroyed, and am therefore apprehensive of some danger from the zealous spreading of such doctrines, especially as they make it equally necessary to admit the preaching up no religion, and no civil establishment whatever.

Seeing that there are such grounds of apprehension, I think that we have cause to be on our guard, and that every man who has enjoyed the sweets of British liberty should be very anxious indeed to preserve it. We should discourage all secret assemblies, which afford opportunities to the disaffected, and all conversations which foster any notions of political perfection, and create hankerings after unattainable happiness. These only increase the discontents of the unfortunate, the idle, and the worthless.—Above all, we should be careful to discourage and check immorality and licentiousness in every shape. For this will of itself subvert every government, and will subject us to the vile tyranny of the mob.

XI. If there has ever been a season in which it was proper to call upon the public instructors of the nation to exert themselves in the cause of Religion and of Virtue, it is surely the present. It appears from the tenor of the whole narration before the reader, that Religion and Virtue are considered as the great obstacles to the completion of this plan for overturning the governments of Europe—and I hope that I have made it evident that these conspirators have presupposed that there is deeply rooted in the heart of man a sincere veneration for unsophisticated Virtue, and an affectionate propensity to Religion; that is, to consider this beautiful world as the production of wisdom and power, residing in a Being different from the world itself, and the natural object of admiration and of love.—I do not speak of the truth of this principle at present, but only of its reality, as an impression on the heart of man. These principles must therefore be worked on—and they are acknowledged to be strong, because much art is employed to eradicate them, or to overwhelm them by other powerful agents.—We also see that Religion and Virtue are considered by those corrupters as closely united, and as mutually supporting each other. This they admit as a fact, and labour to prove to be a mistake.—And lastly, they entertain no hopes of complete success till they have exploded both.

This being the case, I hope that I shall be clear of all charge of impropriety, when I address our national instructors, and earnestly desire them to consider this cause as peculiarly theirs. The world has been corrupted under pretence of moral instruction.—Backwardness therefore, on their part, may do inconceivable harm, because it will most certainly be interpreted as an acknowledgment of defeat, and they will be accused of indifference and insincerity.—I know that a modest man reluctantly comes forward with any thing that has the appearance of thinking himself wiser or better than his neighbours. But if all are so bashful, where will it end? Must we allow a parcel of worthless profligates, whom no man would trust with the management of the most trifling concern, to pass with the ignorant and indolent for teachers of true wisdom, and thus entice the whole world into a trap. They have succeeded, with our unfortunate neighbours on the continent, and, in Germany (to their shame be it spoken) they have been assisted even by some faithless clergymen.

But I will hope better of my countrymen, and I think that

our clergy have encouragement even from the native character of Britons. National comparisons are indeed ungraceful, and are rarely candid—but I think they may be indulged in this instance. It is of his own countrymen that Voltaire speaks, when he says, "that they resemble a mixed breed of the monkey and the tiger," animals that mix fun with mischief, and that sport with the torments of their prey.—They have indeed given the most shocking proofs of the justness of his portrait. It is with a considerable degree of national pride, therefore, that I compare the behaviour of the French with that of the British in a very similar situation, during the civil wars and the usurpation of Cromwell. There have been more numerous, and infinitely more atrocious, crimes committed in France during any one half year since the beginning of the Revolution, than during the whole of that tumultuous period. And it should be remembered, that to all other grounds of discontent was added no small share of religious fanaticism, a passion (may I call it) which seldom fails to rouse every angry thought of the heart.——Much may be hoped for from an earnest and judicious address to that rich fund of manly kindness that is conspicuous in the British character—a fund to which I am persuaded to owe the excellence of our constitutional government—No where else in Europe are the claims of the different ranks in society so generally and so candidly admitted. All feel their force, and all allow them to others. Hence it happens that they are enjoyed in so much peace— hence it happens that the gentry live among the yeomen and farmers with so easy and familiar a superiority:

*————————Extrema per illos*
*Justitia excedens terris vestigia fecit.*

Our clergy are also well prepared for the task. For our ancestors differed exceedingly from the present Illuminators in their notions, and have enacted that the clergy shall be well instructed in natural philosophy, judging that a knowledge of the symmetry of nature, and the beautiful adjustment of all her operations, would produce a firm belief of a wisdom and power which is the source of all this fair order, the Author and Conductor of all, and therefore the natural object of admiration and of love. A good heart is open to this impression, and feels no reluctance, but on the contrary a pleasure, in thinking man the subject of his government, and the object of his care. This point being once gained, I should think that the salutary truths of Religion will be highly welcome. I should think that it will be easy to convince such minds, that in the midst of the immense variety of the works of God, there is one great plan to which every thing seems to refer, namely, the crouding this world, to the utmost degree of possibility, with life, with beings that enjoy the things around them, each in its own degree and manner. Among these, man makes a most conspicuous figure, and the *maximum* of his enjoyment seems a capital article in the ways of Providence.——It will, I think, require little trouble to shew that the natural dictates of Religion, or the immediate results of the belief of God's moral government of the universe, coincide, in every circumstance of sentiment, disposition, and conduct, with those that are most productive of enjoyment (on the whole) in social life. The same train of thought will shew, that the real improvements in the pleasures of society, are, in fact, improvements of man's rational nature, and so many steps toward that perfection which our own consciences tell us we are capable of, and which Religion encourages us to hope for in another state of being. And thus will "the ways of Wisdom appear to be ways of pleasantness, and all her paths to be peace."

Dwelling on such topics, there is no occasion for any political discussion. This would be equally improper and hurtful. Such discussions never fail to produce ill-humour. ——But surely highest complacence must result from the thought that we are co-operating with the Author of all wisdom and goodness, and helping forward the favorite plans of his providence. Such a thought must elevate the mind which thus recognises a sort of alliance with the Author of nature.——Our brethren in society appear brethren indeed, heirs of the same hopes, and travelling to the same country. This will be a sort of moral patriotism, and should, I think, produce mutual forbearance, since we discover imperfections in all creatures, and are conscious of them in ourselves—notwithstanding which, we hope to be all equal at last in worth and in happiness.

I should gladly hope that I shall not be accused of presumption in this address. There is no profession that I more sincerely respect than that of the religious and moral instructor of my country. I am saying nothing here that I am not accustomed to urge at much greater length in the course of my professional duty. And I do not think that I am justly chargeable with vanity, when I suppose that many years of delightful study of the works of God have given me somewhat more acquaintance with them than is probably attained by those who never think of the matter, being continually engaged in the bustle of life. Should one of this description say that all is fate or chance, and that "the same thing happens to all," &c. as is but too common, I should think that a prudent man will give so much preference to *my* assertion, as at least to think seriously about the thing, before he allow himself any indulgence in things which I affirm to be highly dangerous to his future peace and happiness. For this reason I hope not to be accused of going out of my line, nor hear any one say, *"Ne sutor ultra crepidam."* The present is a season of anxiety, and it is the duty of every man to contribute his mite to the general good.

It is in some such hopes that I have written these pages; and if they have any such effect, I shall think myself fortunate in having by chance hit on something useful, when I was only trying to amuse myself during the tedious hours of bad health and confinement. No person is more sensible of the many imperfections of this performance than myself. But, as I have no motive for the publication but the hopes of doing some good, I trust that I shall obtain a favorable acceptance of my endeavours from an intelligent, a candid, and a good-natured public. I must entreat that it be remembered that these sheets are not the work of an author determined to write a book. They were for the most part notes, which I took from books I had borrowed, that I might occasionally have recourse to them when occupied with Free Masonry, the first object of my curiosity. My curiosity was diverted to many other things as I went along, and when the Illuminati came in my way, I regretted the time I had thrown away on Free Masonry. —But, observing their connection, I thought that I perceived the progress of one and the same design. This made me eager to find out any remains of Weishaupt's Association. I was not surprised when I saw marks of its interference in the French Revolution.—In hunting for clearer proofs I found out the German Union—and, in fine, the whole appeared to be one great and wicked project, fermenting and working over all Europe.—Some highly respected friends encouraged me in the hope of doing some service by laying my informations before the public, and said that no time should be lost.—I therefore set about collecting my scattered facts.—I undertook this task at a time when my official duty pressed hard on me, and bad health made me very unfit for study.—The effects of this must appear in many faults, which I see, without being able at present to amend them. I owe this apology to the public, and I trust that my good intentions will procure it acceptance.*

*While the sheet commencing p. 267 was printing off, I got a sight of a work published in Paris last year, entitled *La Conjuration d' Orleans*. It confirms all that I have said respecting the use made of the Free Mason Lodges.—It gives a particular account of the formation of the Jacobin Club, by the Club Breton. This last appears to have been the Association formed with the assistance of the German Deputies. The Jacobin Club had several committees, similar to those of the National Assembly. Among others, it had a Committee of Enquiry and Correspondence, whose business it was to gain partizans, to discover enemies, to decide on the merits of the Brethren, and to form similar Clubs in other places.

The author of the above-mentioned work writes as follows (vol. 3. p. 19.) We may judge of what the D. of Orleans could do in other places, by what he did during his stay in England. During his stay in London, he gained over to his interest Lord Stanhope and Dr. Price, two of the most respectable members of *the Revolution Society*. This Society had no other object (it said) but to support the Revolution, which had driven James II. from the throne of his ancestors.

Orleans made of this association a true Jacobin Club—It entered into correspondence with the Committee of Enquiry of our Commune, with the same Committee of our Jacobin Club, and at last with our National Assembly. It even sent to the Assembly an ostensible letter, in which we may see the following passages:

"The Society congratulates the National Assembly of France on the Revolution which has taken place in that country. It cannot but earnestly wish for the happy conclusion of so important a Revolution, and, at the same time, express the extreme satisfaction which it feels in reflecting on the glorious example which France has given to the world." (The Reader will remark, that in this example are contained all the horrors which had been exhibited in France before the month of March 1790; and that before this time, the conduct of the D. of Orleans on the 5th and 6th of October 1789, with all the shocking atrocities of those days, were fully known in England.)

Nothing would give me more sincere pleasure than to see the whole proved to be a mistake;—to be convinced that there is no such plot, and that we run no risk of the contagion; but that Britain will continue, by the abiding prevalence of honor, of virtue, and of true religion, to exhibit the fairest specimen of civil government that ever was seen on earth, and a national character and conduct not unworthy of the inestimable blessings that we enjoy. Our excellent Sovereign, at his accession to the throne, declared to his Parliament that HE GLORIED IN HAVING BEEN BORN A BRITON.—Would to God that all and each of his subjects had entertained the same lofty notions of this good fortune. Then would they have laboured, as he has done for near forty years, to support the honor of the British name by setting as bright an example of domestic and of public virtue.—Then would Britons have been indeed the boast of humanity—then we should have viewed these wicked plots of our neighbours with a smile of contempt, and of sincere pity—and there would have been no need of this imperfect but well-meant performance.

"The Society resolves unanimously to invite all the people of England to establish Societies through the kingdom, to support the principles of the Revolution (look back to p. 236, of this work) "to form correspondences between themselves, and by these means to establish a great concerted Union of all the true Friends of Liberty."

Accordingly (says the French author) this was executed, and Jacobin Clubs were established in several cities of England, Scotland, and Ireland.

# Postscript.

ALTHOUGH I saw no reason to doubt of the validity of the proofs which I have offered in the preceding pages, of a conspiracy against the dearest interests of every nation of Europe, nor of the importance of the information to my own countrymen, it gives me great satisfaction to learn that it has been received with favor and indulgence. This I may conclude from the impression's being exhausted in a few days, and because the publisher informs me that another edition is wanted immediately. I could have wished that this were deferred for some time, that I might have availed myself of the observations of others, and be enabled to correct the mistakes into which I have been led by my scanty knowledge of the German language, and the mistakes of the writers from whom I derived all my informations. I should, in that case, have attempted to make the work more worthy of the public eye, by correcting many imperfections, which the continual distraction of bad health, and my haste to bring it before the public, have occasioned. I should have made the disposition more natural and perspicuous, and have lopped off some redundances and repetitions. But the printer tells me, that this would greatly retard the publication, by changing the series of the pages. At any rate, I am not at present in a condition to engage in any work that requires dispatch. I must yield therefore to those reasons, and content myself with such corrections as can be made immediately.

I have found, after minute enquiry, that I was mistaken as to the expression of an eminent follower of Dr. Priestly, mentioned before. The person alluded to disclaims all sanguinary proceedings, and my information arose from a very erroneous account which was circulated of the conversation. But I still think the caution equally necessary, which I recommend to the hearers of the frequent and violent declamations made by those alluded to, against all religious establishments.

Except the anecdote of Diderot's library, I do not recollect another assertion in the book, for which I have not the authority of printed evidence. This story was told me by so many persons of credit, who were on the spot at the time, that I have no doubt of its truth.

I also find that I was mistaken in my conjecture that Mr. *Le Franc* communicated his suspicions of the horrid designs of the Free Masons to Archbishop *Gobet*. It must have been to Mr. *Le Clerc de Juigne,* a most worthy prelate, whom the hatred of the Jacobins obliged to fly into Switzerland. The Catholic clergy were butchered or banished, and the Jacobins substituted in their places such as would second their views. *Gobet* was worthy of their confidence, and the *Archbishop of Thoulouse (Brienne)* himself could not have served the cause of the philosophists more effectually, had they succeeded in their attempts to get him continued Archbishop of Paris.

As the poetical picture of unqualified Liberty and Equality, and the indolent pleasures of the patriarchal life, are the charm by which the Illuminators hope to fascinate all hearts, and as they reprobate every construction of society which tolerates any permanent subordination, and particularly such as found this subordination on distinctions of ranks, and scout all privileges allowed to particular orders of men, I hope that it will not be thought foreign to the general purpose of the foregoing Work, if, I with great deference, lay before the Reader some of my reasons for asserting, without hesitation, in a former part, that the British constitution is the only one that will give permanent happiness to a great and luxurious nation, and is peculiarly calculated to give full exercise to the best propensities of cultivated minds. I am the more desirous of doing this, because it seems to me that most of the political writers on the Continent, and many of my countrymen, have not attended to important circumstances which distinguish our constitution from the States General of France and other countries. The republicans in France have, since the Revolution, employed the pains in searching their records, which ought to have been taken before the convocation of the States, and which would probably have prevented that step altogether. They have shewn that the meetings of the States, if we except that in 1614 and 1483, were uniformly occasions of mutual contests between the different Orders, in which the interests of the nation and the authority of the Crown were equally forgotten, and the kingdom was plunged into all the horrors of a rancorous civil war. Of this they give us a remarkable instance during the captivity of King John in 1355 and 1356, the horrors of which were hardly exceeded by any thing that has happened in our days. They have shewn the same dismal consequences of the assembly of the different Orders in Brabant; and still more remarkably in Sweden and Denmark, where they have frequently produced a revolution and change of government, all of which have terminated in the absolute government, either of the Crown, or of one of the contending Orders. They laugh at the simplicity of the British for expecting that the permanent fruits of our constitution, which is founded on the same jarring principles, shall be any better; and assert, that the peaceable exercise of its several powers for somewhat more than a century (a thing never experienced by us in former times) has proceeded from circumstances merely accidental. With much address they have selected the former disturbances, and have connected them by a sort of principle, so as to support their system, "that a States General or Parliament, consisting of a representation of the different classes of citizens, can never deliberate for the general good, but must always occupy their time in contentions about their mutual invasions of privilege, and will saddle every aid to the executive power, with some unjust and ruinous aggrandisement of the victorious Order." They have the effrontery to give the MAGNA CHARTA as an instance of an usurpation of the great feudatories, and have represented it in such a light as to make it the game of their writers and of the tribunes.—All this they have done in order to reconcile the minds of the few thinking men of the nation to the abolition of the different Orders of the State, and to their National Convention in the form of a chaotic mass of Frenchmen, one and indivisible:

> *Non bene junctarum discordia femina rerum,*
> *Ubi frigida puegnabant calidis, humentia siccis,*
> *Mollia cum duris, sine pondere habentia pondus.*

Their reasonings would be just, and their proofs from history would be convincing, if their premises were true; if the British Parliament were really an assembly of three Orders, either personally, or by representation, deliberating apart, each having a *veto* on the decisions of the other two. And I apprehend that most of my countrymen, who have not had occasion to canvass the subject with much attention, suppose this to be really the British Constitution: for, in the ordinary table conversations on the subject, they seldom go farther, and talk with great complacence of the balance of hostile powers, of the King as the umpire of differences, and of the peace and prosperity that results from the whole.

But I cannot help thinking that this is a misconception, almost in every circumstance. I do not know any opposite interests in the State, except the general one of the governor and the governed, the king and the subject.—If there is an umpire in our constitution, it is the House of Lords—but this is not as a representation of the persons of birth, but as a court of hereditary magistrates: the Peers do not meet to defend their own privileges as citizens, but either as the counsellors of the King, or as judges in the last resort. The privileges for which we see them sometimes contend, are not the privileges of the high-born, of the great vassals of the Crown, but the privileges of the House of Lords, of the supreme Court of Judicature, or of the King's Council. In all the nations on the Continent, the different Orders, as they are called, of the State, are corporations, bodies politic, which have jurisdiction within themselves, and rights which they can maintain at their own hand, and privileges which mark them most distinctly, and produce such a complete separation between the different Orders, that they can no more mix than oil and water. Yet the great president Montesquieu says, that the Peerage of England is a *body* of Nobility; and he uses the term *body* in the strict sense now mentioned, as synonomous to corporation. He has repeatedly used this term to denote the second order of Frenchmen, persons of noble birth, or ennobled (that is, vested in the privileges and distinctions of the nobly born) united by law, and having authority to maintain their privileges. The history of France, nay of our own country, shows us that this body may enjoy all its distinctions of nobility, and that the Great Barons may enjoy the prerogatives of their baronies, although the authority of the Crown is almost annihilated.—We have no cogent reason, therefore, for thinking that they will be constantly careful to support the authority of the Crown; and much less to believe that they will, at the same time, watch over the liberties of the people. In the election of their representatives (for the whole body of the gentlemen must appear by representation) we must not expect that they will select such of their own number as will take care of those two essential objects of our constitution.—Equally jealous of the authority of the Crown and of the encroachments of all those who are not gentlemen, and even fearful of the assumptions of the great Barons, the powerful individuals of their own order, they will always choose such representatives as will defend their own rights in the first place. Such persons are by no means fit for maintaining the proper authority of the Crown, and keeping the representatives of the lower classes within proper bounds.

But this is not the nature of our House of Lords in the present day. It was so formerly in a great measure, and had the same effects as in other countries. But since the Revolution, the Peers of Great Britain have no important privileges which relate merely or chiefly to birth. These all refer to their functions as Magistrates of the supreme Court. The King can, at any time, place in this House any eminent person whom he thinks worthy of the office of hereditary magistrate. The Peers are noble—that is, remarkable, illustrious; but are not necessarily, nor in every instance, persons of high birth. This House therefore is not, in any sort, the representative of what is called in France the Noblesse —a particular cast of the nation;—nor is it a junction of the proprietors of the great fees of the Crown, as such;— for many, very many, of the greatest baronies are in the hands of those we call Commoners.—They sit as the King's Councellors, or as Judges.—Therefore the members of our Upper House are not swayed by the prejudices of any class of the citizens. They are hereditary magistrates, created by the Sovereign, for his council, to defend his prerogatives, to hold the balance between the throne and the people. The greatest part of the Nobility (in the continental sense of the word) are not called into this House, but they may be members of the Lower House, which we call the Commons; nay the sons and the brothers of the Peers are in the same situation. The Peers therefore cannot be hostile or indifferent to the liberty, the rights, or the happiness of the Commons, without being the enemies of their own families.

Nor is our House of Commons at all similar to the *Third Estate* of any of the neighbouring kingdoms. They are not the representatives of the ignobly born, or of any class of citizens. The members are the proper representatives of the *whole nation*, and consist of persons of every class, persons of the highest birth, persons of great fortune, persons of education, of knowledge, of talents.

Thus the causes of dissension which refer to the distinctive rights or prerogatives of the different classes of citizens are removed, because in each House there are many individuals selected from all the classes.

A Peer, having attained the highest honors of the state, must be an enemy to every revolution. Revolution must certainly degrade him, whether it places an absolute monarch, or a democratic junto, on the throne.

The Sovereign naturally looks for the support of the Upper House, and in every measure agreeable to the constitution, and to the public weal, exerts his influence on the House of Commons. Here the character of the monarch and his choice of ministers must appear, as in any other constitution; but with much less chance of danger to political liberty.—The great engine of monarchy in Europe, has been the jarring privileges of the different Orders; and the Sovereign, by siding with one of them, obtained accessions of prerogative and power.—It was thus that, under the House of Tudor, our constitution advanced with hasty strides to absolute monarchy; and would have attained it, had James the First been as able as he was willing to secure what he firmly believed to be the divine rights of his Crown.

I do not recollect hearing the lower ranks of the State venting much of their discontents against the Peers, and they seem to perceive pretty clearly the advantages arising from their prerogatives. They seem to look up to them as the first who will protect them against the agents of sovereignty. They know that a man may rise from the lowest station to the peerage, and that in that exaltation he remains connected with themselves by the dearest ties; and the House of Commons take no offence at the creation of new Peers, because their privileges as a Court, and their private rights, are not affected by it. Accordingly, the House has always opposed every project of limiting the King's prerogative in this respect.

How unlike is all this to the constitution consisting of the pure representatives of the Privileged Orders of the Continental States. The self-conceited constitutionalists of France saw something in the British Parliament which did not fall in with their own *hasty* notions, and prided themselves in not copying from us. This would have indicated great poverty of invention in a nation accustomed to consider itself as the teacher of mankind. The most sensible of them, however, wished to have a constitution which they called an *improvement* of ours: and this was the simple plan of a *representation* of the two or three Orders of the State. Their Upper House should contain the representatives of 100,000 noblesse. The Princes of the Blood and Great Barons should sit in it of their own right, and the rest by deputies. The Lower House, or *Tiers Etat,* should consist of deputies from those ignobly born; such as merchants, persons in the lower offices of the law, artisans, peasants, and a small number of freeholders. Surely it needs no deep reflection to teach us what sort of deliberations would occupy such a house. It would be a most useful occupation however, to peruse the history of France, and of other nations, and see what *really did occupy* the Tiers Etat thus constructed, and what were their proceedings, their decisions, and the steps which they took to make them effectual. I have no doubt but that this study would cure most of our advocates for general eligibility, and for general suffrage. I have lately read Velley and Villaret's History of France (by the bye, the Abbé Barruel has shewn that the Club d'Holbach managed the publication of this History after the first eight or ten volumes, and slipped into it many things suited to their impious project) and the accounts of the troublesome reigns of John, and Charles his successor, by authors who wrote long before the Revolution; and they filled me with horror. The only instance that I met with of any thing like moderation in the claims and disputes of the different Orders of their States General, and of patriotism, or regard for the general interests of the State, is in their meetings during the minority of Charles VIII.

With respect to the limitations of the eligibility into the House of Commons, I think that there can be no doubt that those should be excluded whose habits of needy and laborious life have precluded them from all opportunities of acquiring some general views of political relations. Such persons are totally unfit for deliberations, where general or comprehensive views only are to be the subjects of discussion; they can have no conceptions of the subject, and therefore no steady notions or opinions, but must change them after every speaker, and must become the dupes of every demagogue.

But there are other circumstances which make me think that, of all the classes of citizens, the land proprietors are the fittest for holding this important office. I do not infer this from their having a more real connection with the nation, and a stronger interest in its fate—I prefer them on account of their general habits of thought. Almost all their ordinary transactions are such as make them acquainted with the interests of others, cause them to consider those in general points of view; and, in short, most of their occupations are, in some degree, national. They are accustomed to settle differences between those of lower stations —they are frequently in the King's commission as Justices of the Peace. All these circumstances make them much apter scholars in that political knowledge, which is absolutely necessary for a member of the House of Commons. But, besides this, I have no hesitation in saying that their turn of mind, their principles of conduct, are more generally such as become a Senator, than those of *any other class* of men. This class includes almost all men of family. I cannot help thinking that even what is called family pride is a sentiment in their favor. I am convinced that all our propensities are useful in society, and that their bad effects arise wholly from want of moderation in the indulgence of them, or sometimes from the impropriety of the occasion on which they are exerted. What propensity is more general than the desire of acquiring permanent consideration for ourselves and our families? Where is the man to be found so mean-spirited as not to value himself for being born of creditable parents, and for creditable domestic connections? Is this wrong because it has been abused? So then is every pre-eminence of office; and the directors of republican France are as criminal as her former Nobles. This propensity of the human heart should no more be rejected than the desire of power. It should be regulated—but it should certainly be made use of as one of the means of carrying on the national business. I think that we know some of its good effects—It incites to a certain propriety of conduct that is generally agreeable—its honesty is embellished by a manner that makes it more pleasing. There is something that we call the *behaviour of a Gentleman* that is immediately and uniformly understood. The plainest peasant or labourer will say of a man whom he esteems in a certain way, "He is a Gentleman, every bit of him"—and he is perfectly understood by all who hear him to mean, not a rank in life, but a turn of mind, a tenor of conduct that is amiable and worthy, and the ground of confidence.—I remark, with some feeling of patriotic pride, that these are phrases almost peculiar to our language—in Russia the words would have no meaning. But there, the Sovereign is a despot, and all but the Gentry are slaves; and the Gentry are at no pains to recommend their class by such a distinction, nor to give currency to such a phrase.—I would infer from this peculiarity, that Britain is the happy land, where the wisest use has been made of this propensity of the human heart.

If therefore there be a foundation for this peculiarity, the Gentry are proper objects of our choice for filling the House of Commons.

If theoretical considerations are of any value in questions of political discussion, I would say, that we have good reasons for giving this class of citizens a great share in the public deliberations. Besides what I have already noticed of their habits of considering things in general points of view, and their *feeling* a closer connection with the nation than any other class, I would say that the power and influence which naturally attach to their being called to offices of public trust, will probably be better lodged in their hands. If they are generally selected for these offices, they come to consider them as parts of their civil condition, as situations natural to them. They will therefore exercise this power and influence with the moderation and calmness of habit—they are no novelties to them—they are not afraid of losing them;—therefore, when in office, they do not catch at the opportunities of exercising them. This is the ordinary conduct of men, and therefore is a ground of probable reasoning.—In short, I should expect from our Gentry somewhat of generosity and candour, which would temper the commercial principle, which seems to regulate the national transactions of modern Europe, and whose effects seem less friendly to the best interest of humanity, than even the Roman principle of glory.

The Reader will now believe that I would not recommend the filling the House of Commons with merchants, although they seem to be the natural Representatives of the monied interest of the nation. But I do not wish to consider that House as the Representative of any Orders whatever, or to disturb its deliberations with any debates on their jarring interests. The man of purely commercial notions disclaims all generosity—recommends honesty because it is the best policy—in short, "places the value of a thing in as much money as 'twill bring." I should watch the conduct of such men more narrowly than that of the Nobles. Indeed, the history of Parliament will show that the Gentry have not been the most venal part of the House. The Illumination which now dazzles the world aims directly at multiplying the number of venal members, by filling the senates of Europe with men who may be bought at a low price. Ministerial corruption is the fruit of Liberty, and freedom dawned in this nation in Queen Elizabeth's time, when her minister bribed Wentworth.—A wise and free Legislation will endeavour to make this as expensive and troublesome as possible, and therefore will neither admit universal suffrage nor a very extensive eligibility.——These two circumstances, besides opening a wider door to corruption, tend to destroy the very intention of all civil constitutions. The great object in them is, to make a great number of people happy. Some men place their chief enjoyment in measuring their strength with others, and love to be continually employed in canvassing, intriguing, and carrying on some little pieces of a sort of public business; to such men universal suffrage and eligibility would be paradise—but it is to be hoped that the number of such is not very great: for this occupation must be accompanied by much disquiet among their neighbours, much dissension, and mutual offence and ill-will—and the peaceable, the indolent, the studious, and the half of the nation, the women, will be great sufferers by all this. In a nation possessing many of the comforts and pleasures of life, the happiest government is that which will leave the greatest number possible totally unoccupied with national affairs, and at full liberty to enjoy all their domestic and social pleasures, and to do this with security and permanency. Great limitations in the right of electing seems therefore a circumstance necessary for this purpose; and limitations are equally necessary on the eligibility. When the offices of power and emolument are open to all, the scramble becomes universal, and the nation is never at peace. The *road* to a seat in Parliament should be accessible to all; but it should be long, so that many things, which all may in time obtain, shall be requisite for qualifying the candidate. The road should also be such that all should be induced to walk in it, in the prosecution of their ordinary business; and their admission into public offices should depend on the progress which they have made in the advancement of their own fortunes. Such regulations would, I think, give the greatest chance of filling the offices with persons fittest for them, by their talents, their experience, and their habits of thinking. These habits, and the views of life which a man forms in consequence of his situation, are of the utmost importance.

After all these observations, I must still recur to a position which I have repeated more than once, namely, that our constitution, which nearly embraces all these circumstances, has attained its present excellence chiefly in consequence of the innate worth of the British character. About the time of the Conquest, our constitution hardly differed from that of France. But the clashing of interests between the different Orders of the subjects was not so rancorous and obstinate—these Orders melted more easily together—the purity of the principle of Representation in the States was less attended to; and while the French Peers gradually left off minding any business but their own, and left the

High Court of Judicature to the lawyers, and the King
to his Cabinet Council, the Peers of Great Britain, over-
looking their own less important distinctions, attended more
to the State, became a permanent Council to the Sovereign
in the administration and legislation; and, with a patriotism
and a patience that are unknown to the other Grandees of
Europe, continued to hear and to judge in all questions of
justice and property between the inferior citizens of the
State. British Liberty is the highly-prized fruit of all this
worthy conduct, and most people ascribe it to the superior
spirit and independence of the national character. It strikes
me, however, as more surely indicating superior virtue, and
more judicious patriotism; and our happy constitution is
not more justly entitled to the admiration and respect that
is paid to it by all Europe, than to the affectionate and grate-
ful attachment of every true-hearted Briton.

Since the publication of this volume I have seen a very
remarkable work indeed, on the same subject, *Memoires
pour servir a l'Histoire du Jacobinisme, par M. l'Abbé
Barruel.* This author confirms all that I have said of the
*Enlighteners,* whom he very aptly calls *Philosophists;* and
of the abuses of Free Masonry in France. He shows, unquestionably, that a formal and systematic conspiracy
against Religion was formed and zealously prosecuted by
Voltaire, d'Alembert, and Diderot, assisted by Frederic II.
King of Prussia; and I see that their principles and their
manner of procedure have been the same with those of the
German atheists and anarchists. Like them they hired an
Army of Writers; they industriously pushed their writings
into every house and every cottage. Those writings were
equally calculated for inflaming the sensual appetites of
men, and for perverting their judgments. They endeavoured
to get the command of the Schools, particularly those for
the lower classes; and they erected and managed a prodigious number of Circulating Libraries and Reading Societies. M. Barruel says, that this gang of public corruptors
have held their meetings for many years in the *Hotel de
Holbach* at Paris, and that Voltaire was their honorary
President. The most eminent members were *d'Alembert,
Diderot, Condorcet, La Harpe, Turgot, Lamoignon.* They
took the name of ŒCONOMISTS, and affected to be continually occupied with plans for improving Commerce,

Manufactures, Agriculture, Finance, &c. and published from time to time respectable performances on those subjects. ——But their darling project was to destroy Christianity and all Religion, and to bring about a total change of Government. They employed writers to compose corrupting and impious books—these were revised by the Society, and corrected till they suited their purpose. A number were printed in a handsome manner, to defray the expence; and then a much greater number were printed in the cheapest form possible, and given for nothing, or at very low prices, to hawkers and pedlars, with injunctions to distribute them secretly through the cities and villages. They even hired persons to read them to conventicles of those who had not learned to read.\* (See vol. i. 343—355.)

I am particularly struck by a position of Abbé Barruel, *"That Irreligion and unqualified Liberty and Equality are the genuine and original Secrets of Free Masonry, and the ultimatum of a regular progress through all its degrees."* He supports this remarkable position with great ingenuity, and many very pertinent facts. I confess that now, when I have got this impression, I shall find it very difficult to efface it. But I must also say, that this thought never struck me, during all the time that I have been occupied with it; nor have I ever heard it expressed by any Brother, except such as had been illuminated; and such Brethren always considered this as an innovation or improvement on genuine British Free Masonry. I recollect, indeed, that Nicholai, in his account of the German Rosycrucians, says, that the object of Free Masonry in England, since the time of James

---

*The author makes an observation which is as just as it is agreeable. This atrocious gang solicited, with the most anxious assiduity, the participation and patronage of the great ones of the world, and boast of several very exalted names: Frederic II. of Prussia, whom they call the Solomon of the North, Catharine II. Gustavus King of Sweden, the King of Denmark, &c. &c. But in the whole series of their correspondence there is not the least trace of any encouragement or any hopes from our excellent Sovereign George III. Despising the incense of such wretches, and detesting their science, he has truly merited the title of *Philosopher*, by having done more for the real Illumination of the World, by the promotion of true Science, than Louis XIV. with his pensioned Academicians, or than all the present Sovereigns of Europe united; and has uniformly distinguished himself by his regard for true Religion, and every thing that is venerable sacred. This omission is above all praise!

II. is *Toleration* in *Religious Opinions,* as *Royalism* had been the object before that time.

The account which the Abbé gives of the *Chevalerie du Soleil* is very conformable to one of the three rituals in my possession. His account of the *Chevalerie de Rose Croix,* and some others, differs considerably from those in my box. I have reason to think that my materials are transcripts from the rituals, &c. which Rosa introduced into the German Lodges, because the writer of the greatest part of them is an inhabitant of that city.

I think that the Abbé Barruel's account of this matter suggests a pleasing reflection. All the Brethren on the Continent agree in saying, that Free Masonry was imported from Great Britain about the beginning of this century, and this in the form of a Mystical Society. It has been assiduously cultivated in Britain ever since that time, and I believe that the Fraternity is more numerous here, in proportion to the population of the country, than in any other kingdom; yet in Britain the Brethren have never suspected that its principles were seditious or atheistical. While the Free Masonry of the Continent was tricked up with all the frippery of stars and ribbands, or was perverted to the most profligate and impious purposes, and the Lodges became seminaries of Foppery, of Sedition, and Impiety, it has retained in Britain its original form, simple and unadorned, and the Lodges have remained the scenes of innocent merriment, or meetings of Charity and Beneficence. As the good sense and sound judgments of Britons have preserved them from the absurd follies of Transmutation, of Ghost-raising, and of Magic, so their honest hearts and their innate good dispositions have made them detest and reject the mad projects and impious doctrines of Cosmopolites, Epicurists, and Atheists.

> *O fortunato's nimium, fua si bona norint*
> *Anglicolas!*

I have more confidence than ever in the sentiment which I expressed as an encouragement for our moral instructors; and with greater earnestness do I call on them to rescue from corruption and impending ruin a nation so highly deserving of their care.

Mr. Barruel, in the eighteenth chapter of his work, has suggested some reflections, which highly merit attention, and greatly tend to efface the impression which is naturally made on the minds of the unthinking and precipitant, when they observe such a list of authors, whom they have been accustomed to admire, all leagued against Religion. I think, however, that nothing can more effectually remove it, than what I have already shown of the vile and disgraceful tricks which these sophists have been guilty of to support their cause. The cause of this numerous association is distinctly seen in their very procedure. The very first step in their progress is *depravation of manners*. In this they have laboured with as much earnestness as either Spartacus, or Minos, or Bahrdt. It was a treat to me to learn that La Close's abominable book *Les Liasons Dangereuses,* was not merely pandering for his patron Orleans, but also working for his masters at the Hotel d'Holbach. Nothing gives such certain bread to those authors, in the beginning of their career, as immoral and impure writings;—and with such did even their chief set out, and fill his pockets; witness his *Pucelle d'Orleans;* and even after they became the *sages of France,* they continued, either from coarse taste or from serious principle, for the diabolical purpose of inflaming the passions of others, to interlard their gravest performances with impure thoughts and sentiments. Nay, the secret of the Hotel d'Holbach shews us that, for any thing we know to the contrary, the vilest productions of their press may have been the compositions of the octogenary Voltaire, of the sly d'Alembert, or of the author of the *Pere de Famille.* What a pity it is that the *Decline of the Roman Empire* was not all written in England, and that its learned and elegant author, by going into their society, has allowed himself to be drawn into this muddy and degrading vortex!

I should scarcely ask for more to disgust me with the philosophy of these sages, and to make me distrust all their pretensions to knowledge. The meanness of the conduct suited the original poverty of the whole of them; but its continuance strips them of all claims to the name of philosophers. Their pretended wisdom is only cunning—and we must acknowledge that their conduct was clever: for this mean of corruption, concealed or embellished by their talents for sentimental slang (I can give it no better name) made their conversation and their writings most acceptable to their noble patrons.—Now it is that Religion, of necessity, comes on the field; for Religion tells us, that these are mean pleasures for creatures born to our prospects; and Christianity tells us, that they are gross transgressions of *the only just morality*. The progress of the pupil will now be rapid; for he will listen with willing ears to lessons which flatter his passions. Yet Voltaire thinks it necessary to enliven the lessons by a little of the *salaison, quelques bons mots à-propos auprès des femmes*, which he recommends to d'Alembert, who, it seems, was deficient in this kind of small talk.

Surely all this is very unlike to wisdom; and when we see that it is part of a plan, and this an obvious one, it should greatly lessen our wonder at the number of these admired infidels. If we would now proceed to examine their pretentions to science, on which they found their claim to the name of philosophers, we must be careful to take the word in a sense that is unequivocal. Its true meaning is by no means what is commonly assigned to it, a lover of knowledge. It is a lover of wisdom; and philosophy professes to teach us what are the constituents of human felicity, and what are the means of attaining it; what are our duties, and the general rules for our conduct. The stoics were philosophers. The Christians are also philosophers. The Epicureans and the Sophists of France would also be called philosophers. I have put in my objection to this claim already, and need not repeat my reasons for saying that their doctrines are not dictates of wisdom. I shall only add, that their own conduct shows plainly that their principles had no effect on themselves, because we see, from the series of correspondence which Mr. Barruel has laid before us, that they do not scruple to practise villanous and hypocritical tricks, which never fail to disgrace a man, and are totally irreconcileable with our notions of human dignity. Voltaire patiently took a caining from an officer at Frankfort, for having wittily told lies of his scholar Frederic, and his wisdom told him that his honor was cleared by offering to meet the Major, each of them provided with an injection syringe. This was thought sublime wit at Ferney. I do not suppose that the slave Epictetus, or the soldier Digby, would have ended the affair in this manner. Many of the deeds of wisdom of the club d'Holbach were more degrading than even this; and I am confident that the whole of this phalanx of sages were conscious that they were treated by their patrons and pupils as Voltaire was treated by the Solomon of the North, and that their notions of the *vraie sagesse* were also the same with his. He gives this account of it in his letter to his niece: "Le Roi lui avoit repondu; 'j'aurai besoin de Voltaire un an tout au plus—On presse l'orange, et on jette l'écorce.' Je me suis fait repeter ces douces paroles"—(How poor Voltaire would grin!)—"Je vois bien qu'on a pressé l'orange—il faut penser a fauver l'ecorce."

But, as things stand at present, philosopher means a man of science, and in this sense of the word our sages claim great respect. No claim can be worse founded. It is amusing to observe the earnestness with which they recommend the study of natural history. One does not readily see the connection of this with their ostensible object, the happiness of man. A perusal of Voltaire's letters betrays the secret. Many years ago he heard that some observations on the formation of strata, and the fossils found in them, were incompatible with the age which the Mosaic history seems to assign to this globe. He mentions this with great exultation in some of his early letters; and, from that time forward, never ceases to enjoin his colleagues to press the study of natural history and cosmogony, and carefully to bring forward every fact which was hostile to the Mosaic accounts. It became a serious part of the exercises of their wealthy pupils, and their perplexing discoveries were most ostentatiously displayed. M. de Luc, a very eminent naturalist, has shewn, in a letter to the Chevalier Dr. Zimmermann (published, I think, about the year 1790) how very scanty the knowledge of these observers has been, and how precipitate have been their conclusions. For my own part, I think the affair is of little consequence. Moses writes the history, not of this globe, but of the race of Adam.

The science of these philosophers is not remarkable in other branches, if we except M. d'Alembert's mathematics.* Yet the imposing confidence of Voltaire was such, that he passes for a person fully informed, and he pronounces on every subject with so much authority, with such a force of expression, and generally with so much wit or pleasantry, that his hearers and readers are fascinated, and soon convinced of what they wish to be true.

It is not by the wisdom nor by the profound knowledge which these writers display, that they have acquired celebrity, a fame which has been so pernicious. It is by fine writing, by works addressed to the imagination and to the affections, by excellent dramas, by affecting moral essays, full of expressions of the greatest respect for virtue, the most tender benevolence, and the highest sentiments of honor and dignity.—By these means they fascinate all readers; they gain the esteem of the worthy, who imagine them sincere, and their pernicious doctrines are thus spread abroad, and steal into the minds of the dissolute, the licentious, and the unwary.

But I am writing to Britons, who are considered by our neighbours on the Continent as a nation of philosophers—to the countrymen of Bacon, of Locke, of Newton—who are not to be wheedled like children, but must be reasoned with as men.—Voltaire, who decides without hesitation on the character of the most distant nations in the most remote antiquity, did not know us: he came among us, in the beginning of his career, with the highest expectations of our support, and hoped to make his fortune by his Pucelle d'Orleans. It was rejected with disdain—but we published his Henriade for him: and, notwithstanding his repeated

---

*Never was there any thing more contemptible than the physical and mechanical positions in Diderot's great work, the *Systeme de la Nature* (Barruel affirms, that he was the author, and got 100 pistoles for the copy, from the person who related the story to him) that long ago found that Diderot had assisted Robinet to make a book out of his Masonic Oration which I mentioned in page 23. Robinet trusted to Diderot's knowledge in natural philosophy. But the Junto were ashamed of the book *De la Nature*. Diderot seems to have, after this, read Dr. Hartley's book, and has greatly refined on the crude system of Robinet. But after all, the *Systeme de la Nature* is contemptible, if it be considered as pretending to what is received as science by a mechanical philosopher.

disappointments of the same kind, he durst not offend his countrymen by slandering us, but joined in the profound respect paid by all to British science.—Our writers, whether on natural or moral science, are still regarded as standard classics, and are studied with care. Lord Verulam is acknowledged by every man of science to have given the first just description of true philosophy, pointed out its objects, and ascertained its mode of procedure—And Newton is equally allowed to have evinced the propriety of the Baconian precepts by his unequalled success, *suâ Mathesi facem preferente.*—The most celebrated philosophers on the Continent are those who have completed by demonstration the wonderful guesses of his penetrating genius. Bailli, or Condorcet (I forget which) struck with the inconceivable reaches of Newton's thoughts, breaks out, in the words of Lucretius,

> *Te sequor, O magnæ gentis decus, inque tuis nunc*
> *Fixa pedum pono pressis vestigia signis.*
> *Tu pater et rerum inventor, tu patria nobis*
> *Suppeditas precepta, tuisque ex inclute chartis,*
> *Floriferis ut apes in saltibus omnia libant,*
> *Omnia nos itidem depascimur aurea dicta;*
> *Aurea, perpetuâ semper dignissima vitâ.*

After such avowels of our capacity to instruct ourselves, shall we still fly to those disturbers of the world for our lessons? No—Let us rally round our own standards—let us take the path pointed out by Bacon—let us follow the steps of Newton—and, to conclude, let us seriously consider a most excellent advice by the highest authority:

"Beware of false prophets, who come to you in sheep's cloathing, but inwardly they are ravening wolves—BY THEIR FRUITS YE SHALL KNOW THEM—Do men gather grapes of thorns, or figs of thistles?"

THE END.